بسم الله الرحمن الرحيم

KITĀB AL-AMWĀL

By

Abū Ja'far Ahmad Ibn Nasr al-Dā'ūdi
(d. 402/1011)

Edited, Annotated and Translated into English
By
ABU'L MUHSIN MUHAMMAD SHARFUDDIN

KITAB BHAVAN
New Delhi-110002 (India)

Kitab Bhavan
Publishers, Distributors, Exporters & Importers
1784, Kalan Mahal, Darya Ganj
New Delhi - 1100 02 (India)

Phone : (91-11) 23277392 / 93, 23274686, 30906494
Mobile : (91-11) 9910114484
website : www.kitabbhavan.com
Email : nasri@vsnl.com, nusrat@bol.net.in
Fax : (91-11) 23263383

Edition : 2006

ISBN : 81-7151-267-4
Book Code No. K00090

Published in India by :
Nusrat Ali Nasri for Kitab Bhavan
1784, Kalan Mahal, Darya Ganj
New Delhi - 1100 02 [India]

Printed in India at :
Lahooti Fine Art Press
1711, Sui Walan, Darya Ganj
New Delhi - 110002 (India)

CONTENTS

ACKNOWLEDGEMENTS

I express my deepest gratitude and obligation to professor Muḥammad Ṣaghīr Ḥasan Ma'ṣūmī, the former Director of Islamic Research Institute, Islamabad; to Professor Serajul Haq, former Head of the Department of Arabic and Islamic Studies, University of Dhaka, but for whose constant help, guidance and supervision the present work might not have materialised.

I also owe a debt of gratitude to Dr Muin-ud-Din Ahmad Khan, former Reader, Islamic Research Institute, and Dr Ziaud-Din Ahmad for their valuable criticism and constructive suggestions extended to me in course of preparing the work. I have also to acknowledge the kindness of the authorities of Islamic Research Institute, Islamabad, for sponsoring the present work and to the authorities of the Dhaka University for enrolling me as a Research Student.

I should also like to record my thanks for the members of the staff of the Library of the Institute and those of the Dhaka University for their cooperation and assistance rendered to me in making available to me the relevant materials and resources while I was engaged in this study.

A.M.M. Sharfuddin

PREFACE

This work consists of the Arabic text of *Kitāb al-Amwāl* of Abū Ja'far Aḥmad ibn Nasr al-Dā'ūdī al-Mālikī al-Asadī, with explanatory notes, English translation and introduction. The text has been edited for the first time on the basis of a unique manuscript, preserved in the Escurial Library, Madrid, under the title 'Kitāb fīhi'l-Amwāl', MS No. 1165. The title page of the MS mentions the work as 'Kitāb fīhi'l Amwāl' which has been referred to as *Kitāb al-Amwāl* by Qāḍī Ibn Rushd, Qāḍī 'Iyāḍ and 'Allāmah al-'Uqbānī al-Tilimsānī.

The text deals (from the Mālikī point of view) with broad principles of state revenues, military administration, international law of war and peace, and the author's verdicts (*fatāwā*) on the settlements of lands in al-Ifrīqiyyah, al-Maghrib, Spain and Sicily. It also deals with the administration of the properties acquired unlawfully and those abandoned with no legal owners. What is significant is that the work throws light on various kinds of earnings (lawful, disapproved and prohibited) and suggests methods to treat the problems of begging, solicitation of alms and similar aids (lawful, obligatory, and prohibited) and the means to maintain balance in society between various groups of rich and poor people.

As no other copy of the manuscript has so far been traced, I had to rely on the photocopies of the Escurial MS and tried to establish the text by collating it with the parallels found in some of the early works like *Kitāb al-Muqaddimāt* of Qāḍī Ibn Rushd, the *Tafsīr* of al-Qurṭubī and *Tuḥfat al-Nāẓir* of 'Allāmah al-'Uqbānī al-Tilimsānī, etc.

For quotation of the Qur'ānic verses and their numbers, the text of the Qur'ān published by the Tāj Company, Lahore has been used. As for the Prophetic traditions, I have traced them in *al-Muwaṭṭa'* of Imām Mālik, the *Sahīḥ'* of al-Bukhārī and the *Ṣaḥīḥ* of al-Muslim and other compilations of traditions and early works on jurisprudence. For verifying the opinions and events I have collated the text with *al-Mudawwanah* of Saḥnūn, *Kitāb al-Kharāj* of Abū Yūsuf, *Kitāb al-Kharāj* of Yaḥyā ibn Adam, *Kitāb al-Amwāl* of Abū 'Ubayd, Abū Aḥmad Ḥumayd ibn Zanjawayh (MS), *Kitāb al-Umm* of al-Shāfi'ī and the historical works of al-Balādhurī, al-Ṭabarī, Ibn Hishām and others.

Since the MS is very old and it was transcribed about 275 years after the death of the author, some portions of the work are demaged and effaced owing to exposure to sun and moisture, etc. Moreover, the text contains some errors. I have endeavoured to fill the gaps and correct the version of the Manuscript in accordance with the parallels and the theme of the context. Still, there are a number of problems which I could not fully solve. There might also be some lacunae, obscure passages, and illegible words, here and there, in the text which might have escaped my notice. They have been left open with the hope that they will be deciphered later. All the words added in the text have been placed in between the brackets.

The notes added to the Arabic text indicate the versions of the Manuscript, the errors, variations in reading, short biographical notices and description of places, besides the parallel passages quoted from other works.

In the English translation, an attempt has been made to make the translation as literal as possible, and faithful to the original text. For the translation of the verses of the Qur'ān, I have depended on *The Meaning of the Glorious Koran* of late Muhammad Marmaduke Pickthall.

In the Introduction, I have tried to estimate the importance of the present work by comparing it with other similar works and have discussed the life and works of the author. I have also thrown some light on the lives and activities of a number of his disciples through whom his works were transmitted to posterity. Again, I have tried to delineate the significance of the Manuscript and have pointed out how this work influenced the contemporary and later scholars of al-Maghrib.

Lastly, I have summed up the contents of the work in the Introduction. It may be added that the cataloguer of the MS (Escurial) has described it at the end in Latin which I have got translated into English. Both the Latin text and the English translation form the Appendix of the work.

Originally, this work formed a thesis submitted to the University of Dhaka in 1972 for the degree of Ph.D.

A.M.M. Sharfuddin

A NOTE ON TRANSLITERATION

ء medial	:	'	ط	:	ṭ
ء final	:	'	ظ	:	ẓ
ء initial	:	not expressed	ع	:	'
ا	:	a	غ	:	gh
ب	:	b	ف	:	f
ت	:	t	ق	:	q
ث	:	th	ك	:	k
ج	:	j	ل	:	l
ح	:	ḥ	م	:	m
خ	:	kh	ن	:	n
د	:	d	و	:	w
ذ	:	dh	ه	:	h
ر	:	r	ة	:	ah (eg. *sunnah*)
ز	:	z	ـة	:	at (in construct from e.g. *sunnat al-Rasūl*)
س	:	s	ى	:	y
ش	:	sh	ال	:	al- ('l in construct form e.g. Abū'l)
ص	:	ṣ			
ض	:	ḍ			

VOWELS

Short	ـَ	:	a
	ـِ	:	i
	ـُ	:	u
Long	ـَا	:	ā
	ـِى	:	ī
	ـُو	:	ū

DIPHTHONGS

ـَو	:	aw
ـَى	:	ay

Double

ـُوَّ	:	uwwa
ـِيَّ	:	iyya

INTRODUCTION

I. THE WORK OF ABŪ JA'FAR AL-DĀ'ŪDĪ

This work is an attempt to introduce to the readers the *Kitāb al-Amwāl* of Abū Ja'far Aḥmad ibn Naṣr al-Dā'ūdī—a juridical treatise of the fourth century Hijrah, hitherto little known but often referred to by his contemporary and later scholars of al-Maghrib, such as Qāḍī Abū'l-Walīd Muḥammad ibn Aḥmad Ibn Rushd (450/1059–520/1126), the commentator of the Qur'ān, Abū 'Abd Allāh Muḥammad ibn Aḥmad al-Anṣārī al-Qurṭubī (*d.* 671/1273), and the noted jurist Abū 'Abd Allāh Muḥammad ibn Aḥmad ibn Qāsim ibn Sa'īd al-'Uqbānī al-Tilimsānī (*d.* 871/1467).[1]

This treatise contains broad principles of state revenues, military administration, as well as the author's verdicts (*fatāwā*) on the settlements of lands in al-Ifrīqiyyah, al-Maghrib, Spain and Sicily. It also discusses how to maintain equilibrium in society between various groups of rich and poor people.

Abū Ja'far al-Dā'ūdī is not the first author on the subject. A good number of works entitled *Kitāb al-Amwāl* or *Kitāb al-Kharāj* preceded the present work. The subject of revenue administration, the main theme of this work, was dealt with at considerable length in the early compilations of the Prophetic traditions, the juridical books and historical works under different chapters such as *Kitāb al-Maghāzī, Kitāb al-Zakāh, Kitāb al-Siyar, Kitāb al-Jihād, Kitāb al-Ṣadaqah* and so on and so forth.

An independent treatment of the subject appears to have become popular in the early phase of the 'Abbāsid period. The *wazīrs*, *qāḍīs*, *kātibs*, *muftīs* and other officers who were responsible for general administration, including justice, accounts of taxation and disbursement of revenues, are the precursors on the subject. Mu'āwiyah ibn 'Ubayd Allāh ibn Yasār al-'Ash'arī (*d.* 170/786), the famous *wazīr* of the 'Abbāsid Caliph, al-Mahdī (158/775–168/785), is credited with being the first to compile such a work.[2] Soon he was followed by Qāḍī Abū Yūsuf, Yaḥyā ibn Rajab al-Ḥanbalī and others. Out of twenty-seven such works,[3] only five so far seem to have seen the light of the day as chronologically detailed below:

1. Abū Yūsuf Ya'qūb ibn Ibrāhīm (*d.* 182/799) *Kitāb al-Kharāj.*
2. Yaḥyā ibn Ādam (*d.* 203/819): *Kitāb al-Kharāj.*
3. Abū 'Ubayd al-Qāsim ibn Sallām (*d.* 224/839), *Kitāb al-Amwāl.*
4. Abū'l-Faraj Qudāmah ibn Ja'far al-Kātib (*d.* 320/932), *Kitāb al-Kharāj wa-Ṣinā'at al-Kitābah.*
5. Abū'l-Faraj 'Abd al-Raḥmān ibn Rajab al-Ḥanbalī (*d.* 795/1393), *Kitāb al-Istikhrāj li-Aḥkām al-Kharāj.*

In these works, the authors, apart from dealing with the broad principles of revenue administration and other related subjects confine themselves to the problems of the eastern part of Muslim lands, but in his *Kitāb al-Amwāl,* al-Dā'ūdī's main interest lies in the western part of the Muslim lands of his time, namely al-Ifrīqiyyah, al-Maghrib, Spain, and Sicily to which he devoted comparatively, long chapters.[4]

These chapters, in fact, abound in his verdicts on the land settlements which he primarily based on the main principles and outlines of Mālikī *fiqh.* These verdicts provide us with considerable details of the contemporaneous agricultural and economic conditions of the actual owners of the lands in al-Maghrib vis-á-vis the unlawful practices of the rulers of his time who frequently seized and forcibly occupied the public and private properties for their own benefit.

Kitāb al-Amwāl of Abū Ja'far al-Dā'ūdī is, therefore, important for more than one reason; firstly, it can be considered as a significant work on the revenue administration of the early phase of Islam and a unique work of verdicts in the context of the disputes occasionally referred to him on the problems of settlement of lands and administration of properties.

Secondly, by way of comparison with other Ḥanafite and Ḥanbalite works on the subject it gives us a good resumé of the Mālikī law on revenue administration, military organization, land-holdings and land tenure.

Thirdly, for practical purposes, it is undoubtedly an important work of Mālikī law, because we know that the Mālikī school claimed mass adherence in the fourth/fifth centuries of Hijrah in North Africa, Spain and Sicily.[5] The work remained in demand for even five hundred years after the death of our author.[6]

Fourthly, it provides us with authoritative points of comparison with its counterparts in the East. Thus all the relevant works including the present work at hand will provide a comprehensive as well as an exhaustive study on the subject.

Lastly, it is only through this book that we can know such a great author as Imām Abū Ja'far al-Dā'ūdī, whose other works remain untraceable till today.

II. THE AUTHOR

Abū Ja'far Aḥmad ibn Naṣr al-Dā'ūdī lived in fourth-fifth *Hijrah*/eleventh century CE in North Africa. Although we are not in possession of a good chronological account of his life and career, we have at our disposal some authentic and useful data about his life, his students, and his works in the writings of his near contemporary and later authors like the biographer Qāḍī 'Iyāḍ (476/1084–544/1150), the bibliographist Ibn Khayr (502/1108–575/1179), the biographer Ibn Bushkuwāl (494/1101–578/1185) and Ibn Farḥūn (720/1321–799/397), which when pieced together give us an integrated view of our author.

Qāḍī Abū'l-Faḍl 'Iyāḍ ibn Mūsā ibn 'Iyāḍ (476/1084–544/1150), who is proverbially famous for his knowledge of al-Maghrib,[7] provides us with comparatively greater details of the life, activities and works of al-Dā'ūdī. In his biographical dictionary of Mālikī scholars entitled *Tartīb al-Madārik wa Taqrīb al-Masālik li-Ma'rifat A'lām Madhhab Mālik,* he mentions al-Dā'ūdī, belonging to Banū Asad, as an *Imām* of the Mālikī school of law in al-Maghrib. According to him, al-Dā'ūdī hailed from M'sila (al-Masīlah) or Biskarah. He lived in Tripoli (Ṭrabulus) where he wrote his book, *Fī Sharḥ al-Muwaṭṭa'*. Thereafter, he moved to Tlemcen (Tilimsān). Qāḍī 'Iyāḍ further adds that al-Dā'ūdī was a very learned jurist and scholar in various branches of knowledge and an excellent author. He had a good command of Arabic language, *Ḥadīth* and speculative science.[8]

Qāḍī 'Iyāḍ lists the following books of al-Dā'ūdī:[9]

1. *Al-Nāmī fī Sharḥ al-Muwaṭṭa'.*
2. *Al-Naṣiḥah fī Sharh al-Bukhārī.*
3. *Al-Wā'yī fī'l-Fiqh.*
4. *Al-Īḍāḥ fī'l-Radd 'alā'l-Qadariyyah.*
5. *Kitāb al-Uṣūl.*
6. *Kitāb al-Bayān.*
7. *Kitāb al-Amwāl.*

Qāḍī 'Iyāḍ is of the opinion that the learning of al-Dā'ūdī was virtually self-acquired as he was known to have acquired most of his knowledge without sitting at the feet of any renowned teacher (*Imām*). He got his vast knowledge in various sciences through his own efforts. In this connection he narrates a story saying that his contemporary scholars of al-Qayrawān once rejected his verdict on migrating from the realm of Banū 'Abīd on the ground of his having no teacher (*Shaykh*).[10]

Nevertheless, as mentioned by Qāḍī 'Iyāḍ, three pupils of al-Ḍā'ūdī, Abū 'Abd Allāh al-Būnī,[11] Abū Bakr ibn Shaykh Abū Muḥammad ibn Abū Zayd and Abū 'Alī ibn al-Raffā of Couta transmitted (*Ḥadīth* and works) from him.[12] According to Qāḍī 'Iyāḍ, Ḥāṭim al-Ṭarābulisī states that al-Dā'ūdī died in H. 402 in Tlemcen (Tilimsān) and was buried at Bāb al-'Aqbah and that Ḥāṭim could not attend his lectures and that al-Dā'ūdī was alive when Ḥāṭim was at Qayrawān. He further adds that, although he finds in some historical works the date of the death of al-Dā'ūdī mentioned as the year 411, he regards the former date as most probable.[13]

Abū Bakr Muḥammad ibn Khayr ibn 'Umar ibn Khalīfah al-Umawī al-Ishbelī says in his ***Fihrist*** **(entitled *Fihrist mā Rawāhu 'an Shuyūkhihi min*** *al-Dawāwīn al-Muṣannafalī fī Ḍurūl al-'Ilm wa Anwā'i'l Ma'ārif*), in which he enumerates the titles of the early works which he read or heard, with chains of transmission going back to their authors,[14] that he acquired *Ijāzah* (permission) for transmitting Abū Ja'far al-Dā'ūdī's works and Prophetic traditions he had heard from his teachers through six chains of narrators among whom were Imām Ḥāfiẓ Ibn 'Abd al-Barr and Abū 'Abd al-Mālik Marwān ibn 'Alī al-Qaṭṭān al-Būnī, the two leading Mālikite traditionists of al-Maghrib. The text of *Ijāzah* is as follows:

كتاب تفسير المؤطا، لأبى جعفر احمد بن نصر الداودى الفقيه المالكى من اهل المسيلة، وسماه الكتاب النامى، حدثنى به أبوبكر محمد بن طاهر، رحمه الله قال: نابه أبوعلى الغسانى، قال: نابه أبو القاسم حاتم بن محمد الطرابلسي، قال: حدثنى به ابوعبد الملك مروان بن على القطان ويعرف بالبونى.

وحدثنى به ايضا ابو محمد بن عتاب، اجازة قال: حدثنى به ابوعمر بن عبد البر، رحمه الله ، اجازة قال: حدثنى به ابوجعفر احمد بن نصر الداوودى، اجازة منه لى فى جميع ما رواه وألفه رحمه الله.(١٦)

قال ابو محمد بن عتاب: وحدثنى بها ابوعمر بن عبدالبر النمرى الحافظ، قال: كتب الى احمد بن نصرالداوودى باجازة ما رواه والفه.(١٧)

وحدثنى به ايضا ابـو محمـد بـن عتـاب، عـن حـاتم بـن محمـد الطرابلسـى بسـنده المتقدم.(١٨)

تواليف احمد بن نصر الداوودى وجميع رواياته عن شيوخه، حدثنى بهـا ابومحمـد بن عتاب وابوالحسن يونس بن محمد بن مغيث رحمهما الله كلاهما عـن القـاضى ابى عمير احمد بن الحـذاء، عـن ابـى عبدالملـك مـروان بـن على القطـان البونـى، عنه.(١٩)

وحدثنى بها شيخنا الخطيب ابوالحسن شريح بن محمـد المقـرى ، عـن خالـه ابـى عبد الله احمد ابن محمد الخولانى، عن ابى عبـد الملـك مـروان بـن علـى البونـى، عنه.(٢٠)

A. *Ijāzah* for transmitting Abū Ja'far Aḥmad ibn Naṣr al-Dā'ūdī's work *Kitāb Tafsīr* ***al-Muwaṭṭa'*** known as *al-Kitāb al-Nāmī* through Abū Bakr Muḥammad ibn Aḥmad ibn Ṭahīr Abū 'Alī Ghassānī–Abū'l-Qāsim Ḥātim ibn Muḥammad al-Tarābulisī Abū 'Abd al-Mālik Marwān ibn 'Alī'l-Qaṭṭan al-Būnī.

B. *Ijāzah* for all of his works as well as for all of this narrated Prophetic traditions through Abū Muḥammad ibn 'Attāb, Abū 'Umar ibn 'Abd al-Barr–Abū Ja'far Aḥmad ibn Naṣr al-Dā'ūdī.

C. And also through Abū Muḥammad ibn 'Attāb–Abū 'Umar ibn 'Abd al-Barr al-Namarī al-Ḥāfiẓ–Aḥmad ibn Naṣr al-Dā'ūdī.

D. And also through Abū Muḥammad ibn 'Attāb–Ḥāṭim ibn Muḥammad al-Ṭarābulisī–Abū 'Abd al-Mālik Marwān ibn 'Alī'l-Qaṭṭān al-Būnī.

E. And also *Ijāzah* for all of his works and the Prophetic traditions he heard from his teacher through Abū Muḥammad ibn 'Attāb and Abū'l-Ḥasan Yūnūs ibn Muḥammad ibn Mughīth–al-Qāḍī Abū 'Umar Aḥmad ibn Muḥammad ibn al-Hudhdha'–Abū 'Abd al-Malik Marwān ibn 'Alī al-Qaṭṭān al-Būnī–Abū Ja'far Aḥmad ibn Naṣr al-Dā'ūdī.

F. And also through his teacher Abū'l-Ḥasan Shurayḥ ibn Muḥammad al-Muqrī–Abū 'Abd Allāh Aḥmad ibn Muḥammad al-Khawlānī—Abū 'Abd al-Mālik Marwān ibn 'Alī al-Būnī ibn Abū Ja'far Aḥmad ibn Naṣr al-Dā'ūdī.

Besides recording the *Ijāzah,* Ibn Khayr gives an outline of al-Dā'ūdī's life-sketch; He mentions al-Dā'ūdī as a Mālikī jurist of al-Masīlah.[15] He records the testimony of Abū 'Abd al-Mālik Marwān ibn 'Alī'l-Būnī, al-Dā'ūdī's main transmitter and disciple, that he spent five long years with al-Dā'ūdī at Tripoli.[16]

The next transmitter, in the chain of *Ijāzah,* Ḥātim ibn Muḥammad al-Ṭarābulisī gives evidence to the fact that Abū Ja'far al-Dā'ūdī died in H. 402 in Tilimsān. And that al-Dā'ūdī was alive at Tilimsān when he entered the East and that he was unable to visit al-Dā'ūdī on account of difficult sea routes he had to pass by.[17] This, however, supports his earlier statement that al-Dā'ūdī lived upto H. 402 as it has been gathered from other sources that Ḥātim ibn Muḥammad undertook his journey to the East in H. 402.[18]

Abū'l-Qāsim Khalaf ibn 'Abd al-Mālik ibn Bushkuwāl, the noted biographer of al-Maghrib, records the names of as many as eight students of al-Dā'ūdī in his work entitled *Kitāb al-Ṣilah fī Ta'rikh Ā'immat al-Andalus* (The Book of Continuation in the History of the Leading Men of Spain). This work, as the author himself claims, was prepared to supplement the book, entitled *Ta'rīkh 'Ulamā' al-Andalus* (History of the Learned Men of Spain) by al-Dā'ūdī's renowned disciple, Ibn al-Faraḍī.[19]

These pupils either met al-Dā'ūdī in various parts of North Africa, namely Tripoli (Al-Ṭrābulus), al-Qayrawān, al-Masilah and al-Tilimsān or obtained *Ijāzah* from him through correspondence for transmitting his work and Prophetic traditions. These pupils of al-Dā'ūdī later on won name and fame for their knowledge and ability, and some of them even held very important official positions. Ibn Bashkuwāl added sixteen more names to the list of the pupils of al-Dā'ūdī besides the two mentioned above by Ibn Khayr and Qāḍī 'Iyāḍ, as detailed below:

1. Abū'l-Walīd 'Abd Allāh ibn Muḥammad ibn Yūsuf al-Azdī al-Ḥāfiẓ known as Ibn al-Farāḍī. (351/962–403/1013). He was a native of Cordoba. According to Ibn Bashkuwāl, he studied under al-Dā'ūdī at Qayrawān. Ibn 'Abd al-Barr was also one of his pupils.[20]

2. Another student of al-Dā'ūdī as well as the teacher of Ḥāfiẓ Ibn 'Abd al-Barr, mentioned above, was Qāḍī Abu'l-Muṭarrif 'Abd al-Raḥmān ibn Muḥammad ibn 'Īsā ibn Futys ibn Aṣbāgh (348/960–402/1012) of Cordoba. Ibn Bashkuwāl states that from among the inhabitants of Qayrawān, Abū Ja'far al-Dā'ūdī

also gave him permission for transmitting his works. In his later life, Abu'l-Muṭarrif acted as the *Qāḍī* of Cordoba. He was a great traditionist and was such prolific writer that he is said to have engaged six scribes to prepare copies of books for him.[21]

3. Abū 'Abd al-Mālik Marwān ibn 'Alī'l-Qaṭṭān known as al-Būnī (*d.* 440/1048) of Cordoba. As it has been mentioned above, Ibn Bashkuwāl also states that he undertook a journey to the East, remained with Abū Ja'far al-Dā'ūdī for five years and got hold of all the main works and Prophetic traditions he had with him. Ibn Bashkuwāl mentions that al-Būnī wrote a commentary on the *Muwaṭṭa'* of Imām Mālik known as *Fī Sharḥ al-Muwaṭṭa'*.[22] This work was probably either a replica of his teacher's work of the same name or, in a great measure, a projection of his teacher's views with which he made himself familiar during his long five-year association with him.

4. The most illustrious student of al-Dā'ūdī was al-Ḥāfiẓ Abū 'Umar Yūsuf ibn 'Abd Allāh ibn Muḥammad ibn 'Abd al-Barr ibn 'Āṣim al-Namarī (368/978–463/1071). As has been noted above, besides al-Dā'ūdī, Ibn 'Abd al-Barr studied also at the feet of the two pupils of al-Dā'ūdī, namely, Abū 'l-Walīd ibn al-Faraḍī and Qāḍī Abū'l-Muṭarrif. The bibliographist, Ibn al-Khayr also agrees with Ibn Bashkuwāl in stating that Ḥāfiẓ Ibn 'Abd al-Barr was able to acquire permission for transmitting Abū Ja'far al-Dā'ūdī's works and Prophetic traditions he heard from his teacher.[23]

5. Abū Ja'far Aḥmad ibn Muḥammad ibn Muḥammad ibn 'Ubaydah al-Umawī, known as Ibn Maymūn (353/946–400/1010) of Toledo. In 380/991, he along with his friend Abū Isḥāq Ibrāhīm ibn Shinẓīr went on pilgrimage and at Masīlah he sat at the feet of Abū Ja'far al-Dā'ūdī to learn from him. Soon after acquainting himself with knowledge, he returned to Toledo where he settled down permanently to disseminate knowledge. Ibn Bashkuwāl acclaims him as a great scholar, narrator of Prophetic traditions, authority on the views of Imām Mālik and his followers, and a very careful writer leaving little scope for mistakes in his works; and as such, Ibn Bashkuwāl mentions his works as well as those of his friend Ibn Shinẓīr as the most authentic in Toledo.[24]

6. Another student of al Dā'ūdī who rose to prominence was

Abū'l-Muṭarrif 'Abd al-Raḥmān ibn Sa'īd ibn George (368/979–439/1048) of Cordoba. In 399/1009, he moved to the East, performed pilgrimage and on his way back he studied under al-Dā'ūdī at Qayrawān. Upon his return to Cordoba, he served as a member of Advisory Council of the then Government at Cordoba.[25]

7. Abū'l-'Abbās Aḥmad ibn Ayyūb ibn Abu'l-Rabī' al-Bīrī al-Wā'iẓ (360/971–432/1041). He hailed from al-Bīrah but settled down at Cordoba. On his way to pilgrimage he, too, met al-Dā'ūdī at Qayrawān and studied with him. Ibn Bashkuwāl mentions him as a learned scholar as well as a good preacher. He used to deliver sermons at the congregational mosque of Cordoba which attracted a large number of audience, and hence, his epithet *al-Wā'iẓ*.[26]

8. Another student of al-Dā'ūdī who served as a member of the Advisory Council was Abū'l-Qāsim Aṣbāgh ibn Faraj ibn Fārisal-Ṭāyī (*d.* 400/1010) of Cordoba. According to Ibn Bashkuwāl while acting as a member of Advisory Council to the then Government of Cordoba, he proved himself very intelligent, well versed in law, and an authority on the school of Imām Mālik.[27]

9. Abū'l-Walīd Hishām ibn 'Abd al-Raḥmān ibn 'Abd Allāh (*d.* 428/1037), known as Ibn al-Sābūnī of Cordoba.[28]

10. Abū 'Abd al-Mālik Rāshid ibn Ibrāhīm ibn 'Abd Allāh ibn Ibrāhīm ibn Rāshid (*d.* 404/1014) of Cordoba.[29]

11. Abū'l-Ḥasan Kāmil ibn Aḥmad ibn Yūsuf al-Qādisī known as Ibn al-Afṭas (*d.* 430/1039). He hailed from Cadiz but settled down at Seville. Like others, he left for the East and narrated the Prophetic traditions from many traditionists including Abū Ja'far al-Dā'ūdī.[30]

12. Abū Muḥammad 'Abd al-Raḥmān ibn 'Abd Allāh ibn Khāliṣ al-Umawī of Toledo.[31]

13. Abū 'l-Qāsim Aḥmad ibn Muḥammad ibn Mallās al-Fazārī of Seville (370/981–436/1044).[32]

14. Abū 'Umar Aḥmad ibn Sa'īd ibn 'Alī al-Anṣārī al-Qanāṭīrī known as Ibn al-Ḥajjāl of Cadiz (368/979–428/1037).[33]

15. Abū Bakr Aḥmad ibn Muḥammad ibn Ismā'īl ibn Sa'īd al-Qaysī, known as al-Sibtī (349/961–429/1038).[34]

16. Aḥmad ibn Muḥammad ibn Yaḥyā al-Qarashī al-Umawī, known as Ibn al-Ṣiqillī (360/971–419/1028) of Qayrawān.[35]

17. Abū 'l-Walīd Ḥayyūn ibn Khaṭṭāb ibn Muḥammad ibn 'Uthmān al-Kāla'ī of Toledo.[36]

18. Abū 'l-Walīd Ḥajjāj ibn Muḥammad ibn 'Abd al-Mālik ibn Ḥajjāj al-Lakhmī al-Marlishī (369/980–429/1038) of Seville.[37]

Imām Burhān al-Dīn Ibrāhīm ibn 'Alī ibn Muḥammad ibn Farḥūn (720/1321–790/1397) also records details of the life, activities and works of al-Dā'ūdī. In his *al-Dībāj al-Mudhahhab fī Ma'rifat A'yān 'Ulamā' al-Madhhab* (The Golden Brocade on the Knowledge of the Leading Scholars of the School), which he prepared as a biographical work on the leading jurists with special reference to the scholars of the Mālikī school of law. He repeats, almost in the same language, all the details of the life and career of al-Dā'ūdī as given by Qāḍī 'Iyāḍ.[38] Among his writings, Ibn Farḥūn mentions, among others, the following works:[39]

1. *Al-Nāmī fī Sharḥ al-Muwaṭṭa'*
2. *Al-Wā'yī fī 'l-Fiqh*
3. *Al-Naṣiḥah fī Sharḥ al-Bukhārī*
4. *Al-Īḍāḥ fī 'l-Radd 'alā 'l-Qadarīyyah.*

According to Ibn Farḥūn, Abū 'Abd al-Mālik al-Būnī and Abū Bakr ibn Muḥammad ibn Abū Zayd transmitted (*ḥadīth* and his works) from al-Dā'ūdī.[40] Out of these two pupils of al-Dā'ūdī, the former has already been mentioned by Ibn Khayr and Ibn Bashkuwāl and the latter by Qāḍī 'Iyāḍ.[41]

In the light of the above discussion, the life-sketch of al-Dā'ūdī stands as follow: His full name was Imām Abū Ja'far Aḥmad ibn Naṣr al-Dā'ūdī al-Asadī al-Mālikī. He belonged to Banū Asad of north Arabian origin, the scions of which had settled in North Africa. The date of his birth is not known but it can be surmised from the date of the birth of his pupils that he was born in the early half of the fourth century Hijrah.

Among his pupils, we find Abū'l-Muṭarrif 'Abd al-Raḥmān ibn Muḥammad ibn 'Īsā ibn Fuṭys ibn Asbagh ibn Fuṭys ibn Sulaymān (348/960–402/1037) and Abū'l-Walīd 'Abd Allāh ibn Muḥammad ibn Yūsuf al-Azadī (351/962–403/1013). Thus it can be concluded that they were born in the first half of the fourth century Hijrah and the teacher al-Dā'ūdī must have been mature and senior in age at that time. Most probably, he was born at al-Masīlah, the modern M'sila, of eastern Algiers as his biographers, Ibn Khayr and Qāḍī 'Iyāḍ mention him as hailing from al-Masīlah.[42] He travelled extensively throughout northern Africa and lived in different parts of North Africa such as Tripoli, Qayrawān, etc., where his pupils met him, learned from him and obtained from him *Ijāzah* for transmitting his own works as well as Prophetic traditions. However, he spent the last days of his life at Tilimsān, the modern Tlemcen of western Algiers, and died there in 402/1011.

It is however strange that one could become such a great scholar and authority on a school of law without sitting at the feet of any great teacher or going through a regular course of formal instruction. But this was what exactly happened with our author, Abū Ja'far al-Dā'ūdī. He earned such fame as a scholar and teacher that the promising students, who themselves achieved prominance later, crowded around him to listen to his lectures and to obtain *Ijāzah* for transmitting his works and Prophetic traditions on his authority.

Among his pupils, for example, was the famous traditionist of al-Maghrīb, Ḥāfiẓ Ibn 'Abd al-Barr, the historian Ḥāfiẓ Abū'l-Walīd ibn al-Faraḍī, Qāḍī Abū 'l-Muṭarrif and Abū al-Mālik Marwān ibn 'Alī al-Qaṭṭān al-Būnī. Al-Būnī took so much trouble in learning from him that he spent five long years of his life in al-Dā'ūdī's association. Here is the list of those who studied with him or transmitted on his authority.

1. Abū 'l-Walīd 'Abd Allāh ibn Muḥammad ibn Yūsuf al-Azadī, known as Ibn al-Faraḍī (351/962–403/1013).

2. Qāḍī Abū'l-Muṭarrif 'Abd al-Raḥmān ibn Muḥammad ibn 'Īṣā ibn Futys ibn Aṣbagh (348/960–402/1012).

3. Al-Ḥāfiẓ Abū 'Umar Yūsuf ibn 'Abd Allāh ibn Muḥammad ibn 'Abd al-Barr 'Āṣim al-Namarī (368/978–463/1071).

4. Abū 'Abd al-Mālik Marwān ibn 'Alī al-Qaṭṭān al-Būnī (*d.* 440/1048).

5. Abū Ja'far Aḥmad ibn Muḥammad ibn Muḥammad ibn 'Ubaydah al-Umawī, known as Ibn Maymūn (353/964–400/1010).

6. Abū'l-Muṭarrif 'Abd al-Raḥmān ibn Sa'īd ibn George

(368/979–439/1048).

7. Abū 'l-'Abbās Aḥmad ibn Ayyūb ibn Abū 'l-Rabi'ī al-Bīrī al-Wā'iẓ (360/971–432/1041).

8. Abū'l-Qāsim Aṣbagh ibn Faraj ibn Fāris al-Ṭāy'ī (*d*. 400/1010).

9. Abū'l-Walīd Hishām ibn 'Abd al-Raḥmān ibn 'Abd Allāh, known as Ibn al-Sabūnī (*d*. 428/1037).

10. Abū 'Abd al-Mālik Rāshid ibn Ibrāhīm ibn 'Abd Allāh ibn Ibrāhīm ibn Rāshid (*d*. 404/1014).

11. Abū'l-Ḥasan Kāmil ibn Aḥmad ibn Yūsuf al-Qādisī, known as Ibn al-Afṭas (*d*. 430/1039).

12. Abū Muḥammad 'Abd al-Raḥmān ibn 'Abd Allāh ibn Khāliṣ al-Umawī.

13. Abū 'l-Qāsim Aḥmad ibn Muḥammad ibn Mallās al-Fazārī (370/981–435/1044).

14. Abū 'Umar Aḥmad ibn Sa'īd ibn 'Alī al-Anṣārī al-Qanātrī, known as Ibn al-Ḥajjāl (368/979–428/1037).

15. Abū Bakr Aḥmad ibn Muḥammad ibn Ismā'īl ibn Sa'īd al-Qaysī known as al-Sibtī (349/961–429/1038).

16. Aḥmad ibn Muḥammad ibn Yaḥyā al-Qarashī al-Umawī, known as al-Ṣiqillī (360/971–419/1028).

17. Abū'l-Walīd Ḥayyūn ibn Khaṭṭāb ibn Muḥammad ibn 'Uthmān al-Kalā'ī.

18. Abū'l-Walīd Ḥajjāj ibn Muḥammad ibn 'Abd al-Mālik ibn Ḥajjāj al-Lakhmī al-Marlishī (369/980–429/1038).

19. Abū Bakr ibn Muḥammad Abū Zayd.

20. Abū 'Alī ibn al-Raffā.

Works

The sources at hand have so far revealed only seven works of al-Dā'ūdī. The work under study entitled *Kitāb al-Amwāl* is preserved in the Escurial Library, Madrid, as MS No. 1165.[43] That the work *Kitāb al-Amwāl* was extant and known to his contemporary and later scholars is obvious from the fact that constant use was made of the work by the scholar like Qāḍī Ibn Rushd (450/1059–520/1126) who mentioned this work of al-Dā'ūdī by name and referred to some of his views from *Kitāb al-Amwāl.*[44] Of all the works of al-Dā'ūdī, Brockelmann mentioned only *al-Nāmī fī Sharḥ al-Muwaṭṭa'*.[45]

Here is a list of the works of Abū Ja'far al-Dā'ūdī.

1. *Kitāb al-Amwāl.*
2. *Al-Nāmī fī Sharḥ al-Muwaṭṭa'* or *Kitāb Tafsīr al-Muwaṭṭa'*.
3. *Al-Wā'yī fī 'l-Fiqh.*
4. *Al-Naṣīḥah fī Sharḥ al-Bukhārī.*
5. *Al-Iḍāḥ fī 'l-Radd 'ala'l-Qadarīyyah.*
6. *Kitāḥ al-'Uṣūl.*
7. *Kitāb al-Bayān.*

III. THE MANUSCRIPT

The text of *Kitāb al-Amwāl* has been established in accordance with a unique manuscript preserved in the Escurial Library, Madrid, under the title "Kitāb fīhi'l Amwāl": MS No. 1165. Although the work has been mentioned by the scribe[46] on the title page of the MS as "Kitāb fīhi'l-Amwāl", the author's contemporary, near contemporary, and later scholars such as Qāḍī Ibn Rushd (450/1050–1126), Qāḍī 'Iyāḍ (476/1084–544/1150) and 'Al-lāmah al-'Uqbānī al-Tilimsānī (*d.* 871/1467) have described the work as *Kitāb al-Amwāl.*[47] As the citations of the above-mentioned authors correspond to the present MS, this apparent discrepancy of the titles is immaterial and hence the two slightly variant titles, *Kitāb fīhi'l-Amwāl* and *Kitāb al-Amwāl*, should be regarded as relating to the one and the same work of al-Dā'ūdī.

As no other copy of the Manuscript has so far been traced, the Escurial MS stands unique and very valuable. An attempt has been made to decipher the work from the photocopies of the single Manuscript and edit the Arabic text by collating it with the Prophetic traditions, parallel passages found in *al-Mudawwanah* of Saḥnūn al-Tanūkhī, *Kitāb al-Muqaddimāt* of Ibn Rushd, *Kitāb al-Kharāj* of Abū Yūsuf and that of Yaḥyā ibn

Ādam, *Kitāb al-Amwāl* of Abū 'Ubayd and that of Abū Aḥmad Ḥumayd ibn Zanjwayh (MS), *Kitāb al-Umm* of Imām Shāfi'ī, and the commentary of Qur'ān by al-Qurṭubī and so on.

These early works preceded our author and were consulted by him. Again, the names, places, and details of the events mentioned in the work have been verified with the help of the early biographical dictionaries and works on geography and history. A small portion of the work covering from folios 17a to 22a of the Manuscript and dealing with the land settlements in Ifriqiyyah, Spain and Sicily "Dhir Ifrīqiyyah wa'l-Andalus wa Ṣiqilliyyah" appeared in *Études D' Orientalisme Dedicés a La Mémoire De Lévi-Provençal* (Paris, 1962), Tome II, pp. 401–444, with French translation and brief introduction.

By collating the Manuscript with the published portion of the text, a number of errors and omissions have been detected as recorded below:

1.	p. 409	بأيدى مالكها	for	بأيدى مالكيها
2.	p. 409	أن يمسلوا	for	أن يسلموا
3.	p. 410	أعطاهم أولا	for	أعطى هاولاء
4.	p. 412	دمشنو	for	دمشق
5.	p. 415	أفاء الله	for	أفاءه الله
6.	p. 415	فمن ياكل	for	فهل يوكل
7.	p. 415	بقدره بقده	for	بقدره
8.	p. 415	ففشوا	for	فبثوا
9.	p. 420	سرقوسة	for	سوسة
10.	p. 421	الانتقال	for	الزوال
11.	p. 422	وان لم يثبة	for	وان لم يثبت
12.	p. 422	أنه لا يختلق	for	أنه لا يختلف
13.	p. 423	الانتفاع	for	الا الانتفاع
14.	p. 423	أو يبيح له السكنى وأكل الثمرة	for	أو يبيح له السكنى أو الازدراع أو أكل الثمرة

15.	p. 424	تعسيرها	for	تعميرها
16.	p. 424	يقضى له	for	يقضى لك
17.	p. 425	سنها	for	سكنها
18.	p. 426	الاسترداد	for	الاشتراء

On p. 247, the editor has omitted the sentence:

فما كان على المكروه فاشتراء مارفع منه مكروه.

The text consists of fifty-five folios having twenty-three lines a page except the title page and the last one. The title page contains only four lines whereas the last page has seven lines including the colophon. The cataloguer of the Escurial Library has described the MS in Latin in about nineteen lines which have been placed in the Appendix.

The title page indicates the name of the book and that of the author as follows:

كتاب فيه الاموال تصنيف الامام العالم الفقيه الأعرف أبى جعفر أحمد بن نصر الداوودى المالكى رضى الله عنه وأرضاه.

The colophon reveals that the work was completely transcribed by Muḥammad ibn Muḥammad ibn ʻAbd al-Raḥmān al-Maghīlī, for himself on Saturday the 23rd Ṣafar, H. 677.

"كمل الكتاب بحمد الله وعونه والصلوة على محمد نبيه وعبده. وكان الفراغ من نسخة نفع الله به فى يوم السبت الثالث والعشرين لشهر صفر عام سبعة وسبعين وستمائة. ابتداه بالنسخ لنفسه واكمل له محمد بن محمد بن عبدالرحمن المغيلى.

However, it is not known whether the scribe copied from the author's script or from some other copies. It is evident that the work was collated with the original copy by the scribe himself as there are corrections and alterations on the margin by the same hand. The scribe possesses an expert hand in the art of calligraphy and has transcribed the work very carefully and clearly in the Maghribī script as indicated by the peculiar characters of *Fā*, *qāf*, and *Ṭā* etc.

As it is the old practice of writing, the final(ء)' preceded by vowel is generally omitted and *alif* is used in place of *yā* in the final radical of the verb, for example; (ما) for (ماء) (جا) for (جاء) ، (شى) for (شئ) ، (بي) for (مئ) ، (أعطا) for (أعطى) etc. Likewise (ياء اللينة) is used for (همزة) in the middle of the words, for example, (سيل) for (سئل) and (ساير) for (سائير)

In some other places the scribe has very generously added diacritical marks and letter symbols under the corresponding letters to facilitate correct and fluent reading, for example:

(a)	سَبَقَ فِي عِلمِهِ	(fo. 1. b)
(b)	الحشـر	(fo. 6. a)
(c)	اصحاب	(fo. 11. a)
(d)	صلحـا	(fo. 43. b)
(e)	عددا	(fo. 44. a)
(f)	لايعلمون	(fo. 44. b)
(g)	على	(fo. 55. b)
(h)	بحمدالله	(fo. 55. b)
(i)	عونه	(fo. 55. b)

As the Manuscript is very old and was transcribed in H. 677, i.e., 275 years after the death of the author. Some portions of the work have been damaged or faded owing to exposure to sunrays, moisture etc. An attempt has been made to supply the damaged portions with the help of parallel passages and words available in the relevant literature or according to the theme of the context.

For example:

(a)	ثريد مع	(fo. 27 a)
(b)	فدخل عمر	(fo. 27 a)
(c)	ولما جاءه الوفاة	(fo. 28a–28b)
(d)	فاتوه اثنى عشر	(fo. 28 b)
(e)	فالله لخليفة عليكم	(fo. 28 b)
(f)	وأتته امرأة	(fo. 28 b)

(g)	فاخذته رعدة من	(fo. 29 a)
(h)	حتى سقط. فلما خرج قيل له: لو	(fo. 29 b)
(i)	مالك ان عندى	(fo. 29 a, 29 b)
(j)	لمن يليه انى لأرجو	(fo. 30 b)
(k)	يديـه	(fo. 55 b)

The text seems to have some errors committed by the scribe or have been carried from the original copy from which the text was copied. Certain personal names, places, events as well as some views held by some scholars of other schools of law especially those of Imām Shāfi'ī,[48] have not been accurately mentioned in the text. A good number of such errors have been corrected and the versions of the manuscripts have been mentioned in the notes. To illustrate further, a few examples with correct versions are given below:

	MS version	correct version	folio
1.	الذى الذى	الذى	(1–b)
2.	القرى القريبة	القرى العربية	(2–b)
3.	ألم أف لك	ألم (أقل) أف لك	(3–b)
4.	عمـر	أبوبكر	(4–b)
5.	فقال لى المرأة	فقال (هب) لى المرأة	(5–b)
6.	فقلت: ما كشفت لها عن ثوب فبعث بها.	فقلت: ما كشفت لها عن ثوب (فقلت هى لك يا رسول الله قال)فبعث بها.	(5–a)
7.	وهى هذا	ومعنى هذا	(5–b)
8.	صدق يابرسول الله	صدق يارسول الله	(6–a)
9.	سهيل ابن حنيف	عثمان بن حنيف	(9–b)
10.	الدمار	الأسرى	(15–a)
11.	الكرنيين	الكركنيتين	(19–a)
12.	كركنيت	كركنت	(19–b)

13.	لايعدر	لا يعدو	(21–a)
14.	عمـر	ابن عوف	(14–a)
15.	عليها	عليهما	(26–b)
16.	فقالت	فقال	(27–a)
17.	الخون	الخزر	(30–b)
18.	بنو قريضة	بنو قريظة	(30–b)
19.	عثمان	ثابت بن قيس بن شماس	(30–b)
20.	أم الزبير	أم (ابن) الزبير	(33–a)
21.	يدعوا	يدعو	(35–b)
22.	ببنا	بأبنى	(36–b)
23.	بنو النظير	بنو النضير	(38–a)
24.	بالاستيناف	بالاستيلاف	(38–b)
25.	من باع عبد	من باع عبدا	(40–b)
26.	اعتق بعض عبدا	اعتق بعض عبد	(40–b)
27.	كالصدقة التطوع	كصدقة التطوع	(41–a)
28.	فيختار بها	فيختار (رَ) بها	(41–b)
29.	الزكاة الفطر	زكاة الفطر	(42–b)
30.	فان تبتم	وان تبتم	(48–b)
31.	التباعات	ألتباعات	(48–b)
32.	زمنـه	منه	(50–b)
33.	ولا روى أنه	وما روى أنه	(51–a)
34.	ورى مالك	و راىٔ مالك	(51–a)
35.	ويعفوا	ويعفو	(51–a)
36.	بنوا هاشم	بنوهاشم	(52–a)
37.	بيلو	يبلو	(52–b)

38.	ثقت	ثبت	(54–b)
39.	كان ذكرناه	كنا ذكرناه	(54–b)
40.	ولا سكحان	ولا يكون	(55–a)

There still remain some lacunae and illegible words here and there in the Arabic text which have been retained hoping that they may be restored afterwords.

The work consists of four parts (أجزاء) roughly divided into twenty-six chapters (فصول), each beginning with the word *Dhikr*. Fos. 1–b–2–a contain the Preamble.

Fos. 2a–14a supply first part of the work dealing with the subjects such as the rules of the apportionment of war booties, settlements of lands in the conquered territories, laws of granting lands as well as principles of reclaiming waste-lands, limitation of private lands for agricultural, residential and irrigational purposes and also the details of the lands on which *Kharāj* and *'Ushr* were levied.

Fos. 14a–29b form the second part and relate to the precepts of granting stipends during the time of the Prophet, Abū Bakr and introduction of register (*Dīwān*) during the times of 'Umar, definition of the terms, *al-Anfāl, al-Fay', al-Ghanīmah, Jizyah, 'Ushr, Kharāj,* author's verdicts on settlements of lands in Ifrīqiyyah, Spain and Sicily, and precepts of the administration of usurped properties with special reference to the practice of the Prophet, his immediate Caliphs, and views of the close Companions of the Prophet.

Fos. 29b–43b constitute the third part. The fos. 29b–37b are devoted to the general laws of war and peace, whereas fos. 37b–43b relate to *Zakāh* beneficiaries, minimum amount liable for *Zakāh* (*Niṣāb*), rates, *Zakāt al-Fiṭr* and other dues according to properties.

Fos. 29b–55b contain the fourth part dealing with different topics; chapter I is related to the author's verdicts on administration of properties of al-Maghrib, both lawful and unlawful, while the second chapter deals with the practice of begging, and the third chapter discusses, in the light of the Qur'ān and Prophetic traditions, the three economic conditions of human life viz. poverty, self-sufficiency and prosperity.

IV. INFLUENCE OF *KITĀB AL-AMWĀL* ON OTHER WORKS

Of all the works of al-Dā'ūdī, so far known, only the present work has survived. The earliest author to refer to this work, is Qāḍī Abū'l-Walīd Muḥammad ibn Aḥmad ibn Rushd (450/1059–520/1126). In his monumental work on Mālikī *fiqh* entitled *Kitāb al-Muqaddimāt al-Mumahhadāt li Bayān ma iqtaḍathu Rusūm al-Mudawwanah min al-Aḥkām al-Shar'iyyah wa 'l-Taḥṣīlāt al-Muḥkamāt li Ummahāti Masā'iliha' Mushkilāt* (which he, in fact, prepared for explaining the difficult, etymological and legal problems arising out of *al-Mudawwanah,* the fundamental Mālikī legal work of the third century Hijrah). Qāḍī Ibn Rushd made use of this work of al-Dā'ūdī for analysing and elaborating the authentic Mālikī points of view.

As it has been pointed out in the notes of Arabic text, Qāḍī Ibn Rushd refers to al-Dā'ūdī's *Kitāb al-Amwāl* in as many as nine places. Of these, he mentions its name in three places, and in other six places he either quotes almost verbatim from *Kitāb al-Amwāl* or gives its ideas without mentioning his source. A thorough examination of the sections of *Kitāb al-Muqaddimāt* under the heading 'Kitāb al-Jihād': (i) Faṣl fi'l Qawl fi'l Ghanīmah,[49] (ii) Faṣl fi'l-Ḥukm fi'l-Asrā,[50] Kitāb kirā' al-Dūr,[51] and Kitāb al-Zakāt al-Qawl fī Zakāt al-Qirāḍ,[52] dealing with the apportionment of booties of war, the treatment of war captives, discourses on *Jizyah, Zakāh* and the problems of leasing the houses of Makkah on rent, reveals how much Qāḍī Ibn Rushd relies on Abū Ja'far al-Dā'ūdī's *Kitāb al-Amwāl.*

The next author who cites this work of al-Dā'ūdī is the commentator of the Qur'ān, Abū 'Abd Allāh Muḥammad ibn Aḥmad al-Anṣārī al-Qurṭubī (*d* . 671/1273). In his noted *Tafsīr,* this great Mālikī commentator of the Qur'ān of al-Maghrib thus makes use of *Kitāb al-Amwāl* when he comments upon the relevant verses of the Qur'ān. He quotes almost verbatim long passages from al-Dā'ūdī's *Kitāb al-Amwāl* on a number of occasions, such as:

(*a*) Discussing Imām Shāfi'ī's views concerning the nature of division of the booties of war acquired without fighting.[53]

(*b*) Asserting that the verses of *al-Ḥashr* are not conjoined with one another.[54]

(*c*) Analysing the historical decision of 'Umar to retain the landed properties acquired by conquest for the next generations.[55]

Another eminent jurist of al-Maghrib who refers to this work is Abū 'Abd Allāh Muḥammad ibn Aḥmad Qāsim ibn Sa'īd al-'Uqbānī al-Tilimsānī (*d.* 871/1467). In his work, *Kitāb Tuḥfat al-Nāẓir wa ghunyat al-Dhākir fī Ḥifẓ al-Sha'āyir wa Taghyīr al-Manākir,* he quotes al-Dā'ūdī's views taken from this work to elucidate different juridical problems from the Mālikī point of view. He reiterates the views of al-Dā'ūdī in two cases, such as (*i*) assigning the landed properties left in the conquered territories to others[56] and (*ii*) confirming the proprietary rights of the occupants of the lands in al-Maghrib on the statements of the local people.[57]

These facts prove conclusively that Abū Ja'far Aḥmad ibn Naṣr al-Dā'ūdī's *Kitāb al-Amwāl* was widely studied by the scholars and jurists of al-Maghrib and was used as an authentic reference book of Mālikī law for about five hundred years after the death of our author.

V. THE SUBJECT

The book is divided into four parts which in all consist of twenty-eight chapters. The first part contains ten chapters, the second part four, the third part eleven and the fourth part three chapters. The book opens with a preamble which shows the methodology adopted by the author in his juristic treatment of the problems concerning acquisition and appropriation of properties.

To begin with, he pays homage to Allāh and implores Divine blessings and mercy for the Prophet and his family. He then refers to Allāh as the source of all power and embodiment of justice. He quotes a number of verses from the Qur'ān in which Allāh directs the believers to do justice among themselves in respect of their lives, honour and properties. "Allāh commands us", he quotes the Qur'ān, "to obey the Prophet and forbids us to disobey him".

He then goes on to refer to the Prophet's last sermon during the Farewell Pilgrimage in which he declared: "Verily your blood, honour and properties are inviolable to you like the reverence for this day of yours in this month of yours and in this city of yours. So do not turn disbelievers after me smitting the necks of one another." Al-Dā'ūdī, then concludes the chapter projecting the view that lives, properties and honour, except with any lawful authority, are inviolable in accordance with the Qur'ān, *Sunnah* and the consensus of the community.

Part One begins with the rules of the apportionment of the spoils of war which the author mentions as "the properties that fall into the hands of the rulers who possess them for the people". Chapters I–IV deal with the problems of apportioning the booties, distribution of one-fifth of the booty, the method of apportionment of additional shares before or after the war, the definition of the "near relatives" and the details of what was done with the Prophet's properties after his death.

Chapter V, VI and VII cover the settlements of lands in the conquered territories and determination of status of the local people there. In finding out the legal rules of the spoils of war, movable and immovable, al-Dā'ūdī examines elaborately the relevant verses of the Qur'ān, the practices of the Prophet, the decisions of the Four Caliphs immediately after him, the views of his Companions and also the opinions of the early jurists like Imām Abū Ḥanīfah, Imām al-Shāfi'ī, Qāḍī Ismā'īl ibn Isḥāq, Abū 'Ubayd and others.

His critical study of the Qur'ānic verses in the chapter *al-Anfāl*, which lay down rules for the apportioning *al-Ghanīmah,* and those of the chapter *al-Ḥashr* which deal with the disposal of *al-Fay,* lead him to conclude that the relevant verses in these two chapters indicate the same principle of apportionment of spoils of war, whether they were movable or not.

He therefore rejects the idea that the verses in *al-Ḥashr* abrogate those of *al-Anfāl* and hence he refuses to accept new principle of apportionment of spoils of war as different from those contained in *al-Anfāl.* And, likewise, he does not agree with the view that the verses in *al-Ḥashr* are conjoined with one another and as such, disapproves of the practice of retaining the lands of the conquered territories for the next generation without apportioning them among the fighting soldiery. Even al-Dā'ūdī does not agree on principle with the view of 'Umar, the Second Caliph, who, when determined to retain the lands of the conquered territories in the hands of the tillers of the lands, in Iraq, Syria and Egypt, is reported to have interpreted that the verses in *al-Ḥashr* such as– " والذين جاؤا من بعدهم " i.e. "And those who come after them" (59:10) are conjoined with the preceding verses and reserved thereby the right of the coming generations in the conquered lands. Al-Dā'ūdī's arguments may be summed up as follows:

First, the interpretation of 'Umar does not hold good, because the verses in *al-Ḥashr* are independent and are not conjoined with one another.

Secondly, the above interpretation of the verses in *al-Ḥashr* contradicts the rules of distribution of booties as contained in the verses of *al-Anfāl* and followed in practice by the Prophet at Khaybar. Hence, the above interpretation is not valid.

Thirdly, 'Umar's decision to retain the lands on the basis of the above interpretation may not be accepted as argument, because, the senior Companions of the Prophet like Ṭalḥah, al-Zubayr, 'Abd al-Raḥmān ibn 'Awf, Bilāl and others opposed his interpretation and insisted on distributing the lands according to the verses of *al-Anfāl* as well as those of *al-Ḥashr* without taking resort to any interpretation.

Fourthly, in fact, 'Umar acted upon the verses of *al-Anfāl,* and in the conquered lands he recognised the proprietory right therein of the fighting soldiers. He, however, retained the lands in the hands of the tillers to meet the state expenses, both civil and military, after long consultation with the representatives of the *Muhājirūn* and *Anṣār*——the real owners of the lands. He thus took away the lands from them in exchange for something or without anything as the cases might be. So according to al-Dā'ūdī, the lands in the conquered territories may either be apportioned among the fighting soldiers as the verses of *al-Anfāl* and *al-Ḥashr* indicate, or they may be retained for the benefit of the people on their consent, as 'Umar did.

This juridical analysis of al-Dā'ūdī vis-a-vis 'Umar's historical decision was not only novel but was hailed as useful contribution to the commentary of the Qur'ān. To cite, but one example, al-Qurṭubī, the great Mālikite commentator of the Qur'ān, was so much influenced by this interpretation of al-Dā'ūdī that he, while commenting on the relevant verses of *al-Ḥashr,* accepted al-Dā'ūdī's interpretation. He incorporated in his own commentary of the Qur'ān long passages almost verbatim from the work under reference.[58]

Chapter VIII discusses mainly the laws of assigning lands and reclaiming the wastelands. The Prophet and the Caliphs after him assigned lands to the people out of the lands owned by the State or out of the wastelands which had no owners. However, according to al-Dā'ūdī, the objects of common utility such as flowing water, salt, the pasturing field for cattle and the firewood were not allotted by the Prophet to the individuals. As regards revival or reclamation of a 'dead' land, the reclaimer has the right to own the cultivated land and the intruder does not have any right to it.

Chapter IX defines the limitations of private and collective property. On the basis of Prophetic traditions, al-Dā'ūdī holds that one can not lawfully own a vast property which would do harm to others. The following resources are to be owned collectively; (1) water (2) herbage (3) salt (4) flames of fire (5) channels of rivers and riverbeds. Again, according to the early jurists like Ibn al-Musayyib and Ibn Shihāb, privately owned wells, channels and springs have their prescribed boundaries beyond which these can not be extended.

Chapter X sums up briefly the opinions of Imām Mālik, Ibn Sīrīn, Ibn Ḥakam, Ashhab, Saḥnūn and Ibn Wahāb on purchasing *Kharāj*-lands from *Dhimmīs* and Muslims or cultivating such lands on lease. Al-Dā'ūdī disaproves of the practice of retaining the lands in the conquered territories for the benefit of the rulers without distributing these among the fighting soldiers; and he considers the transaction of all such lands as unlawful.

Chapter I of Part Two deals with the principles of disbursement of state allowances. The Prophet generally distributed booties and other state revenues on the spot as soon as these were brought to him. As the system of *Dīwān* (Register) had not come into being, in every tribe the tribal representatives (*'Arā'if*) were entrusted with the task of disbursement of revenues. They kept also the record of those who took part in wars and reported their demands and needs to the Prophet. 'Umar I introduced *Dīwān* containing the lists of the recipients of state-allowances and those of the participants in wars. The emigrants were enrolled in the *Dīwān* on the priority of their relation to the Prophet while the names of *Anṣār* were recorded on the basis of their relation to Sa'd ibn Mu'ādh.

However, in matters of disbursement of state allowances, factors such as relationship to the Prophet and services to the cause of Islam were considered. Ever since the time of the Prophet down to that of 'Umar, the revenues of the state were sound and everyone received his allowances willingly. But as soon as the caliphate shifted from the Companions of the Prophet to others, some unjust collections started pouring in to the *Bayt al-Māl,* and as such, a number of righteous people refused to accept the allowances though others accepted them on condition that the *Bayt al-Māl* should contain mostly the lawful collections.

But gradually when the collection contained mostly unlawful levies, the majority of the *'ulamā'* forbade receipt of these allowances, except, in cases when these collections were surely known as pure and when the recipients were lawfully entitled to these.

Chapter II defines the terms of *anfāl, ghanīmah,* and *'ushr,* and explains the views of Imām Mālik and the opinions of the inhabitants of Kūfah on levying *'ushr* on the lands originally known as *kharāj*-lands or on levying the same on the lands originally known as *'ushr*-lands. According to Mālikī point of view, the decision will be taken according to the classification of the tiller; in case he is a Muslim and free, he shall have to pay *'ushr* and if he is a *dhimmī* or a slave, he is not liable to pay *'ushr.* But the inhabitants of Kūfah hold that the case will be judged according to the category of the land; no *'ushr* will be levied on the *kharāj*-land, while *'ushr* will not be remitted from the *'ushr*-land no matter whether the tiller is a slave or a *dhimmī.*

Chapter III deals with the settlements of the lands in al-Ifrīqiyyah, Spain and Sicily and contains some verdicts of the author which he issued on the basis of the following considerations: (a) Nature of the conquest of these lands by the Muslims; (b) Settlements of the conquering army on the lands; (c) Landgrabbing by others; (d) Ejectment of the owners of the land;

and (e) Reclaiming the waste-lands.

As for Ifrīqiyyah, the author does not know the fact, whether the land was conquered by force, by treaty or by an agreement that the land would belong to the local people. He therefore recognises the proprietary rights of the then occupants of the lands relying on the agreed views of the neighbours to the effect that the lands were not acquired by force or by ejecting the owners.

As for the lands of Spain, the author holds that according to some people the entire country or most of it was conquered by force, but the land was not apportioned among the fighting people. After conquest, some people occupied some parts of the land forcibly without having any authorised allotment from the *Imām*, and thus no piece of land was left for the next generation of the Muslims. In a case like this, al-Dā'ūdī advises the occupants to give up their possession for the benefit of the Muslims and pay the rent of the land to the poor. But if there is none to look after these lands, they may retain these for themselves.

In some parts of Spain the Berber troops received grants of lands from the ruler in exchange for their share in booties. They lived there for a long time and afterwards were ejected by some other ruler. The author confirms the proprietary right of the Berber troops in case they got the grant according to their own rights and the rest of the army were not deprived of their shares. In case of deprivation, the share of such soldiers should be restored to them or to their heirs if they are traceable, otherwise, the lands would be treated like those of the dead whose heirs are not traceable.

However, if out of sheer injustice the lands were allotted to them disproportionate to their share, everyone should give up the possession of the surplus, provided the surplus is known. In any case, the land should be restored to the real owners of the land as discussed above. But, if the owners or their heirs, as the case may be, are not traceable, the occupied land should be treated like the property of one whose heirs are not known.

As for the conquered territories of Sicily, the author relates first the views of Imām Saḥnūn who disapproves of occupying anything of Sicily when it is known that after the conquest, the lands were neither divided into five shares nor retained for the entire Muslim community. However, the author gives different verdicts under different circumstances:

I. In the cases of the conquest of Sicily by force, the inhabitants of some fortresses surrendered to the conquering army after truce but later some of them fled away leaving behind landed properties. In such case, the author confirms the proprietary right of the lands to the remaining inhabitants on the payment of *jizyah* if they had entered into any treaty on condition that the lands would belong to them and that *jizyah* would be imposed on them. But in case of conversion to Islam the lands would belong to them and *jizyah* would be remitted from them. But if the treaty was concluded on payment of *jizyah* both on their heads and the lands they could not sell the lands, and the converts to Islam would own the land with *jizyah* and *kharāj* lapsing from them. According to the terms of former treaty, the lands should be restored to the fugitives or to their heirs if they, their heirs, and their properties are known, otherwise the properties should be treated as *fay'* which Allāh granted to the Muslims.

II. In some other parts of Sicily, where the lands and houses were known to have been retained as *waqf* (endowment) for the entire Muslim community, the author considers the sale and purchase of these as null and void, but if the lands were not retained for the Muslim community and were kept in possession as the strong people occupy the lands forcibly by usurpation without apportioning them according to the rules, the author asks the occupant to give up the possession, and hand over these to the proper authorities in favour of the Muslim community.

III. In some other cases, some Spaniards got allotment for some lands in Sicily for their participation in *Jihād* and for assisting the Muslim troops engaged in war there. But soon they fought among themselves resulting in the extermination of the Spaniards. According to al-Dā'ūdī, if the landed properties of the Spaniards are huge, the occupant should be asked to give up the possession, but if these are meagre, it is praiseworthy to do so.

However, if some one reclaims or settles therein, on lease, purchase, gift or on authorised allotment, while most of the lands belonged to the Spaniards who were not known, the property should be treated like the property of the Muslims.

IV. As to the ownerless waste-lands where the authority forced any people to settle in, the author recognises the proprietary right there of to the new settlers.

V. As for one who planted trees on the public thoroughfares or dug wells therein or turned them mortmain for the mosques, the author acknowledges the right of authority to restore these to *Bayt al-Māl* or to assign these to some other people on lease and the planter will receive only the price of the trees being felled and he shall have to pay the lease of the land for living therein as well as for deriving benefit out of these lands.

VI. The author was asked about a desolate fortress of Sicily which was conquered by the Muslims. A group of people then inhabited it without proper allotment by the then ruler. Then another group came over there from the town and turned the place into the pasture of the townspeople. The original inhabitants thereof opposed them and a war broke out among them. The ruler then came to the help of the former group and drove away the original inhabitants. But soon the former group came in conflict with the authority which ultimately resulted in their externment from the fortress. The ruler then reconstructed the fortress, brought together people from different places, forced them to settle there and assigned the lands and houses to them. The descendants of the original inhabitants known as "girgentian" as well as other people from Ifrīqiyyah came to live along with them. The girgentians then demanded the lands claiming these as their own on various grounds but as they could not produce any document of ownership, the lands were declared as public property in which they had the right of usufruct only. But soon they were externed from the place to other parts of Sicily and had to receive with reluctance only the price of the buildings and the trees being demolished and felled. In such cases, the author gives the verdict as follows:

(*a*) The proprietary right goes to the former group or to their heirs if it has been established that they reclaimed the entire fortress or most of it with a view to settling down there provided they themselves, their whereabouts as well as their inheritance are known. But if some of them are not known, their properties would be treated like the *fay'* granted by Allāh for the Muslims.

(*b*) However, if some parts were reclaimed by the former group while the other parts remained desolate, the waste-lands should belong to the aboriginal people.

However, if they themselves, their properties or their inheritance are not known, the properties again would be treated as *fay'*.

(*c*) If nothing is established and reports vary, the claims will be entertained with convincing evidences. But if the authority forced the people to settle for the benefit of the Muslims and assigned the land for the same purpose, the author considers settlement as well as allotment as lawful. Otherwise, the case is to be determined according to convincing evidences in support of their claims. However, in all such cases the properties should be restored to the real owners provided they themselves, their heirs and the properties are known, but if these facts are not known, the properties would be treated as *fay'* in which no individual can occupy any piece of land without the consent of the real owners of the land or that of the authorities concerned.

Chapter IV dwells on the broad principles of administering properties acquired through unlawful means. The properties acquired through usurpation or any other unlawful means will be treated as debt and as such, will not be subjected to the laws of inheritance. The heir cannot inherit such properties which according to the author should be restored to the claimants, and in case the claimants are not known, these should be considered as *fay'*. Throughout the chapter, the practices of the Prophet, the precepts of his Caliphs and the conduct of the Companions are elaborately discussed to illustrate the model examples of administering the unlawfully acquired properties, to show the ideals of their simple living, and to analyse their careful measures to keep under check the accumulation of wealth in the hands of the rich.

In the Part Three, chapter I–IX are concerrned with the laws of war and peace, while chapters X–XI are related to *zakāh,* its beneficiaries and rates.

Chapters I deals with the treatment of war captives and the apostates. Al-Dā'ūdī appears to be very harsh in dealing with the fighting enemies, war captives and apostates. According to him, the *Imām* cannot cease hostility and start making captives unless and until a heavy slaughter is inflicted on the side of the enemy. On setting the captives free, he recommends that the *Imām* can offer the captives as ransom only in exchange of Muslim captives. He holds that Imām Mālik and most of his followers disapprove of accepting ransom in the form of money, arguing that the Prophet did so at Badr, because he was sure of his victory over the enemies. This, however, does not appear to be a representative Mālikī view on the subject. In his *Kitāb al-Muqaddimāt,* Qāḍī Ibn Rushd quoted this view of al-Dā'ūdī, and refused to accept it as a representative Mālikī view.[59] With regard to the apostates he recommends the capital punishment—the execution. On the heretic tribes of North Africa like Barguātah, Sanhājah, Katāmah, 'Agisah and others who inherited disbelif (*kufr*) from their forefathers, he holds the *jizyah* cannot to be imposed on them. They can be made captives, and be sold out.

Chapter II is related to peace treaties. The peace treaty is to be concluded with the enemy against the amount of money or something else when the Muslim power is weak and the adjoining Muslims are unable to come to their rescue. However, when the Muslims are powerful enough and do not fear the enemy, al-Dā'ūdī does not allow the Muslims to enter into any peace treaty with the enemy. A spy, irrespective of his creed, must be put to death.

Chapter III deals with the circumstances leading to the conquest of Makkah, nature of the conquest, the Prophet's amnesty to the Makkans, leasing of houses in Makkah and sanctity of Ka'bah. Makkah was conquered by force and after the conquest the Prophet declared general amnesty to the Makkans. They were not condemned to slavery. They were asked either to accept Islam or to face execution. The properties and the houses at Makkah were not affected by the conquest. Al-Dā'ūdī further holds that according to Imām Mālik, it is undesirable to lease houses in Makkah at the time of pilgrimage.

Chapter IV discusses wages offered to the fighting army and the voluntary contributions offered to them. 'Umar introduced the system of *Dīwān* by which he maintained the record of the number of fighting individuals of every city and fixed the rates of wages for them. The civil population had to provide the fighting soldiers with the wages. Besides, the civilians sometimes offered some voluntary contributions to the soldiers.

Chapter V relates to *jizyah*, its rates fixed at the time of the Prophet and 'Umar and all about the *jizyah* levied on Banū Taghlib.

Chapter VI deals with the presents offered to the Muslim rulers by the disbelievers, punitive measures for misappropriating the spoils of war and classification of objects which the fighting soldiers are allowed to pick up from the battlefield without the permission of the *Imām*.

Chapter VII discusses how to deal with the properties of Muslims found in the spoils of war or in the possession of a convert to Islam and explains the case of a convert who finds his property which has been taken away from him as the booty in possession of a Muslim and also that of one who offered ransom for a Muslim or for a slave of a Muslim.

Chapter VIII defines the rules of dealing with the inhabitants of the enemy territory who visit the territory of the Muslims, while they hold in possession the Muslims free or slaves, and also deals with the envoys who accept Islam and want to stay in the territory of the Muslims.

Chapter IX discusses different stages of warfare such as invitation to accept Islam before waging war, mode and time of entering the enemy territory and all about guarding the frontier-towns.

Chapter X dwells on the obligatory character of *Zakāh* and defines different kinds of beneficiaries of *Zakāh*.

Chapter XI is related to the classification of the properties liable to *Zakāh*, the rates of *Zakāh*, details of *Zakāt al-Fiṭr* and all other dues accruing from the properties.

Part four contains three chapters each dealing with different subjects; Chapter I deals with the administration of lawful and unlawful properties in North Africa (al-Maghrib). As said above in Chapter III of Part II, al-Dā'ūdī confirms the proprietary right of the lands in al-Maghrib to their occupants on the consensus of the local people of the area to the effect that these occupants acquired these lands by the usual way of ownership and made all sorts of transactions therein as the owners of the lands would do in their own lands.

But about the properties known as *al-Akhmās* (assigned out of one-fifth), *al-Ṣāfiyah* (usurped by the ruler and turned into his private estate), and the properties out of which the owners had fled away because of heavy taxes, or owing to long warfare with the neighbours, al-Dā'ūdī recommends long procedures to restore the lands to the real owners or to their heirs as the case may be. But in case they or their heirs are not known, he suggests that the lands be treated as *fay'* to be used for public good.

Chapter II relates to the practice of soliciting aid (*mas'alah*) and deals with the circumstances in which solicitation of aid is allowed, forbidden and even sometimes it becomes obligatory.

Chapter III deals with the three possible economic conditions of human life, viz poverty (*faqr*), **self-sufficiency (*kafāf*) and prosperity (*ghinā'*).**

After a thorough analysis of these three stages in the light of the Qur'ān and the Prophetic traditions, al-Dā'ūdī argues in favour of self-sufficiency (*kifāf*) and regards the other two stages—poverty and prosperity—as two divine trials through which people are tested and very few from among them can overcome such trials.

NOTES AND REFERENCES

1. See Abū'l Walīd Muḥammad ibn Aḥmad ibn Rushd, *Kitāb al-Muqaddimāt al-Mumahhadāt li-Bayān mā Aqtadathu Rusūm al-Mudawwanah min al-Aḥkām al-Shar'iyyāt wa'l-Taḥṣīlāt al-Muḥkamāt li-Ummahāt Masā 'ilha'l-Mushkilāt* (Cairo, H 1352). Abū 'Abd Allāh Muḥammad ibn Aḥmad al-Anṣārī al-Qurṭubī, *al-Jāmi' li-Aḥkām al-Qur'ān* (Cairo, 1948), and Abū 'Abd Allāh Muḥammad ibn Aḥmad ibn Qāsim ibn Sa'īd al-'Uqbānī al-Tilimsānī, *Kitāb Tuḥfat al-Nāẓir wa Ghunyat al-Dhākir fī Ḥifẓ al-Sha'āyir wa Tājhyīr al-Manākir* (Damascus, 1967) (*Institute, Français de Damas, Bulletin d' études orientales*, Tome XIX Années 1965–66).

A. Ben Shemesh, *Taxation in Islam* (Leiden: E.J. Brill, 1967), vol. I, pp. 3–4.

For the list of twenty-one works see A. Ben Shemesh, *Taxation in Islam* op. cit., pp. 3–6. The titles of the works with the names of their authors are given below:

(i) Mu'āwiyah ibn 'Ubayd Allāh ibn Yasār al-Ash'arī (*d.* 170/786), *Kitāb al-Kharāj*.

(ii) Ḥafṣawayh, *Kitāb al-Kharāj*. According to A. Ben Shemesh, this name might be a corrupted form of Mu'āwiyah; mentioned above.

(iii) Abū Yūsūf Ya'qūb ibn Ibrāhīm (*d.* 182/799), *Risālah fī'l-Kharāj*.

(iv) Yaḥyā ibn Ādam (*d.* 203/819), *Kitāb al-Kharāj*.

(v) Abū 'Alī Ḥasan ibn Ziyād al-Lu'lu'ī (*d.* 204/819), *Kitāb al-Kharāj*.

(vi) Abū 'Uthmān 'Amr ibn Bahr ibn Mahbūb al-Jāḥiẓ (*d.* 255/869), *Kitāb Risālatuhu ilā Abi'l-Najam fi'i-Kharāj*.

(vii) Qāḍī Aḥmad ibn 'Umar al-Shaybānī al-Khaṣṣāf (*d.* 261/875), *Kitāb al-Kharāj li'l-Muhatadī*.

(viii) Abū 'Abbas Aḥmad ibn Muḥammad ibn Sulaymān ibn Bishr al-Kātib (*d.* 270/884), *Kitāb al-Kharāj*.

(ix) Abū 'Abbās, Aḥmad ibn Muḥammad ibn 'Abd al-Karīm, *Kitāb al-Kharāj*.

(x) Abū Sulaymān, Dā'ūd ibn 'Alī ibn Dā'ūd, ibn Khalaf al-Iṣfahānī (*d.* 270/884), *Kitāb al-Kharāj*.

(xi) Qudāmah ibn Ja'far ibn Qudāmah ibn Zayd al-Kātib (*d.* 337/948), *Kitāb al-Kharāj wa Ṣinā'at al-Kitābah*.

(xii) Abū'l Qāsim 'Ubayd Allāh ibn Aḥmad ibn Muḥammad al-Kaludhānī, *Kitāb al-Kharāj*.

(xiii) Abū'l Ḥasan, 'Alī ibn al-Ḥasan (Ibn al-Māshīṭah), *Kitāb al-Kharāj*.

(xiv) Abū'l Ḥasan 'Alī ibn Wāsif al-Kātib, *Kitāb al-Ifṣāh wa'l Tathqīf fi'l Kharāj wa Rusūmihi*.

(xv) 'Abd al-Raḥmān ibn 'Isā, *wazīr* to al-Muttaqī (330/940–333/943), *Kitāb al-Kharāj*.

(xvi) Isḥāq ibn Yaḥyā ibn Surayj al-Naṣrānī al-Kātib, *Kitāb al-Kharāj*. (Two copies).

(xvii) Nasr ibn Mūsā al-Rāzī al-Hanafī, *Kitāb al-Kharāj*.
(xviii) 'Abd Allāh ibn Abū'l-Jarrāh, Abū'l Qāsim Ibn al-Aramram, *Kitāb al-Kharāj*.
(xix) Muhammad ibn Ahmad ibn 'Alī ibn Khiyār, *Kitāb al-Kharāj*.
(xx) 'Alī ibn Ahmad ibn Bustām, *Kitāb al-Kharāj*.
(xxi) Abū'l Nadr, Muhammad ibn Mas'ūd al-'Ayyāshī, *Kitāb al-Jizyah wa'l Kharāj*

A. Ben Shemesh mentions three works besides the works mentioned above.

(i) Abū 'Ubayd al-Qāsim ibn Sallām (*d.* 224/839), ***Kitāb al-Amwāl (Ibid.*** p. 7).
(ii) Abu'l Faraj 'Abd al-Rahmān ibn Rajab al-Hanbalī (*d.* 995/1393), ***al-Istikhrāj li'-Ahkām al-Kharāj***. (*Ibid.*, vol. 11:12).
(iii) Abū Bakr al-Khallāf al-Baghdādī (*d.* 311/923), *Kitāb al-Amwāl*. (*Ibid.*, vol. 11:13).

The following three works have escaped the notice of A. Ben Shemesh.

(i) Qādī Ismā'īl ibn Ishāq (*d.* 282/895), *Kitāb al-Amwāl wa'l Maghāzī*. (See Ibn Farhūn, *al-Dibāj al-Mudhahhab* (Cairo, H 1351), p. 94; and also Ibn Khayr, *Fihrist* (Beirut, 1963), pp. 247–248.
(ii) Abū Ahmad Humāyd ibn Zanjwayh (*d.* 251/865), Al-Zāhiriyyah MS Damascus, No. Hadīth 233 (ii) Kitāb al-Amwāl', parts XIII–XIV.
(iii) Abū Ja'far Ahmad ibn Nasr al-Dā'ūdī (*d.* 402/1011), Escurial MS No. 1165, 'Kitab fini'l Amwāl'.

4. Cf. Esc. MS No. 1165 op. cit., Part Two, chapter III, fos. 17a-22 and Part Four, chapter I, fos. 43a-51a.
5. Ibn Khaldūn, *Muqaddimah*, (Cairo, H 1318) pp. 449–451.
6. *Ibid.*
7. The proverb: is widely current in al-Maghrib: see Al-Qādī 'Iyād ibn Mūsā ibn 'Iyād al-Sibtī. *Tartīb al-Madārik wa' Taqrīb al-Masālik li-Ma'rifat 'Alām Madhhab Mālik*, ed. Muhammad ibn Tāw'īt al-Tunjī (Ribāt, 1383/1965).
8. Al-Qādī 'Iyād, 'Tartīb al-Madārik Ṣadiqiyyah'. MS Grand Mosque Tunis, No. 5132, 6509–10–11, 11:286, quoted by Abdul Wahab (H.H.) and F. Dachraoui, in "Le régime, foncier en Sicile au Moyen Age (IXe Etxe Siècles). Edition et traduction d, un chapitre du "Kitāb al-Amwāl" d, al-Dā'ūdī *Etudes D, Orientalisme DÉDIÉS A LA MÉMOIRE DE LEVIP-ROVENÇAL,*" (Paris. 1962), Tome II:405.

ابو جعفر احمد بن نصر الداؤدى الأسدى : من أئمة المالكية بالمغرب ، والمتسعين فى العلم المجيدين للتأليف ، أصله من المسيلة، وقيل من بسكرة كان بطرابلس وبها أملى كتبه فى شرح الموطأ ثم انتقل الى تلمسان وكان فقهيا فاضلا عالما متفننا مؤلفا مجيداً، له حظ من اللسان والحديث والنظر.

9. *Ibid.*
10. *Ibid.* pp. 405–406. The story runs as follow:

"وبلغنى أنه كان ينكر على معاصريه من علماء القيروان سكناهم فى مملكة بنى عبيد وبقاءهم بين أظهرهم فاجابوه "اسكت لا شيخ لك" . أى لأن درسه كان وحده ولم يتفقه فى أكثر علمه عند امام مشهور و انما وصل بادراكه ، يشيرون أنه لوكان شيخ يفقهه حقيقة الفقه لعلم أن بقاءهم مع من هنالك من عامة المسلمين تثبيت لهم على الاسلام وبقية صالحة للايمان وانهم لو خرج العلماء عن افريقية لتشرق من بقى فيها من العامة آلاف آلاف، فرجحوا خيرا الشرين والله أعلم.

11. Probably, He is Abū 'Abd al-Malik Marwān ibn 'Alī 'l Qaṭṭān al-Būnī. See below.
12. Ṣādiqiyyah MS, *op. cit.*, p. 406.

13. *Ibid.* "وقرأت فى بعض التواريخ: ان وفاته كانت احدى عشرة والأول اصح".
14. Ibn Khayr, *Fihrist*, p. 6.
15. *Ibid.* p. 87.
16. *Ibid.*
17. *Ibid.*
18. Ibn Bashkuwāl, *Kitāb al-Silah*, (Cairo, 1374/1955), vol. I, p. 155.
19. *Ibid.* p. 7, 246.
20. *Ibid.* pp. 246–250.
21. *Ibid.* pp. 298–300.
22. *Ibid.* vol. II, pp. 581–582.
23. *Ibid.* pp. 640–642; and Ibn Khayr; *Kihrist*, pp. 87–88.
24. Ibn Bashkuwāl, *Kitāb al-Silah*, *op. cit.* vol. I, pp. 25–28.
25. *Ibid.* pp. 317–318.
26. *Ibid.* p. 53.
27. *Ibid.* p. 108.
28. *Ibid.* vol. II, 615.
29. *Ibid.* vol. I, p. 184.
30. *Ibid.* vol. II, p. 450.
31. *Ibid.* vol. I, p. 315.
32. *Ibid.* p. 54.
33. *Ibid.* p. 47.
34. *Ibid.* p. 50.
35. *Ibid.* p. 88.
36. *Ibid.* p. 152.
37. *Ibid.* pp. 149–150.
38. Ibn Farhūn, *al-Dibāj*, p. 35 and cf. Sādiqiyyah MS, pp. 405-406.
39. *Ibid.*
40. *Ibid.*
41. See above.
42. Ibn Khayr, *Fihrist*, p. 87 and Sādiqiyyah MS p. 406.
43. Fu'ād Sayyid, *Fihrist al-Makhṭūṭāt al-Musawwarah* (Cairo: Ma'had Ihyā' l-Makhṭuṭāt al-'Arabiyah, 1957), 1:273.
44. Below, notes nos. 55, 56, 57, 58.
45. Brockelmann: *Geschichte Der Arabischen Literatur*, Erster supplement band (Leiden: E.J. Brill, 1937), 1:298.
46. The fact that the name of the auther as well as that of the work is given by the scribe and not by the author is proved beyond doubt by the expression of honorific titles added to the name of the author on the title page of the MS:

كتاب فيه الاموال تصنيف الامام العالم الفقيه الأعرف أبى جعفر أحمد بن نصر

الداودى المالكى رضى الله عنه وأرضاه.

47. For the title of the work quoted as كتاب الاموال See Ibn Rushd, *Kitāb al-Maqadimāt*, 1:278; Ṣādiqiyyah, MS, 11:182; and al-Uqbānī al-Tilimsānī, *Kitāb Tuḥfat al-Nāẓir*, p. 188.
48. See Esc. MS, No. 1165, 2b, 3a, 40a, 42b; and cf. al-Shāfi'ī, *Kitāb al-Umm* (Cairo), IV:67 71; 11:12, 53.
49. Ibn Rushd, *Kitāb al-Muqaddimāt*, 1:269–272 and cf. Esc. MS, fos. 7a, 7b, 9a, 10a, 11b.
50. *Ibid.* 1:2781 and cf. Esc. MS, fos. 29b–30a.
51. *Ibid.* 11:341 and cf. Esc. MS, fo. 32a.
52. *Ibid.* 1:248 and cf. Esc. MS, fo. 39a.
53. Al-Qurṭubī, *al-Jām'i*, XVIII:15 and cf. Esc. MS, fos. 2b, 5b.
54. *Ibid.* XVIII: 21–22 and cf. Esc. MS, fo. 6a.
55. *Ibid.* XVIII: 22–23 and cf. Esc. MS, fos. 9a–9b.

56. Al-'Uqbānī al-Tilimsānī, *Kitāb Tuḥfāt*, p. 188 (153); cf. Esc. MS, fo. 11b.
57. *Ibid*. cf. Esc. MS, fos. 17a, 43b.
58. Above, notes nos. 59–60.
59. Ibn Rushd, *Kitāb al-Muqaddimāt*, 1:278.

PREAMBLE

*In the name of Allāh, the Beneficent, the Merciful.
And may Allāh send down blessings on our chief
Muḥammad and on his family and Companions*

Abū Ja'far Aḥmad ibn Naṣr al-Dā'ūdī al-Mālikī Says: (may God have mercy on him).

All praise belongs to Allāh, the One, Almighty, All-Powerful, the Forgiving, the King, the Omnipotent, the Creator of day and night, who made the creation out of nothing, nor after a similar thing that contained (it), nor with the help of any auxiliary or assistant who could assist Him. So every thing took its course according to the model preconceived by Him. He is the Just in His decree and the Judge in His Commandment. He has chosen Islam as a way of life (*dīn*) for His servants and has revealed a manifest Book wherein He has explained the lawful, and the unlawful (ways), laws and commandments and has warned against committing sins and made it (the Book) a guide and proof for all mankind. Falsehood cannot come at it (the Book) from before or behind. (It is) a revelation from (Allāh) the Wise and the Praiseworthy, One who gave certain instructions to His servants some of which do not admit of abrogation or alteration, nor can His commandment be changed till the Day when they are resurrected.

Islam is one of these (instructions) which means to confess belief in Allāh, in His Angels, His Books, His Messengers, and the Last Day. All that concerning which a report (knowledge) has come from Allāh, the Exalted, and is not to be abrogated, nor can His commandment prohibiting injustice be altered.

Allāh, the Exalted, says: "Lo: Allāh enjoineth justice and kindness" (16:90). And He says: "It is not for a believer to kill a believer unless (it be) by mistake," (4:92) up to His expression; "Whoso slayeth a believer of set purpose his reward is Hell" (4:93). And He says: "For that cause we decreed for the children or Israel, that whosoever killeth a human being for other than manslaughter or corruption in the earth, it shall be as if he hath killed all mankind, and whoso saveth the life of one, it shall be as if he hath saved the life of all mankind" (5:32).

So Allāh has held its punishment as well as its reward as great. He says: "And slay not the life which Allāh hath forbidden save with right" (17:33). And He says: "And kill not one another. Lo: Allāh is very Merciful unto you" (4:29), And He says: "Neither backbite one another" (49:12). He says: "Lo: as for those who traduce virtuous believing women (who are) careless, cursed are they in the World and the Hereafter (24:23), up to the end of the verse. And He says: "And eat not up your property among yourselves in vanity" (2:188).

Allāh has commanded (us) to follow His Book, and has made it a guardian on all His revealed books and has abrogated with it whatever He desired out of the previous books.

Allāh has commanded (us) to obey His Messenger and has forbidden to disobey his Commandments. He therefore says: "And this is a blessed Scripture which We have revealed. So follow it" (6:156). And he says: "Follow that which is sent unto you from your Lord" (7:3). He says: "O, ye who believe: obey Allāh and His Messenger and turn not away from him when ye hear (Him speak)" (8:20). He says: "We sent no messenger save that he should be obeyed by Allāh's leave" (4:64). He says: "whoso obeyeth the Messenger obeyeth Allāh" (4:80). He says: "And let those, who conspire to evade orders, beware, lest grief or painful punishment befall them" (24:63). He says: "And whatsoever he forbiddeth, abstain from it" (59:7), upto the end of the verse.

He says "And We have revealed unto thee the Remembrance that thou mayest explain to mankind that which hath been revealed for them, and that haply they may reflect" (16:44). He says: "Nor doth he speak of (his own) desire. It is naught save an inspiration that is inspired" (53:3–4). So the Messenger of Allāh, may Allāh bless him and keep him in peace, has explained whatever was revealed from Allāh.

He elaborated what was general, and delivered the message with which he, may Allāh bless him and keep him in peace, was sent with, gave good advice to his followers, enlightened them, gave them good tidings, cautioned them and warned them. Allāh then selected for him whatever was available to him and He took him up to Him while he was profusely praised, lamented, blessed and rightly-guided. May Allāh bless him and grant peace to him, his family, his wives and his offspring.

The Messenger of Allāh bless him and keep him in peace, said, on the sacred day in the sacred month, in the sacred city, on the day of Sacrifice, at Minā: "Verily your blood, honour and properties are inviolable to you like the inviolability of this day of yours, in this month of yours, and in this city of yours. So do not turn disbelievers after me smiting the neck of one another. Have I delivered the message? O, Allāh: You bear witness." He added: "So do not adhere to anything against me; I do not declare any thing lawful except that which has been made lawful by Allāh and I do not declare anything forbidden except that which has been prohibited by Allāh," that is to say, he does not say anything but that with which he has been commanded. So blood, properties, and honour, except with any right, are declared inviolable in accordance with the Qur'ān, *Sunnah* and the consensus (of the community) (Bukhārī, *al-Jāmi' al-Ṣaḥīḥ*, Kitāb al-Maghāzī).

PART ONE

Chapter I

ON PROPERTIES THAT FALL INTO THE HANDS OF THE RULERS WHO POSSESS THEM FOR THE PEOPLE, AND DISCUSSION OF ONE-FIFTH OF THE BOOTY (*AL-KHUMS*)

Allāh, the Exalted, says: "Lo: Allāh commandeth you that ye restore deposits to their owners" (4:58). The Messenger of Allāh (peace be upon him) says: "Many a person who meddles in the property of Allāh without any right, shall have the hell fire."* Allāh also says: "And know that whatever ye take as spoils of war, Lo: a fifth thereof is for Allāh, and for the Messenger and for the Kinsman (who hath need), and orphans and the needy, and the wayfarer" (8:41). He also says: "And that which Allāh gave as spoil unto His Messenger from them, ye urged not any horse or riding-camel for the sake thereof but Allāh giveth His Messengers lordship over whom he will" (49:6).

It was, therefore, usual with a land from which the disbelieving owners had migrated without fighting, that Allāh made it exclusive for His prophet. But the Prophet never appropriated it for himself to the exclusion of his *Ummah* and never deprived them of it. He used to take out of it the annual provision for his family and spend the rest thereof on mounts and weapons as military equipment for the cause of Allāh.

Allāh has also said: "That which Allāh giveth as spoil unto His Messenger from the People of the townships, it is for Allāh and His Messenger and for the near of kin, and the orphans and the needy and the wayfarer" (49:7) upto His expression, "they are the loyal" (49:8). So, whatever Allāh has conferred on His Messenger, as mentioned in this verse, the same as that which has been mentioned in the chapter of *al-'Anfāl*, while He has added in this verse, "For the poor fugitives who have been driven out from

* Bukhārī, *al-Ṣaḥīḥ*, Kitāb Farḍ al-Khumūs.

their homes and their belongings" (49:8) and they are the same as "the needy" mentioned in the verse of *al-Khums*.

Some people interpret (saying) that Allāh's expression, "Those who entered the city and the faith before them" (49:9) upto His expression: "And place not in our hearts any rancour toward those who believe, Our Lord, Thou art full of pity, Merciful" (49:10), is conjoined with his expression "For the poor fugitives". But the explicit meaning of the verses indicates something contrary to this interpretation, since the sentence ends with His expression *al-Mufliḥūn* "successful" (49:9) and begins again with "Those who entered the city and the faith" (49:9) and completes the statement with His expression: "They love those who flee unto them" (49:9) with which the sentence ends. Then, again begins with His expression: "And those who came (into the faith) after them (49:9)" and completes the statement with His expression: "They say, our Lord: forgive us and our brethren who were before us in the faith" (49:10).

Ibn Idrīs says that the Arabian villages conquerred by the Prophet without fighting were divided into five shares, out of which four shares went to the Prophet. This is a view which according to our knowledge was never held by anybody before him. He further says: "All that is realized from the people of 'protection' (*ahl al-Dhimmah*) and the people of enemy-territory (*Dār al-Ḥarb*), when they have travelled to us, and the personal effects (*aslāb*) will be divided into five shares, out of which four shares will be given to the fighting personnel." But this is an arbitrary decision without any authority and is not therefore lawful for anybody.

The *'Ulamā'* have agreed that the whole lot of what has been taken by the army as spoils of war and carried to their camp except personal effects and food, the one-fifth thereof, shall be divided according to what Allāh, the Exalted, has mentioned in the verse on *al-Khumus*, and the four-fifth shall be distributed among the free individuals of the army with the exception of those who are minor and unable to fight, and women; they shall have no share. However, if the *Imām* considers to give them something as small gift out of *al-Khumus*, he can do so. But this concerns only the things other than personal effects (*asbāb*), and garments, weapons and the mounts which are taken from the polytheists.

There has been a disagreement concerning personal effects; some say these belong to the slayers. Others say that these will be divided into five shares along with the booty and the four-fifths thereof will go to the army. Ibn Idrīs says: the personal effects (*asbāb*) will be divided into five shares out of which the slayers will be given four-fifths. He also says: the share of the "near relations" (*Dhawi'l Qurbā*) will be divided among Banū Hāshim and Banū'l Muṭṭalib according to their number irrespective of their minors and adults and males and females, who will get equal shares.

The share will be divided among those who take part in fighting and will be inherited by their heirs and they will be given one-fifth of *Khumus* according to the Qur'ān, and every group along with others of the same group will be given *Khums*.

This view does not make any real sense and any division according to it will not be valid. Moreover this entails him (Ibn Idrīs) that he should assign the shares of orphanage to the orphans. He further argues saying that the Prophet gave excess out of the *Khums* of Khaybar for the sake of family and children of the recipients, although there has been much discussion on his mentioning of the family. Ibn Idrīs justifies himself by saying that the Prophet means by "those who were from them" (*man kāna minhum*), "the people themselves" (*min al-qawm anfusihim*). But the Prophetic traditions with which he has argued contain (the reports) that the Prophet gave to Ṣafiyyah fifty *wasaq,* to Banū Ja'far, who were three, fifty wasaq; and to Fāṭimah, one hundred. He also mentions that Fāṭimah demanded the service of a slave; and that the Prophet gave to 'Abbās one hundred and fifty, while the children of 'Abbās in those days were more in number than those of 'Alī.

Thus all these facts prove something contrary to his view. He has, moreover, narrated stories the like of which he does not accept from others. Again, he has attributed these stories to those people whom he does not name. He prefers silence concerning those who bear evidence against him. Even if the story is established in accordance with what he has narrated, it surely indicates the opposite of what he has held.

It has been established that the Prophet gave to majority of those, whose hearts needed reconciliation, one hundred camels. Ṣafwān said: "I stood before the Prophet while to me he was most disagreeable but he continued to give me till he became to me the most beloved of the people," and he (Ṣafwān) adds that if any Lord was indispensable, the Lord of the Quraysh was better than that of the Thaqīf. He (Ṣafwān) says: "What was given to him in that battle reached three hundred camels."

Ismā'īl says that it is lawful to deprive some of them of the booty and to divide the *Khums* among the rest of the people.

Ibn Idrīs says that there has been disagreement concerning the share of the Prophet. Some say it will be assigned to those who have been mentioned with him. Ibn Idrīs says that this is so, because, when a group of people of *ṣadaqāt* are not available, the *ṣadaqāt* are assigned to the rest of the people. He (Ibn Idrīs) further says that this is a good opinion. But if there is an excess, *al-fay'* will be divided among those who are other than those who get *ṣadaqāt*. Some others say that it will be spent on horses, mules and weapons. He (Ibn Idrīs) prefers that it should be employed for purposes most useful for Islam such as sealing the border-towns, preparing horses, mules and weapons. He has hereby illustrated (the problem) with an example which was not so in his opinion.

It has been mentioned on the authority of Nu'mān that the share of the orphans, the needy and the wayfarer would be assigned to them, and the share of the Prophet */fol. 3-b/* together with the share of the near relations will be spent on mounts and weapons on account of a *ḥadīth* narrated by Qays ibn Muslim on the authority of al-Ḥasan ibn Muḥammad ibn 'Alī which says that they disagreed (on their problem), some urged to assign the share of the Prophet to the Caliph after the Prophet and the share of the relations to the near relations of the Caliph. But, later on, they agreed to spend it on war preparations and horses. This was the case during the Caliphate of Abū Bakr and 'Umar.

But this is not established. What is established indirectly is the fact that Banū Hāshim were entitled to one-fifth of *al-Khums*, while the Caliphs had held that they would get out of it to the extent of their needs. In fact, 'Alī and 'Abbās disputed only concerning what was left by the Prophet from the spoils of war that had fallen into his hands without using a horse and a riding-beast.

As for the share of the near relations (***Dhawī'l Qurbā***), there is neither a verse concerning it, nor a *Sunnah* to be argued with in favour of turning the share away from them, and the report, like the one preceded, cannot be advanced as an argument against what has been established by the *Kitāb* (the Qur'ān), the *Sunnah*, and what has been confirmed by the fact that the Caliphs gave them and offered them that which sufficed them, but the Near Relations refused to accept anything save one-fifth of *al-Khums*.

'Alī asked a man, who had found a treasure (*kanz*), to deduce its *Khums* and take away its four-fifths. He then asked him to distribute the *Khums* among the needy. This proves the soundness of the view of Mālik. It has been mentioned that this was a remnant of the wealth of Khosroes and Caesars.

It has been argued by what has been reported that in the battle of Mu'tah, an auxiliary soldier hid himself behind a rock to ambush an infidel and all of a sudden, his horse got hamstrung and fell down. The auxiliary soldier, thereupon, killed him and took hold of his horse and personal effects. When the battle was won by the Muslims, Khālid sent for him and took hold of the personal effects. 'Awf ibn Mālik, thereupon said to him "Don't you know that the Messenger of Allāh left the decision of giving away the personal effects with the slayer?" He said "Yes, but I consider it too much." He said, "You must return it." But Khālid refused. Then 'Awf mentioned the incident to the Messenger of Allāh who asked Khālid, saying "O Khālid, What made you do this?" Khālid said, "I considered it too much."

The Messenger of Allāh asked Khālid to return whatever he had taken from him. 'Awf thereupon, said "Beware, O Khālid, did I not tell you the same?" On this, the Messenger of Allāh enquired, "What was that?" Khālid then told him the story. The Messenger of Allāh became angry and said; "O Khālid, Don't return it to him. Are you going to leave behind my chiefs so that for you will be the best of their commandments, and against them is the turbidity thereof?"

Ismā'īl says that this indicates that the *Imām* cannot give away the personal effects. He can only give them on exercising his personal discretion (*Ijtihād*). And this also shows that it is a part of the *Khums,* because the four-fifths are to be divided in place of booty, and only the *Khums* is to be carried to the Prophet. Now, when four-fifths went to those who acquired the booty, there was no place left for personal effects save to be included in *al-Khums*. It may be assigned to Allāh as He says: "And know that whatever you take as spoils of war its one-fifth is surely for Allāh and for the Messenger" (VIII:41) Now, anything concerning which *"lillāh"* (for Allāh) and *"lil-Rasūl"* (for the Messenger) are used, is not to be considered by itself, it is only to be executed through *Ijtihād.*

Ismā'īl adds that this has been indicated *[fo. 4-a]* also by the saying of the Prophet: "Whoever kills a person (enemy) and has an evidence for it, has the right to his personal effects." It is, therefore, concluded from this, that when one does not produce an evidence, the personal effects would be distributed among the Muslims. However, when everyone has his own case (i.e. a supporting case), the decision will be delayed till the slayer is known.

Aḥmad says that as for his saying: "the four-fifths shall go to those who have (fought) and acquired booty," it expresses a general meaning. It gives a particular sense as has been explained by the Prophet. Now, as for his expression: "Had the case been definite for every one, the evidence would not be demanded," the evidence is only made binding, because sometimes the victim is killed by his own weapon, and sometimes, he is killed by some-one who dies after his death, while others make claims of having killed him.

In that battle, there had accompanied the Prophet even those who had not embraced Islam, and those who had not accompanied the Prophet in any battle from among those who embraced Islam, on the day of the conquest of Makkah. Do you not see him giving it to Abū Qatādah by the recommendation of one who was with him inspite of his claim? This supports our view, since, when one who possesses acknowledges the claim of the slayer, the thing becomes as if it is in his own possession and thus the person becomes the defendant. What is more explicit is that the Prophet did not ask to estimate its value in counting as a part of the *Khums*.

It is also possible that the Prophet had asked him not to return what he had ordered him to give, because he declared the refusal of Khālid as an executed decision, which was not to be rebutted, just to make 'Awf know that Khālid interpreted that rare practice which had preceded from the Prophet in this context, and that his exercise of *Ijtihād* was appropriate for a person who can apply it in case when there is no *naṣṣ* (explicit text) for it. This also shows that the personal effects were (declared) for the slayers before the battle of Ḥunayn, as the battle of Mu'tah took place before the battle of Ḥunayn, and His saying, "The four-fifths are to be distributed among their claimants and the personal effects are a part of the *Khums*". It is also possible that since it was not known earlier that the personal effects would be divided into five shares, Khālid returned them. Now, they would be either returned to the slayer or would be amalgamated with the *Khums* also. The *ḥadīth* of Abū Qatādah indicates that the Prophet had asked the person who had held the personal effects in his possession to hand them over to Abū Qatādah without estimating their value to be counted in the shares.

Ismā'īl ibn Isḥāq says: Sulayman ibn Ḥarb narrates on the authority of Ḥammād ibn Zayd, on the authority of Ayyūb, on the authority of Muḥammad, on the authority of Anas, that al-Barā' fought a duel with a Persian noble and killed him, and sent his two bracelets and the belt (to Madinah). Thereupon, one day 'Umar said, "Abū Ṭalḥah has committed a sin. We formerly used to treat the personal effects as *nafal*. Now, the personal effects of al-Barā' constituted a treasure and I consider that I must divide it into five shares." It was said to Muḥammad, "Did he ('Umar) divide it into five shares?" He said, "I do not know." Ismā'īl says that this saying of 'Umar proves that he used to act according to his personal discretion (*Ijtihād*), and this is quite clear.

Aḥmad says: on the contrary, 'Umar's saying indicates something different, because he did not consult Abū Ṭalḥah on any matter concerning whith the decision had been taken earlier. He ('Umar), however, stated *[fo. 4-b]* that they used to treat the personal effects as *nafal*. He, therefore, apologised to Abū Ṭalḥah when he intended to act contrary to the precedent, because he considered these personal effects enormous. Had it been a case in which he had the right to make decision he would have executed it on the basis of the previous case and would not have been in need of making any apology. This also proves that the decision of personal effects was known beforehand.

Isma'il says: Muhammad ibn 'Abd al-Malik, reported on the authority of Abū Ṣāliḥ on the authority of al-Layth ibn Sa'd, on the authority of 'Aqīl, on the authority of Ibn Shihāb from Sālim, from his father (who relates) that the Messenger of Allāh used to give *nafal* to everyone whom he sent on petty expeditions (*sarāyā*) over and above the share of the general army. He added that the *Khums* in that was compulsory. He further says that the action of the Prophet shows that it was not done in general.

Aḥmad has criticised the *sanad* of the *ḥadīth*, and has said, "Even if it was established, it would bear no evidence, for Ibn 'Umar did not attend all the expeditions so as to attest all cases. He therefore attested what he observed. His evidence would have been a proof had he said that the Prophet did not offer the personal effects as *nafal*. His saying, 'In all these cases there is *Khums*', indicates that it (personal effects) is other than the *Khums*." It also proves that *nafal* is to be given at the time of advance and at the time of retreat, as had been narrated. But the personal effects (*aslāb*) were not mentioned there.

He says: 'Abd al-Wāḥīd ibn 'Ubādah relates on the authority of Ḥammād ibn Salmaḥ, from Isḥāq ibn 'Abd Allāh ibn Abū Ṭalḥah from Anas that on the day (battle) of Ḥunayn, the tribe of Hawāzin came along with children, women, camels and goats which they arranged in arrays to show that they excelled in number and fought fearlessly. Whereupon the Muslims turned away retreating. The Messenger of Allāh, then, said, "O, servants of Allāh, I am Allāh's servant and His Messenger." He then added, "O, the people of Anṣār, I am Allāh's servant and His Messenger." So Allāh routed the polytheists, and the Prophet did not strike anybody with his sword or spear. The Prophet then said "Whoever slays a disbeliever, shall get his personal effects." Abū Ṭalḥah, then, killed twenty men and obtained their personal effects. Ismā'īl adds: "This shows that had it been a known fact, the Prophet would not have argued therein with such a statement."

Aḥmad says: "His argument is baseless, because this battle was attended by those who were neither old converts to Islam, nor had they fought earlier; so, he (the Prophet) wanted to let them know what had remained unknown to them." He also said in this *ḥadīth*: "Abū Qatādah said, 'O,

Messenger of Allāh, verily, I struck a man on the chord of his shoulder while his mail-coat lay on him, but I was in too much hurry to take it off, so see with whom it lies?' I took it, said a person, and so requested the Prophet to make him contented without it. But the Messenger of Allāh kept silent. He was never asked for anything but gave him the same. At this Abū Bakr said, 'No, by Allāh, Allāh grants it as *fay'* to one of the lions of Allāh and will he (the Prophet) give it to you?' The Messenger of Allāh then laughed and said: 'Abū Bakr has spoken the truth.' "

Aḥmad says: "This is no argument in this case, because had it belonged to the Prophet, he (the Prophet) would have given it to the seeker, while Abū Bakr did not say: *[fo. 5-a]* "He (Allāh) grants it as a *fay'* to His Messenger", rather, he had said "He granted it as a *fay'* to the slayer", and the Prophet did not reject it.

Ismā'īl says: 'Alī relates on the authority of Fuzārī on the authority of Abū Malik al-Ashja'ī, from Na'īm ibn Abu Ḥind, from Ibn Samurah, from his father, that the Prophet said: "Whoever slays a man will get his personal effects." He (Ismā'īl) says, " 'Abd Allāh ibn Rijā relates on the authority of 'Ikrimah ibn 'Ammār on the authority of Iyās ibn Salmah who said that his father related saying: 'We made a raid against the tribe of Hawāzin. We were taking our lunch while our riding beasts were weak, and at this time there came a man mounting a camel. He made his camel kneel down and then bound it. Thereafter, he came forward and ate with the people and observed their condition. He then got up and remounted his camel and lo: he was a vanguard of the disbelievers.' "

Salmah adds, "Then I followed him till I killed him and brought his mount dragging it forward. The Messenger of Allāh received me alongwith the people. He enquired as to who killed the man. They replied, 'Salmah'. The Prophet said, 'He will get the entire personal effects.' "

Ismā'īl says this indicates that Salmah had killed him before the battle, because the place where Salmah had killed him was separated by the enemy-territory (*Dār al-Ḥarb*) from the country of Islam (*Dār al-Islām*). The Hawāzin had only advanced from their places as Anas described earlier. The Prophet then proceeded from Makkah and they met at Ḥunayn, a valley of Tihāmah, at a distance of about ten miles from Makkah. Aḥmad says, "What he has argued is baseless, because the booty becomes necessary only because of actual attack with mounts and confrontation, and this had really happened."

Salmah says that the Messenger of Allāh appointed Abū Bakr chief of the Muslim army. "We then made a raid. When we came near (the destination) we alighted at late hours of night and performed our morning prayers. Then he ordered us to march and we fell upon them and met together near the water. I, then, saw a group of people consisting of children and women. I thereupon went ahead and overtook them before they could reach the mountain, and brought them to Abū Bakr. Among them there were a woman from the tribe of Fuzārah, and her daughter, who was the most beautiful woman of the Arabs. Abū Bakr, then, gave her to me as a *nafal.* Later on, I came to Madīnah while I had not yet removed clothes from her. We met the Messenger of Allāh who said, 'Hand over the woman to me'. I said, verily she has fascinated me and I have not yet removed her clothes from her. He (the Prophet) then kept quiet and then called on me the next morning and said, 'Hand over the woman to me, may your father be blessed by Allāh.' I said: 'I have not yet put her clothes off,' and then I said 'She belongs to you, O Messenger of Allāh.' The Prophet then sent her to Makkah and offered her as a ransom for the Muslim prisoners of war."

Ismā'īl says that this goes in favour of excercising *Ijtihād,* personal discretion (by the *Imām*), concerning *nafal;* that is to say, it may be offered in the beginning as well as at the end of the battle. Aḥmad says: "This argument does not hold good even if the tradition is proved genuine, rather this and what has been mentioned, that the Prophet used to give *nafal* in expeditions (*Sarāyā*) in the beginning *[fo. 5-b]* and at the end thereof, one-third after *Khums,* and according to a different *ḥadīth,* in the beginning, one-fourth after the *Khums* and on return one-third, after the *Khums,* strengthen the contention that personal effects belong to the slayers.

Ismā'īl says that Ibrāhīm ibn Ḥamzah has related to us on the authority of al-Mughīrah ibn 'Abd al-Raḥmān from Sulaymān ibn Mūsā from Makḥūl from Abū Salām al-Jayshānī from Abū Imāmah al-Bāhilī from 'Ubādah, that the Prophet used to dislike giving *nafal* saying that the Muslims having strong horses should return these to the weak.

Aḥmad says that, if it was correct, it was only at a time when the Muslims were weak and the booty was meagre since the case of *Anfal* was too well-known to be contradicted by such a *ḥadīth* like this. Ibn al-Musayyib has been mentioned saying that there is no *nafal* after the Prophet. Aḥmad says: "This means, if it was correct, that Islam had become strong and those whose hearts needed reconciliation would not be given that which they used to get from the Prophet."

Ismā'īl says, "There related to us Muḥammad ibn Kathīr, on the authority of Sufyān, from Ibn 'Awn, from Ibn Sīrīn, from Anas, that a certain chief intended to give him some *nafal.* He asked him, 'Have you divided it into five shares?' 'No', replied the chief. Anas, then refused to accept it." Aḥmad says, "It means that Anas was not in the army. He, therefore, enquired as to whether the affair was carried out therein according to its rules, so that he would accept it, not on the fact that personal effects were to be divided into five shares as was held by some people." Ismā'īl says, "This is lawful whether he gives *nafal* or not."

Ibn Idrīs says, "It should be divided into five shares, because he (the Prophet) had granted it to the slayer." He adds, "What is exclusively for the Prophet, is to be divided into five shares." He also thinks that the thing concerning which the expression is made dubious carries more emphasis than what is made exclusive for him. Had it been so, Allāh's words: *"khāliṣatan laka min dūni'l-Mu'minīn,"*[a privilege for thee not for the (rest of) believers] (33:50), would prove that the dedicating women were lawful for other than the Prophet; and Allāh's words: *"khāliṣatan yawm al-Qiyāmati"* [purely theirs on the Day of Resurrection] (7:32), necessarily would mean making others share with them to enjoy association in these, and thus the meaning would be altered and made emphatic what is not emphatic. He opines that *Kharāj* of the land is to be divided into five shares: *Jizyah* is also to be divided into five shares, and whatever is taken from the inhabitants of the enemy-territory when they come to us, is to be divided into five shares. He adds that whatever Allāh confers on His Messenger out of that on which "neither a horse nor a riding beast has been used" is to be divided into five shares. He says this expression has been taken from Arabic meaning that what was for those who attacked (with their mounts) would belong to the Messenger of Allāh.

This is from him a quite arbitrary decision and substantiation of a claim without any evidence and is not intelligible in the language of the Arabs. Things are not to be changed from their face values due to the evil propensity of the souls. Inspite of this, there is no report in all this bearing any *sanad* which he would mention, nor does he know any such report. Moreover, he thinks that this is contained in the Book of Allāh and the *Sunnah* of His Messenger. But he does not quote or mention any explicit text (*naṣṣ*) in this regard.

The Qur'ānic verse that he followed and in which he is confused *[fo. 6-a]* is Allāh's saying: "And know that whatever ye take as spoils of war, lo, a fifth thereof is for Allāh" upto the end of the verse (8:41). Now this is addressed to the believers and not to the Prophet (peace be upon him). He holds that the verses in *al-Ḥashr* are all conjoined with one another. Had he thought over it and looked into it, he would have found it against what he held. For Allāh, the Exalted, says, "He it is who hath caused those of the people of the scripture who disbelieved to go forth from their homes unto the first exile. Ye deemed not they would go forth, while they deemed that their strongholds would protect then" upto His saying: *al-Fāsiqīn* (Evil-Doers) (59:2-5). He has, thus, informed about Banū'l-Naḍīr and Banū Qaynuqā'. Afterwards, He says: "And that which Allāh gave as spoils unto His Messenger from them ye urged not any horse or riding-camel for the sake there of, but Allāh giveth His Messenger lordship over whom, he will" (59:6) So, He informs that surely that goes to the Messenger of Allāh, because nothing was exerted on it when they abandoned it and there did not precede among them any fighting and cutting down of their trees as they turned away from it and the affair was over. Then, Allāh says: "That which Allāh giveth as spoils unto His Messenger from the people of the townships is for Allāh, and for the Messenger, and for the near of kind and the orphans and the needy and the wayfarer" (59:7). This is a sentence which is not conjoined with the first one; therefore, that which Allāh has conferred on His Messenger as *fay'* is for Allāh and for His Messenger as long as no riding beast was used for attacking it.

Ismʻīl says: what comes after this verse is conjoined with it, but the fact is not as he says, since Allāh has brought in the verse some *mubtadā'* (subject) of the sentence and its *khabar* (predicate). Each verse, therefore, is disjoined with what precedes it. Now, the *aḥādīth* which have been narrated to prove that the verse of *al-Khums* was revealed after the battle of Badr concerning the Banū Qurayẓah and that it cannot be considered sound concerning the *nafal*, nor can the like of them be made a reliable source of one of the most important laws of Islam. On the contrary, it is established that the verse was revealed on the occasion of the battle of Badr. As regards the wealth (*amwāl*) of Banū Naḍīr which the Prophet distributed, it related only to things other than their dwellings, because it has been confirmed that that was the only thing Banū'l-Naḍīr, left behind.

THEY HAVE DISAGREED CONCERNING THAT WHICH IS GIVEN BY THE *IMĀM* AS '*NAFAL*'

Ibn 'Umar says: "We went out on an expedition towards Najd in which our shares were eleven or tweleve camels, and they (the fighters) received one camel each as *nafal*." This indicates that they were given *nafal* from the *Khums*. It is also established that 'Alī said, "I had two aged she-camels of which I received one as my share in the battle of Badr and the other was given to me out of the *Khums* on the day of Badr." The Prophet said on the day of Ḥunayn, "Whoever kills a person and has a witness to it will get his (the slain man's) personal effects." Whereupon Abū Qatādah reported to the Prophet that he had killed a person. Then a man said that in reality he had spoken the truth. He told the Messenger of Allāh that the personal effects of the man were with him. So he prayed to the

Prophet to please make him contented without it. Abū Bakr thereupon said, "By Allāh, it is not possible. The Messenger of Allāh will not do injustice to a lion out of the lions of Allāh who fights for Allāh and his Messenger, while you will be given his personal effects." The Messenger of Allāh said, "He has said the truth, so you give it to him." And he did.

Mālik says: "Had it been so that the personal effects belonged to the slayers, this would not have remained unknown to Abū Qatādah, who was one of the prominent Companions of the Prophet so that he had to mention the case to the Messenger of Allāh. Again, had it been a regular case, he would have surely known it. The Messenger of Allāh surely did it in some of his battles, but it has not reached me that the Prophet did it in all of his battles."

Aḥmad says that the two sones of 'Afrā' disputed over the personal effects of Abū Jahl on the day of Badr, Each of them claiming that he had killed him. The Prophet, then, asked them to show him their own swords. When the Prophet looked at their swords, he said, "Both of you (killed him)", and gave them his personal effects as *nafal,* It has been reported through a chain of narrators of which there is some doubt that Ibn Mas'ūd received the swords of Abū Jahl as *nafal,* because he had beheaded Abū Jahl.

On the day of Badr the Muslims were divided into three groups; one group had surrounded the Messenger of Allāh so that he might not be overtaker unawares. Another group was fighting against the enemies and the third group was busy in collecting the booty. When the fighting was over, each group from them claimed that they had better claim to the booty than others.. Those who had surrounded the Messenger of Allāh argued saying that they had better claims because they had guarded the Prophet. The other claimed that they were better entitled to the booty because they had driven away the enemy. Thus, the personal effects became the bone of contention among those who had taken hold of them and those who had killed (their owners). Allāh thereupon revealed: "They ask thee (O Muḥammad) of the spoils of war, say: the spoil of war belong to Allāh and the Messenger. So keep your duty to Allāh, and adjust the matter of your difference," upto His words: "If you are believers" (8:I), meaning thereby that the decision concerning it lay with Allāh and His Messenger and this was in fact a test of their obedience to Allāh. They, thereupon, expressed their agreement and submission.

Allāh then, revealed: "And know that whatever ye take as spoils of war, Lo: a fifth thereof is for Allāh, and for the Messenger," upto the end of the verse (8:41). So the Prophet assigned four-fifth of the booties after the personal effects for the army, giving every man one share and every horseman two shares. In this battle, there were three horses with them, one horse belonged to Zubayr, the other horse to Abū Murthad al-Ghanawī and the third to Miqdād ibn 'Amr, known as Ibn al-Aswad.

The '*Ulamā'* have agreed that two shares are to be given to the horse, except Abū Ḥanīfah who does not like to prefer the horse to its rider, and (according to him) only one share will be given to the horse. They have disagreed concerning a man who keeps more than one horse. Some hold that only one share will be given for one horse. Some others are of the opinion that two horses shall have shares and nothing will be given to more then that. All these views have been reported from the Prophet.

They have disagreed with regard to the hackneys. Mālik and many other scholars hold that when the ruler (*al-wālī*) allows their use, hackneys will be treated like horses. Some think *[fo. 7-a]* that a hackney is entitled to one share and a horse to two shares. Some others say that no share will be prescribed for the hackneys. The first view is more correct as the word *khayl* (horse) is applied to it.

Chapter II

ON WHAT IS AWARDED BY THE *IMĀM* AS ADDITIONAL SHARE (*AL-NAFAL*) BEFORE FIGHTING

Scholars have disagreed on the question whether the *Imām* should give anything as additional share (*al-nafal*). The Syrians and others report that those who were sent on expeditions used to receive one-fourth as *nafal* during their advance and one-third on their return, out of the principal booties. And this is the view of the majority of the inhabitants of al-'Irāq. Mālik, however, dislikes it saying: one should not fight for the sake of the world, and he (Mālik) interprets this according to the *ḥadīth*: "All actions surely depend upon intentions and one only deserves that for which one intends. So, whoever migrates for the sake of Allāh and His Messenger, his migration will be, therefore, towards Allāh and His Messenger, and whoever migrates for the sake of the world which he attains or for a woman whom he marries, his migration is towards that for which he has intended." For this reason Mālik does not like that the *Imām* should promise that whoever slays anyone will get this and that and whoever fights in a certain place will get this and that. He (Mālik) says that if he (*Imām*) does say such things or mentions any *nafal* before fighting, it is to be executed according to what he says, because it is a commandment concerning which they have disagreed; hence it is like a decision that has been enforced.

Those who permit it, argue with what has been substantiated from the Prophet that he said to 'Amr ibn al-'Āṣī, "Shall I send you in any army, may Allāh keep you hale and hearty and give you booty and I desire for you good amount of wealth." He ('Amr) replied, 'My migration is not for the sake of wealth, I migrate only for the sake of Allāh and His Messenger.' The Prophet rejoiced and exclaimed: 'How excellent this wealth is for the excellent man.' "

They say that the Prophet would not have given him that which was not lawful for him. Moreover, when the action is done for the sake of Allāh, here is no harm in seeking wealth as well as that which he earns out of the grace of Allāh. The Prophet Noah (Nūḥ) said: "Seek pardon of your Lord, lo! He is ever Forgiving. He will let loose the sky for you in plenteous rain" (71: 10–11), and Hūd (the Prophet) said: "Ask forgiveness of your Lord, then turn unto Him repentant: He will cause the sky to rain abundance on you and will add unto you strength to your strength" (9: 52).

Chapter III

ON THE METHOD OF DIVISION OF ONE-FIFTH OF THE BOOTY *(AL-KHUMS)* AND ON DETERMINATION OF 'NEAR RELATIONS' *(DHAWŪ'L QURBĀ)*

Scholars have differed about the modality of the division of one-fifth of the booty (*al-Khums*). Mālik and many other *'Ulamā'* are of the opinion that it is to be divided according to one's personal discretion (*Ijtihād*) and not in accordance with the number of the group of people mentioned in the Qur'ānic verse. A similar view has been narrated from the Four Caliphs except 'Alī who in this regard followed the policy of his companions, because the two had interpreted this verse (in their own way). He, therefore, treated it like a decision that comes into force. His ('Alī's) view and the opinion of Banū Ḥāshim was that the *Khums* was to be divided among the five groups.

They had interpreted that Allāh's expression *lillāh* was the opening of the speech, and for the messenger is a share, and every group of people would have a share. It is also confirmed that 'Alī said: "I asked the Messenger of Allāh to give me one-fifth of the fifth *[fo. 7-b]* so that nobody could dispute with me in that," and the Prophet did accordingly. And this continued till the end of the Caliphate of 'Umar. 'Alī added: "I then said to 'Umar: 'This is needed by the general people while we do not need it, so, please distribute it among them.' " 'Alī continued, "When I came out, al-'Abbās, who was a farsighted person, said to me. 'You have taken out from our hands something which will never come back to us.' " 'Alī said: "I was not invited to it afterwards."

Aḥmad says thiṣ was something which he considered at a time when he divided the landed property, but had it been a usual matter, Banū Ḥāshim would have argued with it as evidence and the Caliphs could not have accused them of falsehood concerning what they had related. When 'Alī became caliph, Banū Ḥāshim wanted him to spend it according to their interpretation. But 'Alī agrued: "People have already interpreted and we have also interpreted, but we in our interpretation are no better than that of theirs and I do not like that 'Alī should be blamed for opposing the two (Abū Bakr and 'Umar)." When he arrived in **Kūfah**, he said, "I have not come here just to undo a contract made by 'Umar." The Jews submitted to him a letter which he had written recommending their cases to 'Umar for not banishing them, and they said, "Notwithstanding your letter and recommendation, 'Umar banished us." Thereupon, 'Alī said, "Woe to you, 'Umar was rightly-guided in the matter; however, I am not going to alter any decision taken by 'Umar."

A group of people holds that *al-Khums* is to be divided into six shares; the share of Allāh is to be spent for some good cause, and one share for the Messenger of Allāh, and one share for each one of the groups mentioned in the verse. Another group says that a handful of the *Khums* will be taken and put into the Ka'bah for its maintenance, and this is the share for Allāh, and the rest will be divided into five shares; one for the Messenger of Allāh and one share for each of the groups. Yet, another group holds that it is to be divided into five shares; and we have already mentioned them. But a different group holds that it is to be divided into four and Allāh and His Messenger alone have the right to give their decisions in the matter because both this world and the world Hereafter belong to Allāh while He is not in need of the two. These are the six views. Ismā'īl says that *Khums* belongs to the entire Muslim community and Allāh has mentioned the categories of people in the Qur'ānic verse only to put emphasis on the affairs (of the Muslim community). So these are the seven opinions.

THEY HAVE DISAGREED AS TO WHO ARE THE NEAR RELATIONS (*DHAWŪ'L QURBĀ*)

Some say that (the Near Relations) are the whole tribe of Quraysh. And this is wrong. Some hold that they are Banū Hāshim and Banū'l Muṭṭalib. Ibn Idrīs has argued for this view with a *ḥadīth* which is not confirmed by way of transmission: that the Prophet gave Banū Hāshim and Banū'l Muṭṭalib out of the fifth of the one-fifth of booty. 'Uthmān and Jubyr ibn Muṭ'im, thereupon, went to him and said, "O Messenger of Allāh! you gave to Banū'l Muṭṭalib although we and they stand before you on the same footing." Thereupon the Messenger of Allāh said: "Banū'l Muṭṭalib and Banū Hāshim are one", and he interweaved his fingers. This he said because of the fact that they were persecuted for the sake of Allāh and His Messenger. The unbelievers of the Quraysh entered into a pact (of social boycott) against them including Banū *Hāshim* that they would not mix with them, nor cooperate with them. *[fo. 8-a]* The matter became grave against them and a few years later, when their suffering reached its climax, people from a group of Quraysh made an effort to break this pact. What is established by way of transmission (*ḥadīth*) is that the Prophet gave Banū Hāshim and Banū'l Muṭṭalib out of one-fifth, and that there was no mention of one-fifth of fifth. They had one share in the *Khums* which the Prophet gave them out of it and treated them (Banū'l Muṭṭalib) and Banū Hāshim equally, and out of the same he gave to those whose hearts needed reconciliation (*Mu'allifah Qulūbuhum*), on the day of Ḥunayn. He gave to al-Aqra' ibn Ḥābis and 'Uyaynah ibn Ḥiṣn one hundred camels each. He gave to Abū Sufyān, al-Ḥārith ibn Hishām, 'Abd al-Raḥmān ibn Yarbū' of Makhzūm clan, Suhayl ibn 'Amr, Ḥuwayṭib ibn 'Abd al-'Uzzā, 'Alqamah ibn 'Allathah, Abū Sufyan ibn al-Ḥārith, Mālik ibn 'Awf, al-'Alī ibn al-Hārithah and 'Abbās ibn Mirdās, fifty camels each. 'Abbās ibn Mirdās, thereupon, said:

> These were the spoils of war which I got by my repeated charge riding the clot through the sandy ground. And I urged the people to keep awake from their sleep. When the people slept, I did not sleep. Do you make my spoils of war and that of 'Ubayd, like the spoils of war of 'Uyaynah and Al-Aqra'? Neither Ḥiṣn nor Ḥābis ever excelled Mirdās in a gathering of the people. And I am not inferior to either of the two, and he whom you demean today will never be exalted. And I have never been in the war at the time of defence. I have never been therefore given anything, nor have I been prevented from any thing, except a few small she-camels which were given to me according to the number of their four feet.

By this he meant that he was not given what he deserved.

Dhawū'l Khuwayṣirah said to the Prophet, "Do Justice". He added, "This is a division by which the pleasure of Allāh was not intended." Thereupon, the Prophet said to him, "Woe to you: who will do justice if I do not do justice? surely you will be disappointed and will be in great loss." This has been reported in a lengthy *Ḥadīth*.

Then, some Anṣār also talked a great deal and the Prophet gathered them in a pavilion and said: "Did I not find you going astray and Allāh guided you aright through me? Did I not find you split up into groups and Allāh united you through me? You were weak and humiliated and Allāh made you strong through me." He, then, continued: "If you so desire, you can say, 'Did you not come to us a fugitive and we gave you shelter, frightened and we gave you security, and forsaken and we helped you?' They said, 'Yes, gracious bestowal suits Allāh and His Messenger.' "

The Prophet thereupon, said, "Don't you feel happy that people will go back to their abodes with goats and camels, while you will return to your abodes with me?" They replied, "We do feel happy." The Prophet declared: "*Anṣār* are my companions and my family. Had there been no migration, I would have surely been a man of the *Anṣār*. If people walked into any other valley or mountain, I would surely walk into the valley and the mountain of the *Anṣār*."

It was said to him, "You have given *[fo. 8-b]* 'Uyaynah and al-Aqra' while you have left Ju'ayl ibn Surāqah al-Ḍumarī." He replied; "Beware of Him in whose hand is the soul of Muḥammad, indeed Ju'āyl is the best of the entire men of the world like 'Uyaynah and al-Aqra', but I make alliance with them so that they become sincere Muslims, and I have entrusted Ju'āyl to his Islām."

When the Prophet's Companions showed their back on the day of Ḥunayn, he called out, "O People of *Anṣār*." They said: "We respond to you, O Messenger of Allāh, are we not with you?" Then he turned to his left and said; "O People of *Anṣār*," and they responded in the same words, while the Prophet was riding a mule which continued in keeping its speed in advancing and Abū Sufyan ibn al-Ḥārith was holding its reins. The Prophet continued saying, "I am the Prophet, and am not a false one, I am son of 'Abd al-Muṭṭalib." 'Abbās, who possessed a loud voice, was with him. The (Prophet) asked him to summon (the people) calling them as the people of the gum-acacia-tree. 'Abbās thereupon called out loudly, and the people turned to the Prophet just like a she-camel which hastens to her younglings. The Prophet, thereafter, took up a handful of pebbles which he threw at the enemy saying, "Their faces may be deformed", and the polytheists were routed.

THEY HAVE DISAGREED AS TO THE POLICY WITH REGARD TO THE PROPHET'S SHARE IN *AL-KHUMS* AFTER HIS DEATH

The majority of the *'ulamā'* holds that it will belong to those who have been mentioned along with him in the Qur'ānic verse. Another group of scholars think that it will belong to his successor who will use it in the right cause. In this connection a Prophetic tradition has been narrated to the effect that when Allāh assigns anything to any Prophet as means of subsistance *ṭu'ma,* it belongs to his successor after him.

They have also differed as to whom belongs the share of the Near Relations after the death of the Prophet. It has been established by the (policy of the) Four Caliphs, and it is held also by majority of the *'Ulamā'*, that the Four Caliphs divided it among the Near Relations of the Prophet.

A group of scholars says that it shall go to the Near Relations of the Caliph. The scholars, in general, hold the former view, because the Prophet gave it to them in place of *Zakāh* since they were deprived from accepting *Zakāh* to which they were not entitled as it was taken to be the dirt of the people. And Allāh, the Exalted, has assigned the *Khums* and booty to the Prophet as these were the best kind of earnings while he did not say the same concerning *Zakāh*. The relations other than the Banū Hāshim were not declared prohibited from *Zakāh*. Abū Sufyān and Mu'āwiyyah belonged to the group of *Mu'allifah Qulūbuhum* (those whose hearts need reconciliation) who will be mentioned in the chapter on *Zakāh*.

Chapter IV

ON THE SPOILS OF WAR THAT BELONGED TO THE PROPHET AND ON THE WEALTH HE LEFT BEHIND

Some of the scholars hold that Allāh made some spoils of war for His Prophet exclusive as He so willed. So, of all that was made exclusive for him was that for which neither horses nor camels were ever used. Whenever the Prophet attended the division, he had the choice spoils of war (*al-Ṣafāyā*), one share along with the people in the four-fifths and another in one-fifth.

The choice booty is taken first, before the others take their shares. But if the Prophet was not present at the time of distribution, he had his share of one-fifth and one share like the people in the four-fifths. *[fo. 9-a]* The Messenger of Allāh says: "I have nothing out of that which Allāh has given you as *fay'*, except the *Khums*, and the *Khums* is again returned to you", that is to say, the *Khums* which Allāh has given to them, not that which is conferred on him.

When the Messenger of Allāh passed away, his wives intended to sent a representation to Abū Bakr concerning their inheritance from the Prophet. 'Ā'ishah, thereupon, said to them; "Has the Prophet not said, 'We the Prophets do not leave any inheritance? Whatever we leave behind is a *ṣadaqah.*' " In a different report related by Abū Hurayrah, the Prophet said: "My heirs will not share a single *dīnār,* whatever I leave behind after meeting the maintenance expenses of my wives, and the wages of my worker (*'āmilī*) will be treated as *ṣadaqah.*"

There has been disagreement concerning his expression *wa ma'ūnatu 'āmilī*. Some say that it is the wages of one who digs his grave. Some others hold that it is for the labourers (*'ummāl*) working in his enclosures. Ibn

'Uyaynah mentions that his wives would inherit him since they devoted themselves entirely to him. But this is not correct, since the first view is established and well-known and its chain of narrators is strong. Thus, Mālik has reported it from Ibn Shihāb, from 'Urwah, from 'Ā'ishah and from Abū'l Zinād, from al-A'raj from Abū Hurayrah, and also from Ibn Shihāb, from Mālik ibn Aws fromd 'Umar, 'Alī, 'Abbās, Ṭalḥah, Zubayr 'Abd al-Raḥmān and Sa'd, and similarly 'Uyaynah and a number of prominent '*Ulamā*' have reported it.

It has been reported that 'Umar offered choice to the Mothers of the Believers, the wives of the Prophet, saying if they so chose, he could provide them with maintenance by giving eighty *wasaq* from dates and twenty *wasaq* from barley, and if they so chose, he could give them that which would yield so much crop by assigning to them the lands which would yield them equal to that, and they would have therein their proprietary rights. But I do not consider it to be correct in respect of transmission (of this report).

Chapter V

ON THE POLICY REGARDING THE ENEMY-LANDS CAPTURED BY THE MUSLIMS

Mālik relates on the authority of Zayd ibn Aslam from his father that 'Umar said: "Had there been none to come from the later generations, I would have surely distributed every village that I have conquerred just as the Messenger of Allāh had distributed Khaybār."

According to the reports which come from several sources, 'Umar retained the *Sawād* of 'Irāq, Egypt and the lands of Syria which he had brought under his sway in order to pay allowances to the fighters, and maintenance of their dependants and the progeny. Bilāl and other Companions of the Prophet wanted him ('Umar) to divide among them all that was conquerred, but 'Umar disapproved of the idea that had come from them.

There has been disagreement concerning the action of 'Umar in this connection. Some say that 'Umar wanted to obtain the consent of the army. So, whoever agreed to give up his share without any price in order to retain it for the Muslims, he accepted it, and whoever refused, he ('Umar) gave him the price of his share. It has been narrated that a woman of 'Irāq whose father was in the army said; "I shall not agree unless you fill my sleeve with *dīnārs [fo. 9-b]* and give me a red herd." So he ('Umar) gave her eighty *dīnārs* and a herd and then she agreed.

'Umar sent 'Uthmān ibn Ḥunayf, who surveyed the land, and it reached to two hundred thousand (200,000) *jarīb*. 'Umar taxed forty-eight *dirhams* on each *jarīb* of wheat, twenty-four on each *jarīb* of barley and twelve on each *jarīb* of dates. It is said that he fixed twenty-four on the *jarīb* of wheat, twelve on the *jarīb* of barley and six on the *jarīb* of dates.

He sent 'Abd Allāh ibn Mas'ūd to 'Irāq to lead their prayers and be in charge of *Bayt al-Māl* (Public Treasury) and to make judicial decisions.

among them. He sent 'Ammār ibn Yāsir to command the army, and 'Uthmān to survey the land, and fixed for them a goat daily, half of the goat with its lower parts for 'Ammār and a fourth part for either of his two companions. I think he preferred 'Ammār only for his large family or for the great volume of his work. He says; "Every village out of which one goat is taken every day is sure to hasten to its destruction." 'Umar appointed Ḥudhayfah ibn al-Yamān along with 'Uthmān ibn Ḥunayf for the survey of the land.

Now whoever holds that 'Umar retained the land only after winning the consent of the people, considered his action like the action of the Prophet, as the Prophet divided Khaybar, because his ('Umar's) purchase of the land and renunciation of those who gave up their shares willingly was as good as the division of Khaybar. It is said that 'Umar had retained it without any price having been handed over to him by the army.

It has been reported that 'Umar had interpreted his action by the Qur'ānic verse: *li'l-Fuqarā-i'l Muhājirīna* upto *Rabbanā innaka Ra'ūf al-Raḥīm*. It is said that 'Umar summoned the *Muhājirūn* and the Anṣār and consulted them concerning the conquerred lands and said to them; "You all ponder over it tonight, and come to me next morning." He himself thought over it at night and it became clear to him that these verses were revealed in this context.

When they visited him the next morning, he said: "Last night, I carefully recited the verses of *al-Ḥashr;*" and he then read out: "That which Allāh has conferred as spoils unto His Messenger from the people of the township" (59: 7) upto the verse "and (it is) for the poor fugitives" (59: 8). When he came upto the verse. "They are the sincere ones" (59: 8), he said these are not for these people alone. Next, he recited: "And those who entered the city and the faith before them", upto the verse such are they who are successfull (59: 9), he said these are not for these people alone. Next he recited. "And those who come after them (into the faith)" (59: 10) upto the verse: "Full of pity, very Merciful" (59: 10). He then said, afterwards not a single Muslim remains excluded from this.

I have already mentioned in the beginning of the book the arguments of those who had disagreed with him from among the Companions of the Prophet.

Abū 'Ubayd says that the verse of *al-Anfāl* and the verses of *al-Ḥashr* are decisive (*Muḥkamāt*) nothing of which is abrogated. The Imām may act according to either of the two decisions by using his personal discretion (*Ijtihād*); if he (the *Imām*) so chooses, he can act according to the policy of the Prophet in Khaybar, *[fo. 10-a]* and if he (the *Imām*) so desires he can act as 'Umar did.

Ismā'īl ibn Isḥāq says that this view does not make any sense. How can the *Imām* be given choice in matters of legal decisions? Ismā'īl, on the contrary, opines that the verses mentioned in *al-Ḥashr* abrogate those of *al-Anfāl*. The charge brought by Ismā'īl against Abū 'Ubayd does not stand, because it cannot be denied that Allāh has entrusted the Prophet and the *Imāms* after him with their exercise of personal discretion in a case when they can execute according to their opinion, since our view and the view of Ismā'īl agree on this that *Khums* and *Zakāh* are to be divided only in accordance with the personal discretion of the *Imām*. Hence, any group of the beneficiaries will be preferred and the number is also included in it, while he holds that the *Imām* may not give as *nafal,* there being no difference between this (view of Ismā'īl) and what has been used to differentiate between the two (the view of Ismā'īl and the view of Abū 'Ubayd).

But the argument goes against Abū 'Ubayd from other point of view. For the verse in *al-Anfāl* has already been explained and needs no interpretation. It has been explained by the Prophet by his action in Khaybar. Those who claim that these (the verses of *al-Anfāl*) mean other than the landed-property, do not have any support from the verse which is literally above any interpretation, nor from the action of the Prophet while the verses in *al-Ḥashr,* on the contrary, bear an interpretation other than the one offered: and they are better (understood) without any interpretation, as I have discussed earlier in the beginning of this book, and for the disagreement recorded from 'Umar as to how he retained the land. If it is, however, established, as has been reported, that he won the consent of the people he only accepted the verse of the *al-Anfāl*; and what is in *al-Ḥashr* remained in accordance with the interpretation as mentioned earlier.

Now, what is of this category cannot be considered as abrogator of what has been declared by the Qur'ān, and acted upon by the Messenger of Allāh. In this sense is to be understood the expression of 'Umar, "Had there been nobody to come, I would have not conquerred any village but I would have divided it, as the Messenger of Allāh divided Khaybar," and his expression: "O Allāh, my soul is satisfied with abandoning it." Had it not been so, he would not have consulted the people concerning abandoning the division or would not have given them anything in this context. Nothing of the Qur'ān is abrogated, nor is any verse specified except commandment that does not admit of any interpretation.

Chapter VI

ON THE TERMS ACCORDING TO WHICH 'UMAR RETAINED THE LAND

The scholars in general are of the view that 'Umar retained the land as the (common) possession of the entire Muslim community out of which their fighting people were given their allowances, their border-towns were sealed, and subsistence was given to those who looked after them from among their officials, judges, the disbursing officers, all other officials and those who *[fo. 10-b]* needed them. Then, whatever there remained in excess was distributed among the needy till they became rich, and, then, whatever there remained was divided among the rest of the Muslim community.

If the *Imām* decides to divide it immediately, he can do so, and if he considers to retain it for the future needs and circumstances of the Muslims, he can do so in accordance with his own discretion, good intention, and his conviction in consultation with the people of wisdom and experience from among those who are available to him.

There has been disagreement concerning the modality of division. The Prophet (peace be upon him) used to distribute on the basis of revelation. Abū Bakr used to make equal distribution among the people saying, "Those who preceded in accepting Islam by their activities, were sure to get their reward from Allāh, but this property was only a means of living in which people were equal." 'Alī did so. 'Umar and 'Uthmān used to give on the principle of priority. 'Umar used to give grant to the early converts. He used to say that one must blame only the kneeling place of one's riding beast alone. 'Umar, therefore, fixed for the wives of the Prophet (peace be upon him) twelve thousand *dirhams* each except Ṣafiyyah and Juwayrīyah. It has been mentioned that he gave them six thousand each, as both of them had suffered captivity.

He fixed for the early *Muhājirūn* five thousand each and he himself was like one of them. He fixed for Ḥasan, Ḥusayn and Usāmah ibn Zayd the like of it, while he fixed for his own son 'Abd Allāh three thousand and five hundred. Thereupon, 'Abd Allāh said to him, "Do you give me less then Usāmah?" 'Umar replied "Usāmah was dearer to the Prophet than you, and his father was dearer to him than your father." He gave to the *Anṣār* four thousand each, and the freed *Muhājirūn* three thousand each, and the freed *Anṣār* two thousand each. He gave to the *Muhājirūn,* of the conquest of Makkah, four hundred each. He used to provide the bedouins alongwith the women and children and those who were unable to join the army with generous sustenance. He fixed for a newly born baby one hundred *dirhams*.

In the early phase of his administration he had not prescribed any amount for them. But, it so happened that one night he passed by a woman whose child was crying and a man was asking her to suckle the baby. She said: " 'Umar does not prescribe anything for the newly born baby till the baby is weaned." 'Umar, thereupon, said, "By Allāh, I was about to kill the baby." He prescribed allowances for the newly born baby from that day. He used to begin with the needy.

A group of the people of Kūfah say that when the *Imām* retains the lands, the lands become the possession of their cultivators on whom he will impose *Kharāj* forever whether they accept Islam or not. They argue that 'Umar fixed a specified amount on a *jarīb* of dates every year. They say that *[fo. 11-a]* if it was not legal to do so, it would not be lawful to buy the dates before their appearance.

Some of those who hold the first view say that the entire land was originally without trees, and differences arose only for those plots which were thought good for cultivation. Now, whoever hires what is conducive to the cultivation of wheat, the tax will be fixed for it according to the measurement of wheat, and if he hires what is conducive to the plantation of trees, it will be taxed according to the measurement of that, not on the presumption that there were trees in the land on that day.

Some of them hold that the cultivators of these lands were taken as captives and they were captured by force, therefore, they became the slaves of the Muslims who imposed a tax on them. The *Jizyah* which was imposed on them was in fact *Kharāj*, the payment of which was made binding upon them. The first view, "that the land would be treated without trees" is correct, because most of the *'ulama'* hold that the slaves are not to pay *Jizyah*. And, had the *Kharāj* been paid by the slaves it would have been imposed upon women, and children who could run, but 'Umar had imposed it only on the adult free-men, and I do not know any authority ever holding the view as held by the people of Kūfah. 'Umar and 'Alī had already prohibited buying of any thing from these lands.

There has been disagreement concerning the land of Egypt. Some say it was conquered by force, while others hold that it was conquered by treaty, as has been related by al-Layth on the authority of 'Ubayd Allāh ibn Abū Ja'far and Yazīd ibn Abū Ḥabīb. And it was for this reason that he and others tended to consider the tilling thereon lawful. Some others hold that it was conquerred by treaty which was later on broken by them. 'Amr ibn al-'Āṣī then fought against them and occupied it by force.

There has been disagreement concerning the title by which al-Layth entered (and occupied) the land. Some say he occupied the land after purchasing it, while others hold that he held the land by hiring it, and, yet, others say that he held it by allotment (*iqṭā'*-grant). What is well-known is the fact that he entered (occupied) Egypt by hiring it. His saying that it was taken by treaty, and his insistence on the fact that it was not taken by force indicated his view that what was taken by force was to be divided into five shares, as was done by the Prophet at Khaybar, and that it was not lawful to retain what was taken by force. Had it not been his view, he would not have said, "We know our town, it was conquerred only by treaty." Moreover, he said; I was informed of this by two Jews of the town Yazīd and 'Ubayd Allāh", meaning that the treaty was concluded on the condition that the lands would belong to the Muslims as the Prophet did with some parts of the Ḥijāz, not on the condition that it would be retained by the (original) possessors, because that (second condition) would not permit anybody to enter therein (and occupy the land).

Chapter VII

ON WHAT IS OWNED BY THE TILLERS OF THE LAND AND WHAT IS INHERITED FROM THEM, AND ON THE RULE CONCERNING THEIR WOMEN

Aḥmad says: I have mentioned the difference of opinion concerning the lands retained in their (tillers) hands. Now, as for the purchase of the abodes and other places, which were held in possession of some individuals and that of the wealth they had earned, if the occupants were captured and their lives were spared for the cultivation of the land, as 'Umar has been reported to have done, the majority of the *'ulamā'* hold that they themselves, their women and children are free and that retaining them alive would be treated as grace as exhorted by Allāh in the verse; "And afterwards either grace or ransom" (47: 4).

As regards that which they have earned out of the land not left in their hands, that with which they seek help therein and all that they have produced, will be their possession revolving around them by demarcation, purchase and sale, inheritance or offering in gift, or by any other means by which they owned it. All the lands retained in their hands together with its tools will be treated as mortmain falling in their hands.

Those who consider them slaves, consider all that is in their hands, what they have earned and what remained in their hands as belonging to the entire Muslim community. They also consider their women and children as slaves as long as they are not born of free women; and they treat them like the slaves in respect of all their conditions. But, a few are those who hold this view. The people of Kūfah consider that, what had remained in their hands and what they had earned, were their own property (*milk*); and that they themselves, their women and children were free (*aḥrār*).

Chapter VIII

ON FOUNDING OF TOWNS, GRANT OF LANDS AS FIEFS (*IQṬĀʿ*) AND REVIVAL OF 'DEAD' LANDS (*MAWĀT*)

The Prophet, and the Caliphs after him, used to grant lands to the people from the territory from which their inhabitants were driven out without fighting, from one-fifth of the booty, from unpopulated plots and from uninhabited lands. The Prophet used to write deeds (of grants) for anyone who approached him for the land before it was conquerred. For Example, he wrote a deed of allotment of two villages for Salmān before they were conquerred.

These villages were conquerred by treaty during the time of 'Umar who sanctioned for him the *Kharāj* of those villages. He used to allot to the people only those deserted fields which had not been trampled by the hoofs of camels for pasturing. He would allot neither openly flowing water, nor salt, nor those places from which people gathered their fuel, nor those places where their cattle used to graze, lest this might harm them. He as well as other Caliphs after him, gave grants of mines which in course of time became the possession of those to whom those were granted.

'Umar founded the towns of Baṣrah, Kūfah and towns in Egypt. He granted the land of these places to those who wanted to build structures for themselves which became their possession. He alloted the land of these places to many Companions of the Prophet. Zubayr got an allotment of fourteen houses in these towns. Baṣrah was founded in the year fourteen (H). All of a sudden they discovered a white piece of stone at the time of laying its foundation and they cried out, "Baṣrah: Baṣrah:" (limestone: limestone:) Hence, it was called Baṣrah. Kūfah was built in the year seventeen (H). *[fo. 12-a]* When people got conjested therein, they said, "In this town, we are in Kūfān (the thicket of reeds)". Hence, it was called so.

Egypt was conquerred in the year twenty (H). Its biggest town was Alexandria. There was a place at the spot of the present-day al-Fusṭāṭ near which Zubayr had set up his camp at the time when 'Umar had reinforced 'Amr ibn al-Āṣṣ with him alongwith twelve thousand soldiers. He had, at first, sent 'Amr with three thousand and five hundred soldiers, but afterwards he pitied him and reinforced him with Zubayr and others who were with him. Now, since the city was founded on the spot of the camp (*al-Fusṭāṭ*), it was called so.

It has been reported that the Prophet said: "Whoever revives a 'dead' land it belongs to him, and an unjust occupier has no right." Some *'Ulamā'* hold that there are four (unjust) occupiers; two are explicit and two are implicit. The explicit ones relate to plantations and buildings, and the implicit ones relate to fountains and wells. Mālik says that this concerns deserts and the places which are far away from the human habitation. It appears that Mālik thereby alludes to the Prophetic tradition: "What was not trampled by the hoofs of camels." Ibn al-Qāsim holds similar views.

There has been disagreement concerning the dead or wastelands which are in the vicinity of the inhabited areas. Some scholars think that these are to be included in the rights of inhabited areas. Others hold that these should be distributed among the people of villages who deserve them most. Mālik has also said that nobody has the right to revive a piece of (dead) without the permission of the *Imām*. This is also one of the two views of Ibn al-Qāsim. Ashhab holds that the land belongs to one who revives it without the permission of the *Imām*. But, if he gives permission, the land will belong to him.

They have disagreed concerning the limitation of distance. Mālik says what has been mentioned. Abū Ḥanīfah says: "It will be determined by the device that a man shouts at the one end of the habitation and his voice is not audible to one who is at the other end." Some say, "What is in the midst of the villages will be treated as the right of the villagers in respect of the shares of the inhabitants in accordance with their rights in these villages." It has been proved that the Prophet said, "There is no reserved land (*Ḥimā*) except for Allāh and His Messenger. So, he used to reserve the deserts belonging to none as the property of Allāh. The Caliphs after him retained this practice.

'Umar said, "By Allāh, had it not been the fact that camels belonged to the property of Allāh upon which I make the people ride on the way of Allāh, I would not have reserved even a span of their land, because they fought for it in the days of ignorance and accepted Islam on it. 'Umar used to provide riding beasts for forty thousand. He mounted two persons of 'Irāq and one person of Syria upon a camel. He had put a man Hānī by name in charge of pastures and said to him to lower his side for the believers (i.e. to be lenient), and to include the owners of small herds of camels and sheep in these and to keep away from the cattle *[fo. 12-b]* of Ibn 'Affān and Ibn 'Awf. For, in case, their cattle perish they would turn to dates and crops, but if the cattle of the owners of small herds of camels and sheep perish they would come to me with evidence saying, 'O Amīr al-Mu'minīn! O Amīr al-Mu'minīn!' So; Water and herbage are more convenient for me than gold and silver. Am I therefore going to abandon them; may you have no father?"

Chapter IX

ON THE BOUNDARY OF WELLS, ON HERBAGE, WATER, FIRE, FIRE-WOOD, AND SALT

It has been reported that the Prophet said: "The benefit from the well is not to be withheld." There is disagreement concerning this benefit (*naf'a*) as to what it means. Some say that it means surplus water, while others hold that it means the place wherein the sweepings are thrown. Yet others say that it is the outlet of its flowing water. It is, again, said "the surplus water is not to be withheld, so as to prevent herbage", meaning thereby that if those who have settled over a well of the cattle, prevent others from its surplus water, they in fact prevent others from herbage because water is indispensable for the cattle.

When the Prophet granted al-Dahnā to the Companion of Qīlah, she said: "Surely al-Dahnā is the stable as well as the resting place for the cattle of Banū Tamīm; and the women of Banū Tamīm live behind it." The Prophet, then, took it back. Similarly, when he alloted some plots to a man, it was said to him, "You have alloted the flowing water which is indispensable for the people"; he then took the plots back.

People are, therefore, partners in five things: in water, as they consume it and derive benefit out of it by taking bath and all that is necessary for them and for the drinking of their animals; in herbage, which is not in the possession of any individual; in salt, which nobody can preserve exlusively in his mines; and flames of fire, as nobody can prevent others from enkindling with his flame.

As for fishing in water, they have disagreed concerning what has been reared in water. Some say that one has no right to prevent others from fishing therein. Others say that one has the right to prevent others from fishing therein.

As for the ownerless lands and the thing lying in their river beds and rivers, none has the right to preserve anything out of it, and prevent others from it. If anybody needs water which is in the possession of somebody else, he should fulfil his need. If one refuses, the needy person can take that by force or by any means he can apply even if he has to fight against the owner for it. If the needy person dies out of thirst, his blood-money will be realised from the preventor with severe punishment. Some say that it will be realised from his property, and others say that it will be taken from the relations of his father's side. The discussion of all other circumstances which compel people to do such things, *[fo. 13-a]* will be dealt with in its right place, if Allāh so wishes.

The Prophet granted to Bilāl ibn al-Ḥārith the mines of al-Qabaliyyah in the suburb of Far' which he inhabited along with its surrounding places. When Abū Bakr became Caliph, he said to him, "Surely the Prophet assigned to you so much land which you could not revive, so, allow me to assign out of it to somebody else." Bilāl then allowed him; whereupon he left for him what he could revive and assigned the rest to others.

There is disagreement concerning the enclosure of the wells. Mālik says that it has no fixed limit but such an area should be left to their owners so that it would not harm them. It has been reported on the authority of Ibn al-Musayyib, who said: "The enclosure of the new well is twenty-five cubits on all sides and that of an old well is fifty cubits. Ibn Shihāb says that the enclosure of the well is three hundred cubits and the enclosure of the spring five hundred cubits, and the enclosure of river is one thousand cubits, that is to say, on all sides for those who would revive any piece of land in these wastelands.

There is disagreement concerning the extension of courtyards, the owners of which want to increase any portion thereof. Some say that he can do so as long as it is not harmful to the people. Those who hold this argue that Abū Bakr built a mosque in the courtyard of his house at Makkah before migration, and he used to perform his prayers there. Some others hold that it is not permissible for anybody to make extension on the thoroughfares of the Muslims and on the places from which they derive any benefit.

Chapter X

ON CULTIVATING *KHARĀJ* LANDS, APPROPRIATING THESE BY THE RULERS (*UMARĀ'*) IN THE LATER PERIOD, AND ON THEIR TURNING THE PROPERTY OF ALLAH INTO THEIR PRIVATE ESTATES

It has been reported that the Prophet said: "When the family of so and so reaches thirty men, they take over Allāh's property as (their personal) estates and reduce Allāh's religion to corruption, and make Allāh's servants as their slaves." He also said, "Irāq would withold her *dirham* and *qafīz,* Egypt her *dīnār* and *ardab,* Syria her *dīnār* and *mudd* and you would turn into the same position from which you had started." Meaning that this would happen towards the last days, He also said: "Many a person who meddles in the property of Allāh without any right, will incur Hell-fire." It has also been reported that the Prophet said: "Whoever has incurred or taken *Kharāj,* has indeed incurred or taken humiliation and whoever has incurred or taken humiliation does not belong to us."

It has also been reported that the Prophet said: "Whoever is satisfied with *Ṭisq* from which Allāh has freed him, will have to bear disgrace and humiliation of the people of the two books; which means taking away the land from a *dhimmī* with its tax of *Kharāj.* Many *'Ulamā',* including Mālik, disapprove of hiring the *Kharāj* land on rent because of the *ḥadīth* which refers to this subject. Mālik has explained clearly the idea for which he disliked hiring of *Kharāj* land. He said: "They would want to make the land of the Muslims cheap. *[fo. 13-b]* Some other people allow it and interpret that the meaning of this *ḥadīth* is that whoever takes away this land from a *dhimmī* and transfers to himself its *Jizyah,* he takes it from the authority (*Sulṭān*) while the authority is competent to lease it, there is no harm in taking the land on hire from it or to give the usufruct when he is a deserving person, for a debt that is due to him, or on account of poverty, or due to the big size of the family, or on account of service indispensable for the cause of Islam or for looking after the affairs of the Muslims.

This is held by Ibn Sīrīn, al-Layth, Ashhab, Muḥammad ibn 'Abd al-Ḥakam and many earlier and later scholars. It has been disapproved by some due to the fear that because of this many would buy *Kharāj* lands and thus it would be considered lawful by one who did not deserve it. It is not in the sense that the land is prohibited for one who hires it. For, had it been so, this could not have been retained. The famous view of Mālik is to retain all the lands which are conquerred as it was the practice of 'Umar. But, when the *Imām* divides it in five shares and distributes it, his order will be executed and the land will belong to one who has occupied it, and it will be his possession.

Ibn Wahab was asked about getting (purchasing) the land of Egypt. He disliked to do so. It was thereupon said to him that Ashhab was cultivating the land in Egypt, he said, "Who would do like Ashhab?" Ashhab used to multiply the amount of *ṣadaqah* and offered in alms the multiplied amounts of rent (*Kirā'*).

Saḥnūn says: "Famine broke out in Egypt. I saw him giving *dīnārs* in alms from morning to evening, and offering in alms whatever food he had with him." Al-Layth used to earn four thousand *dīnārs* from his crops, but at the end of the year he had nothing out of it in his hand. He gave to Manṣūr ibn 'Ammār one thousand *dīnārs* and said to him: "Protect with this the wisdom which Allāh has conferred on you." Nāfi' came to Egypt and al-Layth gave him some money. Al-Layth owed Muḥammad ibn 'Abd al-Ḥakam a huge amount (as rent). Then, the governor went out on pilgrimage and al-Layth kept his company like his attendant. When the people dispersed, he asked al-Layth to go away, but he remained with him continuously. He again said to him, "Go away, O Abū 'Abd Allāh", but he prolonged his stay. Muḥammad ibn 'Abd al-Ḥakam then stood up and said: "Do you need anything?" He replied; "I have incurred such an amount as rent of the land." He asked him, "What do you want then?" He replied; "You please put it away from me." He said: "The amount is large, O Abū 'Abd Allāh." He said, "This is not at all a large amount from a person like you for a person like me." He said, "I have waived it."

If the army commanders appropriate the booty for themselves and deprive the soldiers of it, our earlier authorities do not consider it lawful to buy anything out of it. Whoever, then, comes across such a thing he shall have to give in alms four-fifths of it for his accepting from it. Some of them have reported to the effect that he should give in alms the entire price *[fo. 14-a]* by way of caution. Those who oppose us including some of our later scholars hold that he has got the right to sell it. The injustice exists in the prices only. It is, therefore, permissible to buy from him. It is argued by others that by selling, he is agreeing on usurpation, and not on the fact that he can do with the price whatever he likes.

Abū Muṣ'ab considers lawful to buy something out of the expedition in which booty was obtained while *Khums* was kept concealed from the authority with the intent that the buyer would give away *Khums* as charity. I think that he considers this only when the authority does not spend properly what comes to him from Allāh's property, so it is lawful for one who is capable of spending it in its proper way to do so.

THE FIRST PART *ENDS HERE.*
ALL PRAISE BELONGS TO ALLAH, THE LORD OF THE WORLDS.

PART TWO

Chapter I

ON REGISTER (*AL-DĪWĀN*) AND RECEIVING STATE-ALLOWANCES

Ka'b ibn Mālik says: "When the Prophet started for Tabūk, I was one of those who remained behind. We thought that the case of those who remained behind would remain unknown, because we were many in number and there was no register for us. It became impossible for me to gather some equipments for fighting. Every morning I came out to have it, but it became difficult for me to have it; so I said to myself: 'I will get it tomorrow.' This went on till the Prophet left. Then I said to myself: 'Surely I will meet him tomorrow.' And, afterwards, I inclined to the shades (of trees). It, however, grieved me to see that no one remained behind except one who had some excuse or one who was deep in hypocrisy.

"When the Prophet returned and it was announced that he would be entering the city the next morning, I began to recollect what excuse I should make by which I would possibly escape his displeasure. When the Prophet arrived he came to the mosque and performed two *rak'ahs* of prayer as he was accustomed to do this on his arrival." And then Ka'b mentioned the rest of the *Ḥadīth*.

When the people grew in number during the time of 'Umar, he ordered the preparation of a register (*al-Dīwān*) for receiving the allowances as well as for sending expeditions. Thereupon, they registered Banū Ḥāshim, the Banū Taym and then Banū 'Adī, and submitted the register before him. At this, 'Umar said: "You want to please me. Write those who are nearer to the Messenger of Allāh and place 'Umar where Allāh has placed him." They did so. Then 'Abbās came to him and expressed his gratitude for this.

'Umar then ordered to begin with the *Anṣār* on the basis of their relationship with Sa'd ibn Mu'ādh. The allies (*mawālī*) of every group were recorded with them and then the names of the rest of the people were enlisted. He said to Ibn Arqam, who was in charge of the *Bayt al-Māl,* when the latter submitted the Register to him: "Go away and write all the names. Perhaps, you have left somebody whom you did not register." *[fo. 14-b]* Meaning thereby to include everybody. He added, "Everyone without any exception has right in this wealth even if he or she were a shepherd or shepherdess at Adan."

The reason of his selecting 'Abd Allāh ibn Arqam is said to be that one day 'Umar found him present while a letter had come to the Prophet. The Prophet enquired as to who would reply on his behalf? Ibn al-Arqam said, "I shall reply on your behalf, Sir." Ibn al-Arqam expressed what was in the heart of the Prophet. 'Umar kept this in his heart. When he became caliph, he wanted to make use of his honesty and judgment. He often consulted him in dealing with the affairs. 'Umar sent him to 'Irāq to enquire into the complaint when the inhabitants of 'Irāq had complained against Sa'd, but Allāh, however, acquitted Sa'd of the charge they had brought against him.

'Umar appointed some elderly people as tribal representatives (*'Urafā*), assigning one representative to every group who looked into their affairs at the time of sending expeditions and at the time of receiving allowances. They used to submit to him their needs. The Prophet used to appoint representatives for detachments of troops at the time of his going out for battle.

When Banū Hawāzin came to him repenting after he had waited for them for more than ten nights, they said, "You are like our father and we are like your children," or they said, "You are like our child and we are like (your) father, you are the most compassionate to relations and the most righteous in behaviour." The Prophet replied saying, "I have with me those qualities which you see, the best discourse to me is the truest one. I have already waited for you for more than ten nights, so you choose either of the two: either the captives or the cattle (wealth)." They said, "We do not consider anything equivalent to our noble descent."

The Prophet called his Companions and said, "Your brothers have come to me repenting, and I have already given them the choice of either of the two; either the captives or the cattle. They say, they do not consider anything equivalent to their noble descent. So, he whose soul is pleased with the spirit of granting favour it is well and good, otherwise, he will get out of the first booty which Allāh will confer on us." They said: "We agree". The Prophet said, "I do not know who has consented and who has not, you all go away, and let your representatives report to me." The representatives reported to him that they gave their consent and that they yielded.

Thus, the Prophet settled this for them in that way. According to some other reports, Aqra' ibn Ḥabīs and 'Uyaynah ibn Ḥiṣn said, "We are not satisfied." The followers of one of them said like this while the followers of the other said in one voice that they were satisfied. They were, therefore, given something in exchange of what had fallen in their shares. So, one of them got one scabby camel. It also reported that 'Abbās ibn Mirdās said what they said.

Aḥmad says that this is not correct, because although the spoils of war of Hawāzin were in plenty, the Prophet gave to those whose hearts needed reconciliation out of *Khums* and they were more than *[fo. 15-a]* forty men. He gave one of them one hundred camels. When Banū Qaynuqā' and Banū'l Naḍīr were expelled, the Messenger of Allāh divided their properties among the *Muhājirūn* excluding Anṣār except three from Anṣār for whom he assigned shares. They were: Sahl ibn Ḥanayf, al-Ḥārith ibn Ṣummah, Abū Dujānah Sammāk ibn Kharashah on account of starvation they suffered from.

Some say that Prophet divided some parts of the landed property and retained some, but I do not consider it correct. For, had it been so, it would have been mentioned in the genuine *ḥadīth*.

The Prophet had already laid down the condition to the Anṣār when he took the oath of allegiance from them at 'Aqabah at Makkah that they would support those *Muhājirūn* who came to them. The Anṣār, said: "O Messenger of Allāh, we shall share with them in roots (date-palms)." The Prophet said, "The *Muhājirūn* have no knowledge of the work of date-palms, so you give them sufficient provision and share with them the expenses," and they did accordingly.

When Allāh conferred on them the wealth of Banū Qaynuqā' and Banū'l Naḍīr, the Prophet said, to the Anṣār: "If you so desire, you may remain on your condition and I shall divide this wealth among you along with your brothers: but if you so desire, I shall return to you your wealth and let me divide the booty among them by excluding you." They then accepted it (the latter). The Prophet was more generous in giving wealth than the swiftly blowing wind, and he was most generous in the month of Ramaḍān when Gabriel used to come to him.

When the booty of Baḥrayn was brought before the Prophet and it was indeed the largest amount of wealth ever brought before him in his life—eighty thousand *Dirhams*. The Anṣār then heard about it, so they gathered around him in the morning-prayer, coming to him from the remote corners of al-Madīnah. Looking at them the Prophet smiled and said, "I think you have heard of the arrival of Abū 'Ubaydah and of the fact that he has brought something?" They said: "Yes" He said: "Then rejoice and be full of that which pleases you, By Allah, it is not poverty which I fear for your sake. But I fear the world which will be opened for you as it was opened to the people before you, and you would vie with one another for it as they vied with one another, and the world will destroy you as it destroyed them."

'Abbās came to the Prophet and said: "I have redeemed myself, Faḍl and Aqīl and I do require that which Allāh has promised as He said, 'Say unto those captives who are in your ḥands: if Allāh knoweth any good in your hearts, he will give you better than that which hath been taken from you' (8: 70)." The Prophet, thereupon ordered him to take (something), and 'Abbās put things in his mantle and then wanted to raise it to his shoulder but he failed. He then sought help from the Messenger of Allāh to raise it to him, but the Messenger of Allāh refused to do so. He then asked him to order somebody to raise it for him. The Messenger of Allāh replied again in the negative. Then he dropped something out of it and intended to lift it up, but he failed again. Then he asked the Messenger of Allāh again to raise it to him, but he refused. Then he said, "Ask someone to raise it." He said, "No". Then he again dropped something out of it and lifted it with much difficulty and went away. The eyes of the Messenger of Allāh followed him in surprise at his covetousness till the time he disappeared from his sight.

After this, the Prophet said to Jābir, "If there comes to us the wealth of Baḥrayn, I shall give you so much and so much," *[fo. 15-b]* he encompassed his two hands. And the wealth of Baḥrayn came after the demise of the Prophet. Jābir then mentioned this to Abū Bakr, but Abū Bakr kept silent. He again mentioned it but Abū Bakr kept quiet. The he said; "Either you will give me or you will be niggardly with me." Abu Bakr then replied, "Which disease is more sickening than niggardliness? Had you not spoken to me once I would have given it to you, and he gave him a handful. Then he asked him to count, and on counting he found five-hundred *dirhams*. He afterwards asked him to count one thousand over and above this.

'Umar saw a golden set of clothes placed for sale near the gate of the mosque, whereupon, he said, "O Messenger of Allāh, if you could buy this for wearing for the delegations when they come to you and for the Friday prayer." The Messenger of Allāh said: "Only those who have no share (in the Hereafter) will wear it." Afterwards some sets of clothes of the same stock reached him, one of which he gave to 'Umar. 'Umar thereby said: "O Messenger of Allāh, you clothe me with this set of clothes while you had remarked concerning the set of golden clothes what you remarked." The Messenger of Allāh replied: "I have not given it to you to wear it."

'Umar thereupon sent it to his polytheist brother who was at Makkah. He gave it to him so that he could wear it.

Ḥakīm ibn Ḥizām says: "I begged something of the Messenger of Allāh who gave me, then I again asked him and he gave me. I, again, repeated my prayer, and he gave me and said, 'O Ḥakīm, how intense is your begging. Verily this wealth is sweet and fresh, so, whoever receives this with generous soul, he will find it full of blessings, and he who receives this for the sake of ennobling his (lower) soul will be as if he ate but did not feel contented, and surely the best thing for you is not to accept anything from anybody.' " Thereupon, he enquired, "And even not from you?" the Messenger of Allāh replied: "And even not from me." He said, "By Allāh, I shall not accept any thing from anybody after this." And he did not afterwards accept anything from anyone.

'Umar used to present to him his allowance, whereupon, Ḥakīm used to say, "I gave up this in the time of one who was better than you," meaning the Prophet. 'Umar then used to say; "I ask you to bear witness, O Muslims, the Prophet had only said this to Ḥakīm when he saw him ennobling his soul by begging."

The Prophet gave a gift to 'Umar, whereupon, he said to the Prophet, "O Messenger of Allāh! did you not say that it was best thing for anyone of you not to accept anything from anybody." The Prophet replied, "It was only in the case of asking for something. As for that which comes without asking, it is only a kind of sustenance which Allāh has given you." 'Umar then said, "By Allāh, I shall never ask anybody for anything nor I shall refuse anything which is given to me."

Abū Musā says: "I came to the Messenger of Allāh in a group of Asha'rites to ask him for a riding-beast, but we found him busy. The Prophet said: 'By Allāh, I shall not give you a riding-beast.' We therefore turned away: and all of a sudden there came to him thirteen young she-camels. The Prophet then sent for us and gave us some young she-camels with which we moved ahead. Then we talked among ourselves saying: 'We are afraid, the Messenger of Allāh *[fo. 16-a]* surely forgot his oath; did he not swear that he would not give us riding beasts? And he gave us the riding beasts.' We then mentioned this to the Prophet. He said; 'Surely, I shall make you mount the riding-beasts; by Allāh, I surely make you mount the riding-beasts. By Allāh, whenever I do take any oath, and I find afterwards something else better, I offer the atonement for my oath and do the best.' "

Sa'd says: "I was present with the Prophet on the occasion of payment. He gave a man and left out a man who was dearer to me. I then spoke to him secretly, saying 'O Messenger of Allāh, I surely find him a believer (*mu'min*),' " or he said, a Muslim. He says: "Then I sat down, but what I knew of him overtook me and I repeated the same to him." The Prophet then said: "Surely I give a man a gift while somebody else is dearer to me than him fearing lest Allāh would throw the latter headlong into the Hell-Fire." He added, "Verily I give some people and entrust some others to their faith and 'Amr ibn Ḥārith is one of them."

They overwhelmed him by asking for something, so much so that he was forced to lean against an acacia tree which stuck to his mantle, whereupon he said: "Return to me my mantle, by Allāh, I have taken nothing out of that which Allāh has conferred on you, nor even this (and he pointed to a hair of his camel) except *al-Khums,* which is again returned to you. By Allāh, had Allān conferred on you the bounties like the acacia trees of Tihāmah, surely, I would have apportioned them all among you and then you would not find me niggardly or cowardly, nor a liar."

A bedouin pulled his mantle. He was wrapped up in this heavily bordered Najranian mantle. This was done so violently that it left a mark on his neck. The bedouin said: "O Muḥammad, order for me out of the wealth of Allāh which is before you." The Prophet then looked at him, laughed and issued orders to give it to him.

Nobody remained behind from receiving the allowances from him (the Prophet) except Ḥakīm, because of the Prophet's exchange of words with him. Some say that Abū Dharr also refused to receive any allowances on account of his aversion to accumulation of wealth.

The people continued on this upto the death of 'Umar when some of them did not accept any allowance by way of seeking purity and fearing Allāh lest they might receive more than their dues. During the time of 'Umar they were safe from this because of his strict personal discretion, so, the people were in between receiving and giving up the allowance. The recipient did not hold anything in this unseemly, nor did he fear any sin on account of the purity of the collected tax.

However, when the caliphate shifted from the Companions of the Prophet to others, some undesirable levies began pouring in the treasuries. So others remained behind in receiving allowances, as for example, they were Ibn al-Musayyib, Bishr ibn Sa'īd, Ṭā'ūs and others.

Some other people considered receiving allowances lawful as it contained mostly the permissible things, and compared with the permissible things the undesirable ones were very meagre in it. This continued till their desire of receiving the things by the proper way became scanty. What their hands contained consisted of the things collected unlawfully.

The *'Ulamā'*, in general, avoided this and forbade others to receive it except something which was known definitely as good and the recipient of it *[fo. 16-b]* deserved the gift for the reason I mentioned above, then he could receive this. Whoever is employed in a useless work or any help is sought from him for an unjust cause or for something which is not useful for the Muslims, it will not be lawful for him to live on it though the amount paid to him be lawful and good.

Chapter II

ON *ANFĀL, FAY', GHANĪMAH* AND *'USHR* OF LANDS

Allāh, the Exalted, says: "They ask thee (O Muḥammad) of the spoils of war", upto the end of the verse (8: 1). And He says: "That which Allāh giveth as spoils unto His Messenger" (59: 7). And He says, "And know that whatever ye take as spoils of war, lo! a fifth thereof is for Allāh and for the Messenger" (8: 41). So, *Anfāl* means supererogatory gifts since Allāh gave this as a supererogatory gift on and above the victory which He had granted them. His saying continues: "And We bestowed upon him Isaac and Jacob as a grandson (*Nāfilatan*)" (21: 72), and His saying: "And pray in the small watches of the morning: (it would be) an additional prayer (or spiritual profit) (*Nāfilatan*) for thee" (17: 79).

Fāy' is that which Allāh returned to them out of the wealth of the enemy; and *ghanīmah* is that on which they prevailed upon. The names of *fāy'* and *anfāl* both include all kinds of booty.

Some of the jurists have disagreed concerning these terms: some say that *fāy'* is that which Allāh confers on them without fighting, and *ghanīmah* is that which they obtain and prevail upon after coming out victorious, and this is an explanation which has not been traced back (to the Prophet), and this does not make impossible to name *ghanīmah* as *fāy'* because *ghanīmah* is also included in that which Allāh has conferred. Some say that *ghanīmah* is that which they obtain without fighting and *fāy'* is that upon which they prevailed upon; but, this is wrong.

Mālik deferred his view concerning the *Jizyah* taken from land, as to whether it will be treated as *fay'* or as *ṣadaqah;* and he thought that he would investigate into this to know about the real problem. Ibn al-Qāsim says that Imām Mālik tended to think that it would be treated as *fāy'*, and there is no doubt in this. But he (Imām Mālik) deferred his view about it just to avoid sin. As to one who enquired Ibn 'Abbās, he only enquired Ibn

'Abbās of the word itself as to wherefrom it was derived, to which Ibn 'Abbās had replied that it was in a way derived from *al-Anfāl*. He (Ibn 'Abbbās) says that the horse and the personal effects constitute *nafal*. Now, the man repeated the question till he put him (Ibn 'Abbās) into inconvenience.

They have disagreed concerning the *'ushr* of a *Kharāj* land. Mālik and many *'Ulamā'* hold that when a free Muslim cultivates it on payment of *Kharāj*, or it is given to him by way of gift, he shall have to pay along with this (*Kharāj*), *'ushr* also as *Zakāh* of the crops in the lands which are irrigated by flowing water, by the roots of the trees (*ba'l*) and by rain, and half of *'ushr* when the lands are irrigated artificially. Al-Layth and many others hold that neither *'ushr* nor half of *'ushr* is to be imposed on the *Kharāj* land.

They have differed on the *'ushr* land which is owned by the Muslims belonging particularly to each one of them. Mālik and many *'ulamā'* hold that if the land is cultivated by a free Muslim adult or minor *[fo. 17-a]* male or female, he shall have to pay *'ushr;* but if it is cultivated by a *dhimmī* or a slave, who got it on rent or as a gift, no *Zakāh* will be imposed on the (grain) crops.

Some people of Kūfah hold that only the land is to be considered and not its cultivator; If it is a *Kharāj* land, *'ushr* will not be imposed thereon, and if it is the land of *'ushr,* the *'ushr* will not be remitted from its cultivator, whether he is a slave or a *dhimmī*. Al-Layth, however, holds that *'ushr* was not to be imposed on the *Kharāj* land. He himself used to pay this accordingly.

Chapter III

ON IFRĪQIYYAH, SPAIN AND SICILY

(Historical) reports differ concerning the affair of Ifrīqiyyah. Some say it was conquered by (a peace) treaty; other say that it was taken by force of arms, and some others hold that its inhabitants accepted Islam on retaining the lands in their possession.

Saḥnūn says: "I have investigated into its affair but I could not arrive at any decisive conclusion concerning it. A man came to him with a treasure-trove which he had found in a place in Ifrīqiyyah, Saḥnūn divided it into five shares and afterwards divided the four-fifths and gave him half of it and put the other half along with the one-fifth in *Bayt al-Māl*.

Aḥmad says: "The border of Ifrīqiyyah is from Ṭarābulus to Ṭabnah. What is necessary to keep in mind concerning this is to let that continue which has been agreed upon throughout the centuries and let it be retained in the hands of its owners except when it was generally known that it was usurped or its inhabitants were ejected from it.

"So is the case with the places known as *al-Akhmās* which became so famous and the knowledge of which became so well-known throughout the centuries, and thus each place that was inhabited was known to the neighbours without any disagreement and the details of rights thereof were corroborated, and thus the matters like this could not possibly remain unknown to the people of the place and to those who lived in its neighbourhood.

"As to the land of Spain, some people have already entered into it, thinking that Spain, or most of it was conquered by force. It was not divided into five shares, nor was it distributed, except that people occupied some portions thereof without obtaining allotment (*iqṭā'*) from the *Imām*. It was not left out for those Muslims who would come in future. The case being so, it is binding upon the occupant of any portion out of it, to declare himself immune of it so that it might be used for the welfare of the Muslims and he should give away its rent to the needy. However he can use it when there was none to follow its proper course."

It is also said that a group of the Berber troops, who had conquered al-Faraj, proceeded to a place out of the conquered lands and asked its ruler (*wālī*) to hand over the place to them in exchange for their share of booty. The ruler, therefore, gave them the place, and they got it as a grant (of fief). They then remained settled therein for a long time. Afterwards they were summoned to vacate the land by another ruler, but they refused and fought over it till they were ejected from it. (Now the question is) whether it is lawful to dwell therein or to buy the foodstuffs gathered from it?

He (Aḥmad) says that in case the chief of the army (*Ṣāḥīb al-Jaysh*) had already divided the rest of the conquered lands among the entire army and whatever he had given them was to the extent of their rights or little less or more, or little to that extent the like of which might be cheated by the people *[fo. 17-b]* in transactions, or he gave them obviously an additional amount which he counted out of *Khums,* and declared the excess as a *nafal* for them all, these will be sanctioned for them. They have right to defend it against anyone who intends to take hold of it.

But if it was not divided among the troops as it was divided among them (Berber troops) and he had given them to the extent of their rights, they would not be interfered with, since the land which was conquered and out of which a portion was given to them remained intact.

But if the troops are known and, in case of their death, their heirs are known, they would be given out of it to the extent of their rights. But if they are not well known it would be treated as a property the owner of which was dead while his heir was not known. But if it is known that the ruler gave them more than their rights and more than the entire *Khums* with an evident excess in which injustice was known, then everyone of them should surrender the property to the extent of the excess if it was known.

But if it was not known and the matter remains unknown, the bearer can carry as much as he can. They would have what was in their hands except when one observes piety, then, he may withdraw from that which was in his hand, and can give its rent as *ṣadaqah.* But when it is proved that the matter was correct or the matter was unknown, what was taken back from them would be restord to them provided they were available. But if only some of them are found, then what is in his hand should be restored to them. Those who are not found should be searched out. But if tracing is not possible, what he has taken from the property would be regarded as a property the heir of which was not known. We have already mentioned the rule about it.

An enquiry was made of what has been narrated on the authority of Saḥnūn concerning the purchase of portions of Sicily which were conquered by the Muslims. The reporter says concerning what is mentioned (about it) that Sicily was neither divided into five shares, nor was it distributed among the army, nor was the entire of it retained as *waqf* (mortmain) for the Muslims who would come in future as it was reported concerning the practice of 'Umar. People entered therein and its food-stuffs were carried to different parts of Ifrīqiyyah. Saḥnūn disliked this as it belonged orginally to the land (of Sicily).

Some people said to him: "When Sicily was conquered by force, the inhabitants of some fortresses refused to surrender—till they came down after making a peace-treaty. Then some of those who had made peace-treaty ran away while their houses remained intact." He says: "As to those who remained from among those who had entered into a peace-treaty, if they made treaty on the terms that the land would belong to them and that *Jizyah* was to be imposed on their heads, then they would have their lands, doing therein whatever they liked.

"Whoever accepted Islam from among them would be freed from *Jizyah* on their heads and would get their lands. But if they concluded a peace-treaty on the terms that *Jizyah* was to be imposed on both their land and heads, none of them would be allowed to have the right of selling his land because their land was (a source of) strength. Whoever from among them embraced Islam, *Jizyah* would lapse from his head as well as from his land to the extent of the *Kharāj* to be fixed as due against his land which would belong *[fo. 18-a]* to him and he would be allowed to do with the land whatever he liked."

He says: "As for those who were ejected, if they were recognised or their heirs and properties from which they were ejected were known, these would belong to them. But if their properties were not known and those who had settled therein after them were not in doubt and confusion because the property was kept separated and was not used by those who remained there, except that they did not know their own shares separately or knew what belonged to everyone of them (these properties will be *fay'*). But they did not turn up, or the news of their death became known, but it was not known how they were inherited, whether they embraced Islam, or remained disbelievers, so, what remained unknown like this, was to be treated like the *fay'* which Allāh had conferred on the Muslims.

"But if the *Imām* decides to retain it so that what it yields is to be spent for the welfare of the Muslims, he can do so. If he decides to sell it and spend its price in the welfare of the Muslims, he can do so. But if there is no *Imām* to look into the affairs of the Muslims, the just persons of the place will look into the affairs of the Muslims as it would have been done by a just *Imām*."

It was said to him: "Some of the people of these fortresses have run away; they were subdued by the Muslims by killing and choking, and so they ran to Damascus and other places." He said: "If it was done to them by way of oppression while they had not disregarded the treaty, they would be asked to settle in the lands from which they were ejected provided they were available or their heirs were available and were recognised. But, if they remained unknown, it would be treated as *fay'* conferred by Allāh on the Muslims."

It was said to him: "What do you think about the sale of the lands and houses in the island of Sicily after they were conquered and left for all the Muslims?" He said, "If it is proved that the land was retained for the Muslims as it has been reported about the decision of 'Umar concerning the *Sawād* of Iraq and Egypt, their sale would not be allowed and the land would be restored to its former state. If this is not proved and the land remained in the occupation of those who possessed it by means of oppression in the same way as it is said that the powerful people occupied by force many places without dividing them into five shares while the rest of the army received nothing, the occupant should withdraw from it and hand it over to those who would look into it for the welfare of the Muslims."

It was again said to him that the houses and dwellings thereof were divided unequally and the ruler preferred his own groups and gave them a good deal thereof without any right and without their sacrifice for the cause of Islam thus depriving the entire army. He observed that this case was like the one that has preceded.

A group of people from Spain came out to wage *Jihād* on a fleet of boats and reached Sicily where they found that the enemy had already surrounded the Muslims in a fortress. The Spaniards landed to confront them, defeated the enemy and killed them. The Muslims then came forth and the fortress was conquered. The Spaniards behaved arrogantly towards those *[fo. 18-b]* who were in the island. Whereupon they pounced upon the Spaniards and killed them, while the Spaniards had their landed properties along with them which were not recognised in those days.

He says: "If what belongs to the Spaniards is in good quantity but their places as well as their occupants are not known, nor anybody from those at whose disposal the landed properties are could ascertain how these became their exclusive properties out of the holdings of the Spaniards, the occupant should withdraw from his possession.

"But, in case their belongings are scanty, and the affair is not known, nor can anybody know its place and the title of his exclusive possession, then whoever holds something in possession at present should withdraw from these out of piety without any decree upon him to the effect. But if he gives up his possession from a portion thereof to the extent of what belonged to the Spaniards this is surely a praiseworthy act."

Some people question as to the case of a man who inhabits in this kind of land, dwells therein on rent, or by purchase or by a grant offered by the ruler or having a share which the ruler divided among his troops. He says: "If most of the town or its major parts are those areas from which the Spaniards were ejected and the places exactly are not known, nor do the Spaniards of the day know them, the land will be treated as a property whose owners are not known, and will be considered a *fay'* which Allāh has conferred on the Muslims. But if the place from which they were ejected is scanty, the opinion concerning it has already been discussed earlier."

It was then enquired whether in these places the fruits from the old trees or from the trees planted by the Muslims could be taken with or without the permission of the occupants in case when one only eats and carries with him nothing? He says, "If the land is developed today and what has been abandoned by its owners are in plenty, I have already stated to you that it would be treated as a *fay'* which Allāh has conferred on the Muslims. There is no harm if anybody needs it and eats with good intention.

"But if most of the land belonged to those who had remained behind, none will be allowed to consume anything thereof and the occupant will be asked to leave it by way of piety. However if his soul does not approve of this action, he can fix the portion to the extent of their right and withdraw from his occupation to that extent. If they do not do accordingly, any transaction with them should be avoided. One who enters into any transaction with them with regard to that which is in their hands, the transaction will not be binding, he will surely fall into *ḥarām*, the unlawful."

It was said to him that there were people whom the ruler forcibly settled in a place not possessed by any Muslim while the place was desolate having no trees therein. They then spread therein and inhabited and planted (trees) in it, whether it was lawful for them to derive benefit out of it if they so desired? He said that it was permissible for them; they could freely use these as their possession over which nobody had any claim.

It was said to him that if one plants anything on a thoroughfare, or he digs wells there, or constructs mosques and declares them mortmains and then it was seized by the ruler of the time who restored it to *Bayt [fo. 19-a] al-Māl* or offered it to a tenant, would the place be allowed to be inhabited or the fruit grown therein be taken? He said "If the plantation or construction was made therein by way of an encroachment without any doubt he would surely have the price of demolishing and uprooting of the plantation. But, if the ruler uses it for some better purpose and includes it in the welfare of the Muslims, it is permissible to purchase, hire and occupy it by all permissible means.

"As for one who plants trees and raises constructions he is to pay the rent of the portion he dwells in and of the portion he uses. The account will be settled therein in accordance with the price of the crops uprooted."

It was enquired of him about a fortress which was at the distance of three miles from the sea and lying waste at the time of its conquest. The Muslims then inhabited it and it became prosperous. A group of people then proceeded to it and used it as pastures for their cattle without obtaining allotment (*iqṭā'*) from the ruler and settled there for a long time. Another group of people from the town, then, came to them and started using the land as pastures. Now the inhabitants of the place defended the place against them and treated the area as their landed properties and made boundaries all around for them and lived there. This caused a fight among them for the land.

Consequently, those who had settled therein in the beginning killed a number of the people who had driven them out of it. The latter, thereupon, complained to the ruler who sent to them an army. As a result most of the inhabitants of the fortress, who had defended it, were killed and the rest ran away. The fortress, thus, remained in the possession of those who had driven people out of it and in these they got neither permission nor allotment from the ruler. They stayed there for a long time while the rulers continued in succession without challenging them till some of the rulers forced them to cut the wood for the boats to be used for *Jihād* but they refused to cut the wood and said: "Our duty is only to wage *Jihād* and we are not wood-cutters." The ruler, thereupon, sent armies in succession and besieged them till they suffered destitution, and the siege prolonged. The besieged, thereupon, sought refuge with the Christians and a number of them ran away to them but were not helped by the Christians and met their end.

The fortress was vacated by all of them. The ruler then gave orders for inhabiting the fortress to which people were brought from all sides and were forced to settle therein. The fortress was allotted to them. Thus the ruler made them dwell in its houses and many successors of the original inhabitants also dwelt there along with some other people who had come from Ifrīqiyyah. Some of them were rich and some were not rich. Then there rose the progeny of the Agrigento who had been ousted from the fortress along with some early settlers who had survived and said to the ruler that the land was theirs and that he should remove the usurpers from there. The ruler enquired as to how the city belonged to them. Some elderly people said that they had purchased the land from a man known as al-Ṭiflī. The ruler of the period asked to sell to anyone willing to buy. Others *[fo. 19-b]* said that the land belonged to them as they had bought it from Ibrāhīm ibn Aḥmad. And that they had fought along with him at Taormina and had received six thousand as *fay'* with which they had purchased it from him. The ruler then said: "By Allāh, is there any deed or document in your possession?" they replied, "Long time has passed over it, we have nothing of the kind in our hand." He then, said, "This land belongs to the whole community of the Muslims, I am not giving you this because of your claim."

The ruler asked some of the old people of Sicily, who were present at this court, about Agrigento, a man told him that the registers were entirely in the possession of his father who was in charge of the *Khums* as well as *Kharāj* of the land. He was also a trustee over it. He used to read about this fortress recorded in the *Dīwān*. He paid every year for all its stony lands and herbages therein. He paid the tax and was in charge of the *Bayt al-Māl* of the Muslims except that the Register was burnt down in the days of Khalīl ibn al-Ward.

The sons of 'Abd al-Ṣamad said: "We were present with Ibrāhīm ibn Aḥmad and had said to him, 'Sell to us this fortress for six thousand *dīnārs*.' He favoured us but he neither completed the deal, nor we gave him the price, and it remained so upto this day." The ruler thereupon, said to them: "Live along with the people as they lived and nobody from among you should say that this belonged to his father or else I shall cut his tongue. It appears to me that nothing belongs to you."

They, thereafter, settled there on condition that the land belonged to the Muslims in common till an army of the Muslims was sent to the Roman cities, and a group of the army from among the people of that fortress and other places fled away (from the battle-field). By way of punishment, the ruler forced those who had fled away to settle in Taormina, Remitta, Waliyaj and the deserted fortresses in the vicinity of the enemy. They then settled therein as long as Allāh wished. Then some of the elderly people of Agrigento approached the ruler and said: "We are the people of one and the same race so put us in one and the same place. If a calamity overtakes us we shall face it together." He, therefore, put them all in Syracuse and forced all their ancient companions to settle at Susah. They again rose after some time and said to the ruler: "We have landed properties in that fortress." The ruler said to them that the decision had been taken concerning them that they could only live with the Muslims. Now, whoever got his house pulled down or trees uprooted, he could take the price upon proclamation. They, thus, sold their houses and all that brought price for them. Nevertheless, they always used to say, "Our landed properties are not permissible for anyone."

Aḥmad said: "The beginning of your question was different from the end of it. You said in the beginning of your question that a group of people had turned it into pastures *[fo. 20-a]* after it was desolate till it so happened that they were driven out of it by another group of people who again were driven out by the ruler after he had killed most of them, without omitting any possibility of doubt in your question, nor mentioning the source of your information. Then, you mentioned their views and their disagreement; some of them saying that they had purchased from a particular ruler, and others claiming that they had purchased it from another ruler, while some other people gave evidence to the contrary of this.

"The reply to your question is this: if the knowledge of these cases was continuous and was transmitted likewise, the action would be taken in accordance with what has been transmitted continuously (that is to say) if their narration of planting trees and that of resistance of their planters was continuous as you mentioned. Now if the owners of the trees had planted them for residing and making boundaries therein, without any desire of going away from these and also they had inhabited the entire fortress or most of it, they had better claim to the fortress than those who drove them out of it.

"If they themselves, their places and how they inherited them were known, these places would belong to them. But if they all or some of them were not known whereas some were known, the property, the owners of which are not known, would be treated as a *fay'* as conferred by Allāh on the Muslims.

"But if they planted trees in some places while some other places remained vacant, then in the parts inhabited by those who resisted the former group who wanted to eject them as well as the places which remained desolated they had better claim to these. If the areas particularly were known or how they were inherited was known, the case would be settled accordingly. If the owners of the places were not known, nor was it known how they inherited, then it would be a *fay'* which Allāh had conferred on the Muslims. But, in case the transmission of reports was not continuous, and if the statement of those who stated that they used to pay the usual *Kharāj* to the *Bayt al-Māl* was established, this would be settled accordingly and the tax would be spent for the welfare of the Muslims.

"If the ruler made the people inhabit therein after due consideration, this would continue. But if this was not established, nor was the real case known and the stories varied and nothing was transmitted continuously except the statement of the ejection of the people who drove away from these the owners of trees, that the ruler had expelled them from these places, then the place would belong to them. If they confirmed one another therein the matter would be settled in accordance with what they mutually confirmed.

"But if they disagreed and made claims for their own rights against each other, they would be asked to prove their claims. Now whoever proved for himself something with evidence, he would take hold of it, but if there was nothing except a claim, then the object claimed would be divided among *[fo. 20-b]* the claimants on the basis of their oath. Thus, everyone of them would take oath to the effect that what he claimed belonged to him, and then the thing would be divided among them.

"As for the claim of one who says that the registers were at the disposal of his father as well as for the claim of Banū 'Abd al-Ṣamad, these would make nothing binding, because in most of the cases the rulers had transgressed; sometimes they became angry with some people and seized their entire landed property and entered these into their registers.

"Those who asked Ibrāhīm ibn Aḥmad to sell the fortress to them might have summoned to purchase those lands from the ruler which were taken away from them by way of injustice. But it was not possible for them to claim what was taken away by the rulers on account of their position and power and nothing could be relied upon in this case except the continuous transmission, and that two reliable witnesses should give evidence to the effect that they continued listening to the just people who decreed on evidence in the case and that they had acted accordingly.

"So what is established by a continuous transmission would be acted upon as I shall mention to you. But if the matter is proved to be dubious, I shall see that your question does not vary from the fact that the ruler ejected some people from the fortress. I have already explained how the action should be taken in case when they were known or not known, and in case when they are not known what to do with what belongs to everyone of them exactly and how they would inherit their property except that all of their heirs were known.

"If they had made a peace-treaty on something they would not be interfered with. But if they refused to make peace, it would be postponed till they come to terms concerning it. If the matter was as you mentioned and it was proved that it was a free land belonging to none it would be lawful for one, to whom the ruler assigned anything out of it, to derive benefit from it and own it in the way he got it. If the ruler granted itself to him, he would have it, but if the ruler allowed him to drive benefit only it would be so.

"If the matter was difficult, they could be treated as I have mentioned to you that the fortress would belong to those whom the ruler had ejected from it. If they claimed that their rights were well-known, they would not be interfered with and nobody else would be allowed to derive benefit from any part thereof except one who would be allowed to do so by one of the owners who had claimed it for himself without any contest or dispute or permitted him to continue cultivating it, or to take the fruit for a particular period or he makes it exclusively (cut off) for himslelf. Again, it would not be lawful to buy the fortress from them, nor to take it one rent as long as they were prevented from it. It is, however, permissible to accept from them anything they offered without price.

"In case it is not known what belonged to them originally and how they inherited it, it would be treated as *fay'* conferred by Allāh on the Muslims. This would be a lawful possession for those who were favoured by the ruler by way of consideration in a proper way. But if the ruler did not act therein properly and entrusted it to those who did not deserve the same, then, the case would be considered by his successor, or even by just Muslims known for their justice and power in case his successors had not done their duty properly. Contrarywise, nobody will be allowed to eat anything out of it except the needy or those who can accept the property of the Muslims."

It is said about the person who had in his possession some landed property *[fo. 21-a]* from Agrigentum, the original inhabitants who had inhabited it and in which they had planted trees and then abandoned these lands till the trees perished and the land became desolate and "dead". Then, some other people came there and inhabited it and as a result, new trees were planted in place of the old ones and thus they grew into huge wealth. But before they were revived a second time, these were full of plants and the bulls had eaten up all of it. When these lands were inhabited the second time and ten years elapsed the trees became mature and became five hundred *rubā'ī* (i.e. four cubits high) while before their development they were only three *rubā'ī*.

He says: "If it is proved that Agrigentum belongs to the people whom the ruler ejected from it, and that their migration from the place was due to oppression which was meted out to them and that they did not give up what was in their possession, the second group, then, alighted therein on interpreting the difference of opinion concerning the origin of the place, the former will be asked to hand over to the latter a price in between the price of the place as a desolate one and that of its price evaluated on the day when it was decreed for you. If he refuses to do so the reclaimer will be asked to hand over to the former its price in accordance with its value on the day he started reclaiming it. If he refuses, both of them will be treated as partners. The one, in respect of the price of the deserted land and the other in respect of its price in between the prices evaluated before and after its development.

"This is so when the land was reclaimed by plantation only, but if the trees replaced the former ones, he will get the wages of his labour therein. If it is not proved that the land belonged to those whom the ruler ejected from it, rather if it is proved to the effect that it was a case in which lands were to be treated as a *fay'* which Allāh has conferred on the Muslims, the action therein between the planter and those who look into the affairs of the Muslims will be as I have described the action between him and the occupant who abandoned it. But if the Girgentian abandoned it without coming under any oppression and compulsion rather merely out of losing interest in it and with the intent that he would not come back to it though his ownership had already been established as I described and afterwards this man reclaimed it, the land would belong to one who reclaimed it."

He says: "If it is established by the evidence that a Girgentian who reclaimed it first was not the heir of the Girgentian who owned it and it belonged, in fact, to a different inhabitant of Agrigentum and it is also established that Agrigentum actually belongs to those whom the ruler had ejected from it and its owners were known, the matter between them and those who inherited it the second time will be dealt as I have described it to you, and that the other person has no claim over it."

He was asked about those land-owners who died leaving no heir, and whom the ruler had ejected, then a man from Ifrīqiyyah came there and got it allotted (as an *iqṭā'*) to himself and inhabited it with or without the permission of the ruler. He said that if he had inhabited it with the permission of the ruler, it would belong to him and if he inhabited it while it was desolate without the permission of the ruler who, if allowed him to continue his hold over it, *[fo. 21-b]* it would belong to him, otherwise, he would get the price of what he would spend on its reclamation or revival."

Then it was said to him: "What do you think, if the poor are allowed to dwell in the fortress, drink its water, and cultivate its field? Moreover, how it would be lawful for the rich if the ruler forced them not to dwell there and how to buy food-stuff from the fortress, and bring down ships therein, and to load them with their food stuff?"

He said: "If it is proved that the fortress belonged to those who were ejected from it as you have described and they are known, its dwelling would not be allowed for anybody else and the owners should be asked to go back to the fortress. But if they were unknown, nor was it known how they inherited it and what was their property, or it was proved that the fortress belonged to the Muslims, then it is lawful for the rich as well as for the poor to dwell therein. Whenever the ruler assigned as grant (*iqṭā'*) any portion thereof by way of consideration it would belong to him. And whoever was favoured by the ruler with any part of it, it would belong to him. The purchase of any dwelling-place therein from a person who lived therein lawfully and transaction with him will be permissible. But whoever lived therein illegally, the purchase of the crops raised from the place and the fruits plucked from the trees planted therein is disapproved. If the majority of the owners of the fortress are not known while some owners are known, the lands in which the owners are not known will be treated as I mentioned to you, as that which Allāh conferred on the Muslims as *fay'*.

"The *Imām* will issue orders concerning it according to his discretion. He may assign it as an *iqṭā'* or sell it or offer its use to a deserving person. But in case when the owner of the land, his inheritance, and their benefit and their properties are not known it is permissible to take *Zakāh* from it for the poor, because, either it belongs to the occupant, or to the owner of the land and either of them shall have to pay *ṣadaqah* (i.e. *'ushr*) of the crops brought to the floor.

"As for the boats which supply provisions from the fortress, if these or most of these are indispensable for its inmates, it is well and good. But if these or most of these are disapproved, then the supply of the provisions from it is also disapproved."

It was asked whether it is necessary to vacate a frontier-town like this on account of its being doubtful or forbidden while it was the face and controlling part of the city? Some of its inmates do not have anything except that which can only satisfy their hunger or cover their secret parts and if they vacate these parts Sicily will remain desolate. He says,"If what was necessary for the fortress proved to be belonging to those who were ejected from it and they were known, they should be invited to return to it and their properties should be restored to them.

"If there were enough men among them for inhabiting it and for mending its condition they would be considered sufficient, otherewise, there would be added to them those who would inhabit it, and the latter would be given the properties the owner of which were not known. The fortress would be looked after according to what is best for the interests of the Muslims. But if the owners are not known, I have already described that this will be treated as a *fay'* which has been conferred by Allāh on the Muslims.

"The *Imām* can act therein in accordance with what is *[fo. 22-a]* most useful for the Muslims. But, if it is known that some of the owners of the place are known while some others are not known, then in cases the owners are known it is sufficient for them to choose between the lawful and the unlawful.

"As to the food-stuff which the owners of boats and others carry, I have already described to you concerning its origin, as to what is permissible and what is not. Now, what is disapproved of it is also reprehensible to buy anything raised from it and what is contrary to this will be lawful for its buyer and for those who will purchase it from him to sell, and with Allāh lies the right guidance."

Chapter IV

ON RENUNCIATION OF ALLOWANCES (*'AṬA'*) PAID BY THOSE WHO TURNED GOD'S PROPERTY (*MĀL ALLĀH*) INTO PRIVATE ESTATES, THEIR TRANSACTION, DEMAND FOR PAYMENT, THEIR PETTY TRADE AND PROFITS ACCRUING THEREFROM

Allāh, the Exalted, says in the verses of inheritance: "After any legacy he may have bequeathed or debt (hath been paid)" (4: 11). There is no disagreement among the people that whoever usurps wealth or takes hold of it without any right, incurs a debt against him. Allāh has first dealt with the debt before mentioning inheritance. The *Ummah* (Muslim community) is unanimous in holding that debt precedes bequest. So, when this is the case it is not befitting for an heir to take his share while there are others who have greater right than him, no matter whether the deserving one is known or not. In case he is not known, he will be traced out. If his trace is not expected, the property will be treated as a *fay'* which Allāh has conferred on the Muslims. The bequests of a person described above are not lawful.

Whoever purchases an unlawful commodity in exchange of lawful money while the price is cash (*'Ayn*), Ibn al-Qāsim says that there is no harm in purchasing the commodity from him whether the seller knows the impurity of the price or not. Ibn 'Abdūs says: "If the seller knows the impurity of the price, the purchase from him is allowed, but if he does not know the same, the purchase from him is not allowed."

This is a conjecture which has been given without a careful thought, and by this he preferred only the course of piety. This sounds remote from him because he has a better excuse if he does not know than the case when he knows. Saḥnūn does not approve of purchase when the seller knows the impurity of the price. Ibn Idrīs, al-Marwazī, and Ibn al-Mundhir say that if he purchases in exchange of cash (*'Ayn*) the bargain will not be concluded, and will be cancelled. If the commodity has passed through the hands of many persons, every transaction concluded in exchange of the same will be rebutted.

If one purchases and claims the commodity by the contract without making any condition of handing over the money and then he hands over the same money, the contract will be valid and it will be permissible to buy the commodity from the purchaser of the same. But if the same article is purchased in exchange for an unlawful object, the purchase of the commodity is not lawful, because the owners of the commodity who purchased with it have the right of confirming the sale and taking hold of the article or cancelling the deal *[fo. 22-b]* and taking back their money, in the opinion of our authorities as well as in the opinion of others. Any commodity in which the sale is not concluded, the commodity remains in the possession of the seller. So, what is of this nature cannot be purchased.

Whoever sells any unlawful object in exchange for lawful object, whatever he obtains in an unlawful transaction is unlawful; and the unlawful object will be considered so in the hands of its recipient if he knows it.

In the case of a powerful despot who purchases from one who is under his sway, the former takes initiative in demanding the sale, the latter can apply the right of either confirming the sale or rebutting it and taking hold of that with which he was deceived as soon as he is safe because the former is like the usurper. But if the seller himself takes the initiative and requests the former to buy from him, while there was no compulsion or fear in their affairs, nor did he purchase in exchange of an unlawful object, his sale is lawful.

Whoever has debt against one whose responsibility is outstripped by claims of injustice and oppressions while the claimants are innumerable and what he has in his possession is not enough to pay up his debt, nor is it equivalent to the same, and even the limit of his dues is not known, it is not permissible for anyone to demand payment of claim upon him because his wealth is liable to be divided into lots so it is not permissible for him to take hold of anything which is not known whether it is his due or not.

There is no harm for one who had entered into any transaction with him or enjoyed genuine claim against him to have it transferred by the bankrupt or have its security borne by someone else with or without his order, and the recipient is allowed to take it, since he has not taken any thing from him to harm his creditors. It is only permissible to buy lawful article from him because he had already given something to him in exchange for what he received from him. Hence he has not done any harm to his creditors. The demand of payment from him is prohibited because it will harm them. He was not like the attorney (*qā'im al-wajh*) in what he gives decree, in his gifts and in his doing good deeds because he can defend, overcome by force, and is hardly overpowered by others to impose any decision upon him. But when the claims upon him are known it will be most undersirable to demand any payment from him.

When the wealth of some governors (*'Ummāl*) of 'Umar increased, people talked much about it so much so that their poet said:

> We perform pilgrimage (*ḥajj*) when they perform it, and we take part in fighting when they take part. Wherefrom they, then, have abundance of wealth while I have no abundance of wealth? When the Indian trader comes with musk-vesicle, it flows through their parting places of the hair. So take care of the wealth of Allāh wherever you find it, they will soon be satisfied if you give them a share out of yours.

'Umar, thereupon, took half of the wealth of those governers who had it in abundance. He sent Muḥammad ibn Maslamah to 'Amr ibn al-'Āṣ *[fo. 23-a]* in Egypt for taking one half of what he had. 'Amr prepared for him rich food on the first night he came to him. Muḥammad then said: "This cannot be a food for the guest." He swore not to take it. He took half of what he ('Amr) had till he took hold of one of his pairs of shoes, which he set aside. 'Amr thereupon said, "There should not come a time in which the son of Al-'Āṣ served as governor under the son of al-Khaṭṭāb, I had surely found his father clad with the woollen, striped cloth, while my forefathers wrapped with brocade." Ibn Maslamah said to him: "Leave this, your as well as his father are all in the Hell-Fire but he is better than you." 'Amr, then asked him (Muḥammad) to conceal the talk from *'Umar,* and he thereby, did not mention it to 'Umar.

'Umar, said to Abū Hurayrah after he had taken one-half of what Abū Hurayrah possessed: "Will you not accept any employment?" He replied, "No, because I fear that my back will be beaten and my honour will be abused." 'Umar said to him, "Verily, Yūsuf ibn Ya'qūb (may Allāh be pleased with him), who was better than you, accepted employment."

Abū Mūsā came to him ('Umar) along with the delegates of 'Irāq. One of them reported to 'Umar that Abū Mūsā had selected forty girls of the tribe of Usāwirah and had two *sā*'s, two storeys of building and two bowls daily. Al-Aḥnaf ibn Qays was among the delegate. 'Umar asked him about the forty girls of the Usāwirah tribe. He replied, "I feared lest the soldiers might be deceived concerning them and I knew their ransom, so, I paid their ransom and divided it into five shares and distributed these among them." He then enquired of the people, if such was the case, they said; "Yes". He then asked the reporter, if the case was so? He said, "Perhaps". He, then enquired about the two storeys of building. He replied, "I use one for the wealth of the Muslims, and the other for my family." He then enquired of the people if such was the case. They replied in affirmative. He then enquired of the reporter about it who said, "Perhaps and may be". He then enquired about the two bowls of 'Aqīlah meaning the slave-girl of Abū Mūsā. Abū Mūsā kept quiet. 'Umar then wanted the people to express their views. They said, "He is the one who is known to you and you know him better. Moreover, he enjoyed along with you Companionship of the Prophet." 'Umar said: "The leavened bread of 'Irāq is forbidden for 'Aqilah." And he conducted her to al-Madīnah, while he sent Abū Mūsā back to his assignment.

'Umar appointed Ḥudhayfah as Governor of al-Madā'in and wrote in his letter of investiture, "You (people) listen to him, obey him and hand over to him whatever he demands from you." But usually he used to write in his letters of investiture: "You listen to such and such a person and obey him as long as he administered justice among you." People appeared to have refused to accept his appointment and consulted privately among themselves. They then put questions to him. They then decided to ask him, and on their enquiry he said, "(I want) food to eat and the fodder for my donkey." They added: "Do you want anything else?" He said, "No". When he returned, and it was said to 'Umar that he would enter the following morning, 'Umar waited for him from a hidden place and Ḥudhayfah appeared riding on a donkey, sitting on a packsaddle while he had let loose both of his legs on one side. 'Umar hastened to him and held him tight and said, "You are my brother and I am your brother."

When 'Umar arrived in Syria, the Commanders of the troops came to meet him. Whenever anyone of them approached him, he would say, "Send him off". He was mounting a camel and his freed slave *[fo. 23-b]* Aslam was on another camel travelling with him. So every official was sent off. The Syrians who had come out, asked: "Where is the *Amīr al-Mu'minīn*?" Aslam repeatedly said, "In front of you". They therefore proceeded towards his back, while 'Umar continued his journey till Abū 'Ubaydah appeared on a camel, with its rein made of wool. When he approached 'Umar, he made the camel kneel down and got down. 'Umar also got down and saluted him, then they walked together, Aslam was still saying to everyone who enquired about the Caliph, "Go ahead". Thereupon 'Umar said to him, "You have said much", Aslam thereupon said: "This is *Amīr al-Mu'minīn*." They then looked at him bewildered and 'Umar said; "Verily the eyes of these people are acccustomed to (see) the dress of those who have no share (in the Hereafter), hence their eyes belittle us."

When 'Umar entered the locality, he asked Abū 'Ubaydah to take him to his residence. Abū 'Ubaydah enquired as to what he wanted to do with his residence. 'Umar said: "Let us go". When he entered, he found no furniture in the house. Abū 'Ubaydah placed for 'Umar a pillow made of skin and full of fibres of palm trees. 'Umar then wanted some food, and Abū 'Ubaydah brought for him a container made of palm-bough which contained broken pices of barley bread. 'Umar thereupon said: "O Abū 'Ubaydah, the world has changed all the people save you, 'Umar and the family of 'Umar are obedient to Abū 'Ubaydah." 'Umar sanctioned for him two hundred *dīnār*s which Abū 'Ubaydah gave away in alms. 'Umar also ordered for Mu'ādh two hundred *dīnār*s which Mu'adh also gave away in alms.

'Umar noticed the signs of starvation among the people of a village, so he asked them to write down the names of the needy. And they wrote down the name of their Governor at the top of those whom they enrolled as needy.

He looked into the case of Shuraḥbīl ibn Ḥasanah in whom he did not find the ability of chieftainship, so he discharged him from his office. Shuraḥbīl thereupon said to him privately, "O *Amīr al-Mu'minīn,* verily, your dismissing me is disgraceful (for me), so please explain my case to the people." 'Umar, therefore, addressed the people and said: "I did not dismiss Shuraḥbīl out of displeasure, nor on account of embezzlement of money. I found a more suitable person for his post and, therefore, had to discharge him from his office. Had I known anything else I would not have excused him."

The people of a village complained to him about their Governor (*'āmil*) saying that he did not come out to the people till the day was advanced; he had a day in the weak in which he did not come out; and a day in the month on which he did not come out and at night he did not come out though any accident might have happened. 'Umar then said to the Governor: "Why don't you come out till the day is advanced?" He said, "I have my family and children so I do not come out till I see that they have taken their meal, I thus come out without any anxiety." He said: "Even once a week you do not come out." He said, "I stay just to straighten the circumstances of my family." He then enquired about the day in the month, He said: "I was among the polytheists, when they killed Khubayb, they struck him and he shouted loudly. When that time comes I fall in swoon and I think surely Allāh will not forgive me."

'Umar said, "Then what about the night?" He said, "Please excuse me." 'Umar said: "You will have to tell." He said: "Please excuse me, Allāh will excuse you." He ('Umar) said, "I beseech you, you must tell." He said, "I keep the night for Allāh and the day for them, so, I do not like to mix up one work with the other."

It is necessary to deal generously with *[fo. 24-a]* the official and his associates in respect of their livelihood and it was said: "Keep them with sufficient resources so that they are not forced to embezzle money." And he used to treat them like this and he also said, "This is scarce for one who acts with justice and similar is the case with everyone who is entrusted with the affairs of the Muslims."

When the wealth multiplied, he used to import good robes and with them clothed the Companions of the Prophet. Then there came to him some robes out of it and he clothed his companions with it. Out of these he gave two robes to Ḥasan and Ḥusayn but these robes were short for them. He thereupon wrote to his Governor to send him two robes immediately to suit their measurement, as the case had rendered his life unpleasant.

Once some robes were brought before him and he put on one of them. Ibn 'Awf said to him, "How excellent is this!" Then a number of robes were brought before him at the end of the year, and he put on one robe and forgot the remark of Ibn 'Awf. Ibn 'Awf again remarked, "How excellent is this!" And 'Umar, this time, kept this in his mind. Afterwards some other robes were brought before him and he chose the most inferior one and wore it.

Ibn 'Awf again said to him, "How excellent is this!" 'Umar enquired, "Do you like this, O Abū Muḥammad?" He said: "Yes". So 'Umar gave him that particular robe. Afterwards 'Umar brought out other garments and then Ibn 'Awf realised that it was inferior one. He, therefore said to 'Umar, "Was it a deceit, O, *Amīr al-Mu'minīn?*" 'Umar said, "You said what you liked year before last year, you repeated the same last year and then, I did not escape you this year."

He clothed Usayd ibn al-Ḥaṣīr with a robe which he sold in exchange for five slaves whom he set free and said, "He who prefers these two robes to the emancipation of those slaves is surely weak in judgement."

One day 'Umar took an account of himself and said: "I think that the apparent contentment of the people that appears to me is only due to fear from me. Perhaps the case with them is countrary to this." He then thought of one whom he would ask of this and suddenly there occurred to his mind the name of Muḥammad ibn Maslamah. He, therefore, went to him. Muḥammad ibn Maslamah said: "O *Amīr al-Mu'minīn,* why did you not send for me I would have surely come to you?" He said, "Suddenly it came to my mind that people express themselves agreeable to me only because of fear from me. I beseech you in the name of Allāh, tell me what do the people think of me?" He said: "By Allāh, you are just as we like, and you like. Had it been otherwise, we would have straightened you just as the shafts of spear are straightened in its instrument." 'Umar added, "All praise is due to Allāh Who has created among the followers of Muḥammad those who would straighten their ruler when he displayed any crookedness just as the shaft is straightened in its instrument."

Once 'Umar came out on an errand and suddenly a widow followed him saying that Muḥammad ibn Maslamah came to them as a tax-collector but gave her nothing, and not knowing that he was 'Umar himself, she said to him, "Let us go to him". 'Umar asked Yarfa' to call Maslamah. She rejoined: "May Allāh put you aright, if you would come along with me to him, my need would be fulfilled more quickly." 'Umar said; "If he does not come to us, we shall go to him." When Yarfa' reached Muḥammad ibn Maslamah, he enquired as to what did he want. Yarfa' said, "I do not know except that I saw a woman along with him." Muḥammad ibn Maslamah said, "By Allāh, she is one of them."

He then came to 'Umar. 'Umar said, "We were impatient like the itch of the head and were afraid of being snatched away by the people, but when Allāh made us victorious, I sent you as a tax-collector; and you did not give this woman anything. *[fo. 24-b]* Muḥammad ibn Maslamah replied, "Please, do not make haste, O *Amīr al-Mu'minīn,* either she did not come to me, or I omitted her by mistake." He ('Umar) said, Give her, and if you go out afterwards, receive her with kindness." Then, the woman shrank and felt ashamed.

'Umar once, wrote to Mu'ādh and Abū 'Ubaydah, abjuring them by Allāh, to tell him whether he was a king or a caliph. They replied, "If you take a single *dirham* without any right or spend it for an unjust cause you are a king and not a caliph."

State allowances increased during the time of 'Uthmān so much so that a slave-girl was bought according to her weight, a horse for twenty thousand *dirhams*, and a palm tree for one thousand *dirhams*.

The Prophet appointed a tax-collector. When he came back he said, "This is for you and this (object) has been offered to me as a present." The Prophet, thereupon, addressed the people and said, "What is it? I send one of you (as a tax-collector), when he comes back, he says, 'This has been given to me as a present.' Why does he not sit down in the house of his mother and see whether any present is offered to him or not?" He added, "None of you would come carrying anything on his neck but he would bring it carrying on his neck on the Day of Resurrection, be it a grumbling camel or a bellowing cow or a bleating goat."

The Prophet, inspite of what Allāh gave him exclusively out of *Anfāl Ghanīmah* and *fay'*, used to accept food and clothes up to the level of essential subsistence. The best of robes in which he was ever seen was what Anas said that he saw him in a red robe, nothing better than that he ever saw on him. The Prophet put on a black cloak having design in it. Perchance he looked at its design in the prayer and said, "It was about to tempt me, you return it to Abū Jahm and bring for me one having no design known as *Anbijaniyyah*.

The *ḥadīth* of Qaylah contains: "I saw him seated squatting and wrapped in a bed-sheet-like shabby cloak, [a bed-sheet which was a bit worn out]." Al-Mughīrah saw the Prophet in a journey while he had a Syrian gown on him, the sleeves of which were too narrow for his hands. He passed away, may my father and mother be ransomed for him, in a patched garment.

He used to put on shoes of tanned leather without having any hair on it. He used them for making ablution. There was no sieve in al-Madinah during his life, and he did never eat at the table. Whenever food was brought to him he used to put it on the floor. He had luxuriant hair which he let loose as long as Allāh willed, then he parted it, and shaved them off on the occasion of the Farewell Pilgrimage. The Prophet gave half of his hair to Abū Ṭalḥah and divided the other half among his Companions.

The cap of Khālid fell in the course of a battle field in the enemy territory. He then rushed to the midst of the enemy and picked it up. On enquiry he explained that there were some hair of the Messenger of Allāh in the cap. The Prophet consummated his marriage with 'Ā'ishah who was wearing a shirt worth four *dirhams*. The inhabitants of Madinah used to borrow it for their brides to be blessed with it.

The Prophet used to take a year's provision for his family. Once he came out to the mosque and found Abū Bakr and 'Umar. He enquired as to what had brought them out. They replied that hunger had brought them out. *[fo. 25-a.]* He said, "The same thing brought me out. Let us go to Abū'l-Haytham ibn al-Tayhān". Abū'l-Haytham ordered (his people) to bring for them barley which was prepared and he asked for sweet water for them and then slaughtered a goat for them. The Prophet said, "Avoid (slaughtering) the milch-animal." He then said; "You will certainly be asked about the pleasure of this day."

Jābir noticed signs of hunger in the face of the Prophet on the occasion of digging the Ditch. He, thereupon, went to his family and said; "I noticed hunger on the face of the Messenger of Allāh." He, then, ordered for a *Ṣā'* of barley which was prepared, and he slaughtered a domestic animal. Then he came to the Prophet and informed him of this. The Prophet, thereafter, said to his Companions, "Verily Jābir has prepared a meal (meaning a feast), so let us go." The Prophet walked along with his people who were one thousand in number. The Messenger of Allāh entered Jābir's house and then uttered in the food whatever Allāh wished him to utter, and lo: the whole lot of the people ate out of it and afterwards there remained so much food that it sufficed his family and his relations.

Anas says: Umm Sulaym folded a few breads of barely in her scarf and gave back some of them to me and asked me to take them to the Messenger of Allāh, whom I found in the mosque in the crowd of the People. I then stood up before them. The Messenger of Allāh asked me, 'Did Abū Ṭalḥah send you?' I said, "Yes". He rejoined, "With food?" I said "Yes". He, then, asked his Companions to get ready.

They all, then, departed while I walked in front of them and reached Abū Ṭalḥah and informed him. Abū Ṭalḥah then said: "O Umm Sulaym, the Messenger of Allāh arrives along with his people, while we have no food to suffice them all." She said, "Allāh and His Messenger are aware of it." Abū Ṭalḥah then received the Prophet who came in and said. "O Umm Sulaym, bring to me what is with you." She brought the bread.

Then, by the order of the Messenger of Allāh, she crumbled it, squeezed the butter skin with her hand and seasoned it with condiment. The Messenger of Allāh then uttered a prayer over the food with what Allāh desired him to do so. Then he asked Abū Ṭalḥah to allow ten of them to come in. Abū Ṭalḥah sent them accordingly and they all ate to their satisfaction and went out. The Prophet again asked him to allow ten of them to come in, Abū Ṭalḥah sent them in and they all ate to their satisfaction and went out. Thus, the whole party to the last of them. They were seventy or eighty in number.

The Prophet did not arrange any wedding feast with bread and meat for anyone of his wives except Zaynab. He mostly arranged his wedding feast with meal of dates mixed with butter.

Once honey was presented to one of his wives. When he entered upon her she entertained him with it, while there remained its smell with the Prophet. At this, his other wives became jealous. 'Ā'ishah and Ḥafṣah both made an agreement and advised his wives to enquire about the smell which they felt from him saying that perhaps he had eaten Manna. Now Ṣawdah says, "I almost enquired him of this when he was still at the door on account of fear from 'Ā'ishah." The Prophet said, "No, but I drank *[fo. 25-b]* honey with such and such wife." The Prophet said to Ḥafṣah, "By Allāh, I shall not take it," and he asked her to keep it a secret. But she informed 'Ā'ishah of this and both of them divulged it. Thereupon Allāh revealed, "O Prophet: why bannest thou that which Allāh hath made lawful for thee," upto His saying "*wa abkārā*" (and Maids) (66: 1–5). The Prophet then took oath of refraimng from his wives for a month and discontinued his going to them and confined himself to his parlour which was a small room.

'Umar says, 'We used to prevail upon our wives at Makkah, but we found in the tribes of Anṣār that their wives prevailed upon them. Our wives at Madinah, therefore, learned this from their wives. One day my wife answered me back. So, I said to her, 'How does it concern you'. She replied; 'How amazing, O son of Khaṭṭāb, you do not like me to return you answer for answer but your daughter scoffs daily at the Messenger of Allāh." I enquired, 'Did she scoff at (the Prophet)?' " He then said, "I put on my clothes and went to Ḥafṣah and enquired, 'Does anyone of you scoff at the Messenger of Allāh?' She said: 'Yes'. I thereupon said, 'Do not risk yourself; verily 'Ā'ishah is more beautiful and dearer to the Messenger of Allāh than you. Do'nt you fear that Messenger of Allāh will be angry, and consequently Allāh will be angry because of his anger and will direct the Messenger of Allāh to divorce you?' " 'Umar added that he had a friend from among the Anṣār with whom he had arranged to visit the Prophet on alternate days. On his turn he used to visit the Prophet and tell the Anṣārī friend all that he had learned from the Messenger of Allāh, and in his turn, he used to visit him ('Umar) and tell him whatever he had learned about the rumour that the king of Ghassān was making war preparations against them.

"One day", says 'Umar, "my Anṣārī friend knocked at the door violently. I came out and asked him whether the king of Ghassān had arrived. He replied, rather it was more serious than that, the Messenger of Allāh had divorced his wives. I said to myself 'did I not say the same thing to Ḥafṣah?' I then went to Hafṣah and said, 'Did I not tell you? Did the Messenger of Allāh divorce you all?' She replied, 'I do not know, and he is in that parlour.' I then went to the mosque and found the people weeping near the pulpit.

I, too, sat down and wept because of their weeping, but my soul, however, did not remain in peace, so, I went to the parlour and found a black slave at its entrance. I asked him to take permission for 'Umar. Whereupon, he entered, then, came out, and said, "I mentioned your name, but the Prophet kept quiet." I, therefore, returned to the people but my soul did not let me be at peace; so, I came back to the parlour again, and asked the slave to seek permission for 'Umar. The slave entered, and came out, and said, "I mentioned your name but he kept quiet." I again went back to the people, but again, my soul did not let me be at peace, so, I returned and asked the slave to seek permission for 'Umar. He entered, came out, and said, "I mentioned your name but he remained silent." When I turned my back, I was called by him and he said, *[fo. 26-a]* "He has permitted you." I therefore entered and saluted him and the Prophet returned to me his salutation. I found him on the sand-made bedstead which had left marks on his skin. So I stood and said, 'O Messenger of Allāh, we the people of the tribe of Quraysh used to prevail upon our wives. When we came to this tribe of the Anṣār, we found in them that their women prevalied upon them. Our women learned the same from their women.' "

Then, 'Umar mentioned to the Prophet his discourse with his wife and what she had told him and what he had said to Ḥafṣah. The Messenger of Allāh thereupon smiled. 'Umar says: "Then I said, 'O Messenger of Allāh, have you divorced your wives?' He replied; 'No'. I then praised Allāh, took my seat and said: 'O Messenger of Allāh, you are in this condition while the Khosroes and Caesars move about in brocade.' He said, 'O 'Umar, had I prayed to Allāh to turn the mountains of Tihāmah into gold and silver. He would have surely done so. What should I care for this world?' "

Abū Hurayrah says, "One day, I was extremely hungry, so I met Abū Bakr. I asked him to recite a verse of the Qur'ān which I recited so that he might give me something to eat. But he recited the verse for me and went away. Then, I met 'Umar and I behaved likewise. He also acted like Abū Bakr. Then I met the Prophet who asked me to follow him. And I followed him. He then brought out a cup of milk and asked me to call the people of the Ṣuffah whom I called. I said to myself, 'How would it suffice them?' I, however, called them and they all drank out of it and went away. The Prophet then said, 'O Abū Hurayrah, will you drink?' I said: 'I shall drink.' He said, 'Drink then.' I drank and I stretched out my both hands with it to him. He then asked me to drink. I drank and stretched out my hands again to hand it over to him. The Prophet agains asked me to drink. But I said, 'O Messenger of Allāh, by Allāh, I do not find any space for it.' And he drank it."

Ḥafṣah brought to the Prophet something which was presented to her by her sister. The Prophet drank out of it. On another occasion some milk mixed with water was brought to him, while a bedouin was on his right side and Abū Bakr was on his left. He then drank from it and offered it to the bedouin and said; "Begin with the right side, the right side, and the right side."

'Ā'ishah brought to Prophet some food and some home-made condiments, whereupon, the Prophet said, "Did I not see the cooking-pot boiling with meat?" She said; "It has been given to Barīrah as *ṣadaqah,* but you do not eat *ṣadaqah.*" He said, "This is *ṣadaqah* for her, but for us it is a present."

When the Prophet was at Ṣahbā, a place at the lower part of Khaybar, he asked to bring provisions which was nothing except gruel of barley. Then he asked to make soup out of it and they all ate, then rinsed their mouths and performed *Maghrib*-prayers.

'Alī says: "I had two full-grown she-camels. I got one of them as my share of the battle of Badr, while the other I received from the *Khums*. So, I gathered ropes and wooden packs and sought help from some people to bring dry herbage with which I wanted to prepare the wedding feast of Faṭimah and a man came to us and said that Ḥamzah got intoxicated and cut the humps of both the camels and opened their bellies. Then I came to the Messenger of Allāh and said; 'I did not see a scene like today and I mentioned the incident to him.' He thereby took his cloak and accompanied me to Ḥamzah. We found him along with *[fo. 26-b]* a drinking party while he was intoxicated. Ḥamzah then raised his head and said; 'You all are only the slaves of my father.' The Messenger of Allāh then turned back and left the place.

Some prisoners of war were brought to the Prophet. Faṭimah then came to him to ask for a slave. The Prophet said to her, "Shall I not offer you something better than this, you recite *Subḥān Allāh* (Sublime is Allāh) thirty-three times, *Allāh Akbar* (Great is Allāh) thirty-three times, and *al-ḥamdu lillāh* (all praise belongs to Allāh) thirty-four times.? Or he said, you utter *al-ḥamdu lillāh* thirty-four time *Allahu Akbar* thirty-four times and that will be better than a slave, a slave and a slave."

The Prophet was shrouded in three pieces of white clothes of one thread which were folded one upon another. They were made of average (ordinary) sort of cotton clothes.

After his proclamation as Caliph, Abū Bakr went to the market, carrying some clothes. Some people met him and asked him as to where he intended to go and to whom he had entrusted the affairs of the people. He said, "Indeed my people know that my profession is not to be made to shorten the maintenance of my family." People, therefore, prevailed upon him to return and fixed for him one goat. When death approached him, he ordered to take the account of what he had spent out of the *Bayt al-Māl* and it amounted to seven thousand *dirhams*. He thereupon, asked them to deposit into the *Bayt al-Māl* all that he had left behind except the dwelling-houses. It was accordingly deposited into the *Bayt al-Māl*. 'Ā'ishah says, "The Muslims have, thus, earned profit through him while they did not earn profit through anybody else." He was moderate in his dress, in taking food and drinking and all that concerned him.

'Umar used to be moderate in his dress, food, drinking, and he used to patch his clothes. He patched even with three pieces in between his two shoulders matting one upon another. He walked barefoot and slept during the day in courtyards of the walls. He had every day two wooden bowls, over which his visitors used to assemble. It was then suggested to him that he should have richer food than this, He replied, "I am afraid, I would then hasten to exhaust all my excellent foods. Allāh, the Exalted says, 'Ye squandered your good things in the life of the world.' (46: 20). I fear I might adopt the way other than that of my two companions and thus I would be treated in a different manner."

One day, Abū Mūsā attended his meal which contained the bread of barley, vinegar and olive oil. Abū Mūsā ate out of it a little, whereupon, 'Umar reminded him saying, "I found you among the people of Ṣuffah while today you remained behind in eating it; I eat it while I felt of it to be what is in it, certainly, one of these two condiments had sufficed me."

One day 'Amr ibn al-'Āṣ came to him while the people were at the bowl of 'Umar who was standing on their heads, on account of great number of people. 'Umar, thereupon, took a handful of broken bread mixed with meat (*tharīd*) and gave it to 'Amr which he took in his right hand and threw it into his left hand and began to eat out of it sitting in a corner. When 'Amr came out, some people asked him, "What did you do with yourself?" He said, "By Allāh, certainly he knew that I had sufficient food but he intended to test me only. *[fo. 27-a]* Had I refused I would have certainly received punishment from him."

One day 'Umar's son called on his sister Ḥafṣah who offered him broken bread with meat. She said to him, "Would that you had put some olive oil in it to make it more palatable." He said, "I fear lest *Amīr al-Mu'minīn* might enter and I would get punishment from him." She said, "This is not the time of his coming in, so saying, she put some olive oil over it, and 'Umar entered while he was eating. 'Umar exclaimed, "What! Two condiments at a time." He then put on his clothes and started beating him till he became tired.

'Umar used to take a stroll at night to investigate into the affairs of the people. In the year of the famine, one night, he went out and heard some children weeping because of hunger. He then came back and took a load of flour and some fat which a strong man can carry. He put them on his shoulder. Some of those who met him offered their services to carry his load which he refused, saying that only he who had harmed them should carry for them. He then sought permission from the inmates of the house who permitted him to enter. When he entered, he enquired whether they had any cooking-pot. They replied in the affirmative. So, he took the cooking-pot, placed it properly and poured water in it. He then put some fat and salt and began to blow into the fire while smoke was gushing forth through his beard. Then he put some flour into it. When it was cooked, he poured it in a large wooden bowl. He then left them eating and himself waited outside to overhear their conversation. The ate, and then played till they fell asleep.

Some of those who envied him saw him one night in the darkness of night. He said: "I thought ill of him and followed him in a way that he would not see me till he reached a house in ruins wherein he entered. At this, my ill-feeling increased, and he stayed there for a while and then came out. I, thereupon, entered in the ruins and enquired of the inmates and there appeared a person in the house whom I enquired as to who he was. She replied, "I am a poor and blind old woman." Then, I asked about the man who had gone away. She said, "I do not know except that he comes to me every night or on alternate nights and removes the harmful things from me, and leaves near me sufficient food." The man then said to himself, "Where was I led by my evil thought?"

Once 'Umar met a woman carrying a water-skin full of water. He asked her, "Have you not anyone who can do this for you?" She replied, "Had there been anyone, I would not have carried it." He then took it from her and said, "Why did you not, then, go to 'Umar"? She replied, "I am told that he is rough and rude." He said, "Perhaps, he treats only the unjust and transgressor with roughness and rudeness." She answered, "I do not know." When she reached near her place, she said, "This is my place." He gave her the water-skin and said, "No, you must come to 'Umar." The woman then came to his locality seeking guidance from the people and was surprised to see that the bearer of her water-skin himself was the man who issued orders and prohibitions. Realising this, she turned her back and went away. 'Umar then called Yarfa' to call the woman back. He called her and 'Umar gave her a servant.

A man ate with him in the year of the famine and began to wipe off the grease of the dish, whereupon, 'Umar said to him, "It seems that you are *[fo. 27-b]* a destitute." He said, "By Allah, I have not tasted clarified butter, nor have I seen any food prepared with it since such and such period." 'Umar, thereupon, said, "By Allah I shall not take clarified butter till the people have the means of sustence as they had beforehand." He, therefore, used to take olive oil without altering it, so, his complexion changed into brown colour while he was fair. So, whoever saw him only that year described him of brown complexion.

'Umar wrote to 'Amr ibn al-'Āṣ in the year of the famine: "To 'Āṣ ibn 'Āṣ, now after (praise of Allah) surely, you do not worry if you along with your companions are satiated, without taking into consideration the fact that if I myself and my companions remain hungry. So help, help." In reply, 'Amr wrote to him: "At your service: at your service, and at your service, sir. The caravan is sure to reach you, its front part will be near you while its rear part will remain with me and, Allāh willing, I shall soon transport for you through the sea that much which will make those who are near you free from want." On this, some of his companions said to him, "If you open to him the passage of the sea, he will not leave for you anything in Egypt." So, he wrote to 'Umar: "Verily, I have looked into the matter of the sea, but nothing seemed to be right." 'Umar also wrote to him: "Either you will finish that or I shall send somebody else who will do the job while you will be in your house."

'Umar used to send a camel loaded with flour to the family of the Prophet and said to them, "You slaughter the camel, eat its meat and make condiment with its fat, eat the flour and wrap yourselves with the bag." He also entrusted to them some people who would attend to their slaughtering. He also said, "Verily, the bedouins like to keep the camels alive." He said, "I have determined to assign like this to every member of the family of the Prophet. Verily a man does not die on account of half satiation." (This continued) till there reached him the wealth of Egypt.

Once 'Umar went out on a journey. While journeying, 'Alī, Ṭalḥah and a group of the Companions of the Prophet lost their way. When the evening approached, they found some people in a tent whom they asked to send to them somebody to talk. They replied; "This is not possible, we are all naked. We have only a single garment, whoever goes out wears it." They then stood perplexed, and at that time there appeared to them the owner of the tent who drove his emaciated camels including a fat she-camel. On their asking for refreshment he replied, "We have nothing with us except what you see. As for this she-camel, it belongs to 'Umar against whom nobody can dare." They smiled and got hold of the she-camel, slaughtered it, and ate out of it, and asked them to eat its meat, make condiment with its fat and make shoes with its hides. In the morning, they set on their journey, and asked them to meet them at a particular well. When they returned to 'Umar and informed him of all about it, he said, "Why did you not ask them to do so and so?" They replied, "We have already done so."

The man, however, came to 'Umar who gave him one hundred goats and asked him to look after them, to live on their milk, wool, and, then to see him again at a particular well at the end of the year. When the man met him the next year he reported to 'Umar that the goats had reached upto two hundred in number and that they had *[fo. 28-a]* lived on them. 'Umar again asked him to look after them and to live on their milk, wool, and to call on him at the end of the year at a particular well.

The man again met 'Umar and reported to him that the goats had multiplied to four hundred in number and that they had lived on them. 'Umar again asked the man to look after them and live on their milk, wool, and asked him to meet him at a particular well. He met him at the appointed place and reported that they had grown eight hundred in number and that they remained occupied with them while they got hold of a small herd of goats other than these, so, he urged 'Umar to take hold of them. 'Umar said, "These goats belonged to you from the very beginning but you are stupid."

'Umar did not cut off the hands of those who committed theft during the year of the famine as the people were needy. This is the opinion held by Malīk and Awzā'ī concerning those who committed theft on account of hunger. The famine however continued for six years.

'Uthmān was moderate in his food and dress, modest and chaste except that he fell in what the generation urged him to death because of the diffusiveness of the subjects and his old age. He therefore spent wealth among the Muslims, and the affair became of such consequence to him that he sacrificed himself to defend his religion. His death opened the door of civil war and gave rise to schism.

'Alī was moderate in his dress and food. He had inclination towards coarse cloth; and he used to cut both of his sleeves at the upper end of the sides of his fingers. He used to walk on foot through mud or rain and disposed of all that was in his *Bayt al-Māl* every Saturday. Whenever he looked at the contents of the *Bayt al-Mal*, he said, "This is my collection which comprises the best of it, while every other collector has his hands moving towards his mouth. O Red (gold), and O White (silver), you deceive everyone save me." When he died nothing was found in his possession except three hundred *dirhams* which he had arranged for buying a slave.

Once food was brought to Ibn al-'Awf, who said, "Ḥamzah died, he was better than me, he was shrouded in a woollen garment which was drawn on his face while his feet were uncovered, so Idhkhir grass was placed on them. Muṣ'ab ibn 'Umayr died; he too was better than me, they treated him in the same way."

Once Ṭalḥah abused his servant, he then gave fifteen thousand *dirhams* in alms. He was called the hero of the Quraysh on account of his generosity and courage. Al-Zubayr died while he was in debt of one hundred thousand *dirhams* which was paid out of his landed properties. Sa'd and Sa'īd were foremost ascetics and their prayers were always granted by Allāh.

All the four Rightly-Guided Caliphs died and everyone of them had worthy sons who deserved caliphate, had it ever been entrusted to them. But none of them did so out of the fear of Allāh and due to compassion for others.

Mu'āwīyyah spent wealth generously and was forbearing. He granted to Ḥasan four hundred thousand *dirhams*, to Ḥusayn three hundred thousand, to Ibn al-'Abbās two hundred thousand, and to Ibn al-Zabayr one hundred thousand. Often he delivered sermons in patched-clothes. When *[fo. 28-b]* death approached him, he ordered to deposit half of his wealth in the *Bayt al-Māl*, and in this act he followed the practice of 'Umar. When the people other than the Companions of the Prophet took over the administration, the affairs changed a little, till 'Umar ibn 'Abd al-'Azīz became caliph. He admistered justice, righted wrongs and restored to the owners what the chiefs of Banū Umayyah and others had assigned as (*iqṭā'*). They discussed this among themselves.

Hishām ibn 'Abd al-Malik entered upoon 'Umar ibn 'Abd al-'Azīz. Hishām says: " 'Umar was a venerable person, I found him sitting on a mat wearing a white robe." He says, "I kept quiet. When my silence prolonged, he said, to me, 'O Hishām, tell me what do you want?' " He said, "I then said, 'You have changed the practice of your own people and altered their decisions and enabled the critics to criticise them.' He said to me, 'Are you impartial?' I said, 'Yes'. He said, 'By Allah', I said, 'By Allāh'. He again said, 'By Allah', I said, 'By Allah'. He repeated, 'By Allāh', I said, 'By Allah'. He then said to me, 'What do you think of the case when a man entrusts his minor children to a man whom he had appointed trustee over them and administrator of their affairs. The man then usurps their wealth and offers the same as a bequest to his own sons settled them on it, writes for them the deed of ownership therein and makes others witnesses to it.

Then others grow up and demand their property from them. While you happened to be the judge, how would you then decide the case?' " Hishām said, "I shall restore it to its owners." He said, "He had already made a deed duly witnessed in favour of his children and a long time had passed over it." Hishām said, "Even if the case be like this?" 'Umar ibn 'Abd al-'Azīz then said, "By Allāh, what is the difference between your case and between this?" Not even like and he made signs to a little bit of the earth.

Among those who were very much bitter against him on this was Maslamah ibn 'Abd al-Mālik. Once 'Umar said on the pulpit, "I see that schism shall not come to an end till it is transferred into slavery." Maslamah remarked, "Lo! I was not safe from slavery till I saw his grave."

Maslamah said to 'Umar on his death-bed, "Surely you have left your children destitute, and they need what the other people need. Would you then entrust them to me and to my equals from among your family? I shall, on your behalf, suffice them in matters of their provision." 'Umar asked (his people) to make him sit. He, then, said to Maslamah, "As for what you have mentioned that I left them destitute, surely, I did not deprive them of any right that was their due, nor did I give them anything which was not their due. Their case is just like either of the two men; a man who fears Allāh, and in that case surely Allāh will make their affair easy; or they are not so, in that case, I do not like to help them. As for your proposal that I should entrust them to you or to your equals among your people, verily I leave them in the custody of 'one who has sent the *Kitāb* and who is the guardian of the good doors.' " Then he asked them to call his sons.

They, twelve in number, came. His eyes became full of tears and he exclaimed: "There have come a group of people whom I have left behind as destitutes. O my sons, go away, Allāh is the guardian over you. Verily you would not come across anybody from among the Muslims or the *dhimmīs* but he would find for you your right."

A woman from 'Irāq came to 'Umar ibn 'Abd al-'Azīz so that he would fix some allowance for her. When she saw his house she said to herself: "We have come to seek riches from the house of poverty *[fo. 29-a]*. She then entered and 'Umar was then plastering a wall in the house. She sat down beside Fāṭimah. 'Umar looked at Fāṭimah now and then. The woman thereupon said to her, "Verily this labourer looks at you." She said, "He is the *Amīr al-M'uminīn.*" The woman thereupon attired herself with proper clothes and became ashamed. When 'Umar finished his work, he enquired about her need. She said, "I have seven daughters." He said, "I have fixed maintenance for one of them."

She praised Allāh. He said, "We have granted maintenance for the second", and she praised Allāh again and thus he continued granting maintenance for her daughters one by one and she continued praising Allāh up to the sixth daughter. She said, "O *Amīr al-M'uminīn*, may Allāh give you good reward." He said, "Had you continued praising Allāh, I would have surely fixed maintenance for the seventh one also. She will now be with her sisters." He wrote a letter for her. No sooner had she reached 'Irāq than the news of his death reached the place. She, then, handed over the letter to the Governor who executed his order concerning her.

Before he became caliph, 'Umar ibn 'Abd al-'Azīz used to wear beautiful clothes. When he was proclaimed as caliph he became ascetic and shunned the world. Before he assumed caliphate, once a robe was purchased for him for six hundred *dirhams*, but he did not like it. During his caliphate a robe was bought for him for six *dirhams* and he accepted it.

Ibn al-Musayyib was imprisoned and special care was taken about his diet but he refused to take the special diet and said, "Find out those pieces of bread which I used to take." The *Amīr al-Mu'minīn* sent for him five thousand *dirhams* which he refused to accept while he was found quarrelling with his slave over half a *dirham* which he considered to be dearer to him than the former.

Al-Walīd sent some money to Bishr ibn Sa'īd but he refused to accept it. Then al-Walīd said to 'Umar ibn 'Abd al-'Azīz who had mentioned the name of Bishr before him: "You have guided me to a Khārijite. By Allāh, I shall certainly put him to death." 'Umar then said to him, "Perhaps he does not need the money, now I shall guide you to a man like him." And then he guided him to a different man who accepted the offer.

Mālik says: "I often passed unaware of any danger except when Ziyād, the freed slave of Ibn 'Abbās, put his hand on my back between my two shoulders. Then I turned to him and he would say; 'You should be cautious, if the case is just as they say, you will be held in chains, but if it was otherwise you are safe,' " meaning Rabī'ah and Zayd ibn Aslam. When al-Manṣūr banished Rabī'ah to 'Irāq, he ordered for him five thousand *dirhams* but Rabī'ah refused to accept them. Manṣūr had also ordered for him a slave-girl which also he refused to accept. Mālik says that in character he was most ascetic of the people.

Ṭā'ūs entered upon Muḥammad ibn Yūsuf while the former was shivering with cold, so Ibn Yūsuf ordered to put a Persian mantle (*Ṭaylasān*) on him. But Ṭā'ūs began to move his shoulders so violently that it fell down. When he came out *[fo. 29-b]*. It was said to him, would that you had accepted it and given it to somebody in alms. He said, "I am afraid, that afterwards somebody would come forward saying that Ṭā'ūs accepted, so he would accept but would not give in alms."

Ibn al-Qāsim says, "I saw camel-dung burnt in the house of Mālik." He also says, "Mālik said, 'I had a piece of clothes which I wore and performed pilgrimage several times, without washing it.' " It is mentioned that he exhorted Abū Ja'far al-Manṣūr, and asked him to investigate into the condition of his subjects. Manṣūr thereupon said to him, "O Abū 'Abd Allāh, is it not true that when your daughter cries out of hunger, you ask for the two stones of the hand-mill to be moved, so that the neighbours would not hear her cry?" Mālik replied, "By Allāh, nobody other than Allāh knows it." Manṣūr rejoined, "How is it, I know this and I do not know the condition of my subjects?"

A person from Kufah narrated: "I carried some food-stuff to Makkah where Sufyān al-Thawrī had been staying. His sister had sent through me a provision-bag of dates for him, I found him reclining in the mosque, so I saluted him but he returned my salutation in a low vice. I therefore, said to myself, 'Perhaps he is angry with me for carrying the food.' Hence I left him till the people dispersed from him.

"Then I said to him, 'Verily your sister has sent to you a provision-bag of dates.' He asked, 'Where is that?' I said; 'In the litter.' He said, 'Let us go'. So I went with him and brought it out for him. He then uttered the name of Allāh and started eating. Afterwards he enquired of me if I had water, and I then offered him water. He uttered the name of Allāh and drank it.

"Then he asked me about the condition of some particular persons. I, then said, 'I saluted you when I saw you, but you did not make query at that time.' He said, 'I had no food for the last three days. Then, when you mentioned to me my sister I came to know that it was out of this,' meaning spindle and he demonstrated it with his fingers."

Once he was employed by some camel-drivers on their way to Makkah. Sufyān prepared bread for them but he burnt their bread, so they beat him. When he arrived in Makkah one of the camel-drivers came to the mosque and found the people crowded around him. He exclaimed, "This is the person whom we had employed." A certain man said to him "Well, this is Sufyān." He, thereupon, informed his companions of it. They came and as soon as they found him alone, implored him to forgive them. He said, "There is no harm, Whoever burns the food of the people is generally beaten." They then asked him to allow them to keep his company, whereupon, he said, "Provided it is on the former condition, otherwise, not."

THE SECOND PART COMES TO AN END BY THE GRACE OF ALLĀH AND HIS ASSISTANCE: AND BLESSINGS BE ON MUḤAMMAD AND ON HIS FAMILY

PART THREE

Chapter I

ON EXECUTION, RELEASING ON GRACE AND ON RANSOM

Allāh, the Exalted, says: "Now, when ye meet in battle those who disbelieve, then it is smiting of the necks, until, when ye have routed them, then making fast of bonds; and afterwards either grace or ransom till the war lays down its burdens" (47: 4). And He says: "It is not for any Prophet to have captives until he hath made slaughter in the land." (8: 67)

Therefore, it is not desirable for any commander of an army or that of troops to take anyone from among the fighting people as a captive except after making large slaughter. As for one whose return to the battlefield is expected but his mustering power is not feared, if the *Imām* thinks to offer him as ransom *[fo. 30-a]* for the Muslim prisoners, he can do so.

There has been disagreement about accepting their ransom in the form of wealth. Most of our authorities disapproved of this, saying that this was done only at Badr because of the fact that the Prophet was sure of the fact that he would soon come out victorious over them. The Prophet had consulted his Companions concerning them, whereupon, Abū Bakr and a group of his Companions suggested to him to set them free on ransom saying: "They were your relations." He added: "Allāh might deliver them on your account." But 'Umar and 'Alī had suggested to put them to death. 'Umar said, "Hand over 'Aqīl to 'Alī to put him to death, and hand over that particular cousin of him, I shall put him to death." 'Alī said, "They have forced us to follow the common usage of the Arabs, so please enkindle fire for them and burn them with it."

But the Prophet inclined to the view of Abū Bakr and released them on ransom except 'Uqbah ibn Mu'īṭ, whom he killed. When he was brought out for execution he said, "Shall I be put to death in the midet of these people?" "Yes", said the Prophet. He enquired, "What for?" The Prophet replied, "Because of your disbelief in and rebellion against Allāh and his Messenger." He said, "Who will look after my children?" "Hell", was the reply. The Prophet ordered the dead bodies to be thrown into the ditch.

He then stood over them and addressed them, saying: "O, 'Uqbah ibn Rabī'ah, O, Shaybah ibn Rabī'ah," and he named others and said, "Have you found the truth of what was promised by your Lord?" They (the Companions) said, "O, Messenger of Allāh, Do you speak to the dead?" The Prophet replied, "You are not better hearers than they."

The Prophet executed al-Naḍar ibn al-Ḥārith on the way, and said, "Had Muṭ'im ibn 'Adī been alive and prayed to me concerning these corpses, I would have surely released them." Muṭ'im ibn 'Adī was one of those who had tried to destroy the document written by the disbelievers of the Quraysh against Banū Ḥāshim and Banū Muṭṭalib stipulating that they would not have any social contact with the latter till they surrendered the Prophet to them.

The saying of Allāh: "Had it not been for an ordinance of Allāh which had gone before, an awful doom had come upon you on account of what Ye took" (8: 68) is only as Allāh knows best (was revealed) concerning the booties to which the soldiers at the battle of Badr had hastened and their dispute among themselves before the modality of distribution of booties was explained to them, and it does not surely concern them as to what and why they took, as it is held by some people. This is, because, Allāh has already promised them (of giving) one of the two kinds. Moreover, the Prophet would not have given them anything which was not permitted for them.

It is permissible to release two or three prisoners of war in exchange for two Muslim prisoners. Imprisonment is no security of life for the prisoners who do not accept faith. Nobody other than the *Imām* can consider their case when they deserve captivity. Whoever, then, thinks it proper to kill him, he will kill him, and whoever wants to spare his life in order to offer him as a ransom or to enslave him, he can do so, when none shares him.

Abū Mūsā besieged the inhabitants of a certain fort and made a treaty with them on condition that Abū Mūsā would set free one hundred from among them and would do concerning the rest whatever he desired. Their chief, therefore, started releasing whomever he wanted and Abū Mūsā used to say to those around him, "Verily I hope the enemy of Allāh would deceive himself, and he counted one hundred without counting himself." Abū Mūsā, therefore, ordered to smite his neck, whereupon, the chief said, "I am with them." Abū Mūsā replied, "You made the condition of only one hundred."

He, therefore, smote his neck. This is held by a group of the *'Ulamā'* but Saḥnūn holds that one is not liable to execution in case of doubt.

Abū Mūsā sent Hurmuzān as a captive to 'Umar in the care of Anas ibn Mālik. 'Umar asked Hurmuzān to speak. He ejaculated and enquired, whether he would speak like a living one or a dead one? 'Umar replied, "You speak, there will be no harm (to you)." He said, "O, Arabs, as long as Allāh maintained neutrality (among you and us) we enslaved you and ruled over you, but as soon as Allāh sided with you, we lost our sway upon you."

At this 'Umar grew angry and intended to execute him saying, "He is the murderer of my leader al-Barā' ibn Mālik." Anas, thereupon, said to him, "You can not do that." 'Umar enquired, "Why, has he given you something, or have you received something from him?" Anas replied, "Certainly not, you have already allowed him to speak without fear."

In the meantime 'Umar had forgotten what he had said and thereby asked him to bring someone to attest to what he had said or he would start punishing him. Anas, then, found al-Zubayr remembering what 'Umar had uttered. 'Umar therefore set Hurmuzān free. It is narrated that the Prophet executed seventy captives of war after making a large slaughter.

A prisoner of the Khazar tribe was brought before 'Umar ibn 'Abd al-'Azīz. 'Umar said, "Certainly, I am going to execute you." The prisoner said, "This would not decrease the number of the people of the Khazar tribe." 'Umar ordered his execution; and he never executed any other prisoner during his caliphate.

When Banū Qurayẓah yielded to the judgement of Sa'd ibn Mu'ādh, and they were allies of his tribe, and as such, they expected that he would spare their lives. Sa'd had received an arrow in the median vain of his arm on the day of the Ditch (*al-Khandaq*) and had said, "O Allāh, do not let me die till my eyes are pleased to see the doom of Banū Qārayẓah", and the bleeding had stopped. They had induced the combined forces of the disbelievers (*al-Aḥzāb*) against the Muslims. He, therefore, gave his judgement of killing their fighting men and enslaving their children. The Prophet said to him, "You have given the judgement according to the judgement of Allāh," or he said, "According to the 'Judgement of the King' ". Hence, all those who used razors (i.e, were adults) were put to death. 'Aṭiyah al-Qurayẓī says, "I was among them, they looked at me, and I had not grown hair, my life was spared."

Zubayr ibn Bāṭā had a favour upon 'Uthmān, who said to the Prophet,

"Verily Zubayr has a favour upon me. I, therefore, want to make a requital for it." The Prophet said, "I set him free." 'Uthmān informed Zubayr of this. Zubayr said, "How can one live without his family and children?" 'Uthmān reported this to the Prophet who said, "I set his family and children free." 'Uthmān informed Zubayr of this favour, whereupon he said, "How can one live without his property?" And 'Uthmān reported the same to the Prophet, who said, "We have given up his wealth for him." This was informed to Zubayr who, however, enquired of his some particular acquaintances about whom it was said that they were all killed. *[fo. 31-a]* Zubayr then said, "There is now no charm left for me in life. You have done to the best of your capacity." He was, then, executed.

At Badr, those disbelievers of the Quraysh who had no wealth to offer in ransom were set free on condition that they would teach the Anṣār the art of writing.

The Anṣār said to the Prophet that they would forgive the ransom of 'Abbās, their nephew. But the Prophet replied, "No, by Allāh, not even a single *dirham.*" Then 'Abbās said to the Prophet, "Did I not accept Islam?" But this did not do any good to him, as he had not migrated. Whatever was on him was taken away from him. He was of tall stature. So, they sought for him a shirt to cover him. At last, 'Abd Allāh ibn Ubayy ibn Ṣalūl gave him his shirt, and the Prophet in return gave 'Abd Allāh his inner shirt when he died. He was shrouded in it. 'Abbās was tied up with lamb's skin which made him groan at night, this kept the Prophet awake.

Aḥmad was asked about selling and purchasing the inhabitants of Bargouaṭah and booties taken from them, and whether *Jizyah* could be imposed on them if they agreed to pay it after their defeat. He was also asked about some people who were mentioned as disbelievers and settled in the districts of Ashīr. They belonged to the tribe Ṣanhājah. They considered themselves belonging to the Arab stock. He was enquired whether they would be treated like the Arabs; that nothing but Islam would be accepted from them or they would be put to death and what decision would be taken concerning them all.

Aḥmad replied that, if the people from Bargouaṭah were taken as capitives then it was permissible to sell and enslaves them after they were divided into five shares and were distributed (among the people), and *Jizyah* would not be accepted from them if they offered it, since the text with refrence to *Jizyah* only relates to the People of the Scripture and the Magians.

Similar is the case with the Ṣanhājah tribe who hailed from the tribes known as Suwālah and those who fell in the same category in the districts of Katamāh and 'Agīyah. Now, whoever becomes himself a renegade will be put to death and his wealth will go to the Muslims. But, whoever inherits disbelief from his forefathers, is to be treated like Bargouaṭah. They will only be enslaved when they accept Islam and will be forced to accept Islam. As for one who conceals his disbelief is liable to nothing save execution.

Chapter II

ON DISCUSSION OF TRUCE AND, ON APPREHENSION OF BETRAYAL BY ONE WHOSE SETTLEMENT LIES IN BETWEEN THE MUSLIMS AND THE DISBELIEVERS

When the Muslims gain upper hand and have no fear from the enemy, it is not permissible for them to make truce with the enemy on the condition of wealth and without it, since Allāh says, "So, do not falter and cry out for peace when Ye (will be) the uppermost." (47: 35) But when the Muslims are too weak to fight the enemy and it becomes impossible for them to have help from the Muslims of their neighbourhood, they can make truce with them on or without the condition of wealth.

But when the armistice continues between us, and they hand over to us some persons as hostages from among them against the wealth which they promise to pay but afterwards they break the truce, turn into enemy and stop the payment of the amount on which the truce was concluded, there is disagreement concerning their hostages. *[fo. 31-b]* Some say that they will be treated like the wealth in which transaction is allowed till they pay the entire amount of the truce imposed on their companions.

However, some others say that if they want to remain as *Dhimmīs*, nothing of the sort will be taken from them. The first view is preferable. But, if during the period of truce they want to sell their children to us, most of our authorities do not allow the purchase from them, because according to the truce the children have similar rights like their fathers. Some people hold that it is allowed.

When they ask for protection (*Dhimmah*) of Allāh and His Messenger, this would not be given to them, because of the Prophetic tradition that prohibits this. They will, however, be given the protection of those with whom they have made the truce. In case of apprehension of breach of truce from those who have concluded the truce but reside near us and they are settled between us and the enemy territory (*Dār al-Ḥarb*), Mālik and a section of '*Ulamā*' hold that vigilance will be kept on them, they will be exempted from the obligation to fight and the people should be on guard against them. They will not be treated hastily till their treachery becomes manifest and the treaty will be maintained as long as they remain faithful and they will be defended as long as they pay.

A section of the people hold that the treaty will be thrown back to them fairly as "Allāh does not like the treacherous" (8: 58). The spy, be he a Muslim or a disbeliever, will be put to death and his life will in no case be spared as it is feared he might turn to his old habit and he might be followed by others. In case he is a Muslim, his act will be regarded as apostasy.

Chapter III

ON THE CONQUEST OF MAKKAH, RULING ABOUT ITS INHABITANTS, ITS PROPERTIES, LOST AND FOUND, AND ON ALL ITS RELEVANT AFFAIRS

The Prophetic tradition consecutively related to and supported the view that Makkah was conquered by the force of arms; and that the Prophet entered the city having a helmet on his head, lowering his head in submission to Allāh, Glory be to Him. He was reciting the verse: "The Kingdom belongs to Allāh, the Almighty one". The Prophet had ordered Khālid ibn al-Walīd to proceed to the lower part of Makkah and not to begin fighting unless they start it. It was, then, reported to him, "Look, Khalīd has reached upto Ṣafā". Whereupon, the Prophet said, "Perhaps they have started fighting with him."

It has been narrated that when the Qurayshites showed endurance for fighting, the Prophet ordered the Anṣār to be called for him. They all gathered around him. He then asked them if there were any aliens amidst them. They said, not except their nephew (sister's son). The Prophet said, "The nephew of the people belongs to them. Don't you see the Qurayshites who have gathered their rabbles around them? You uproot them by striking the sword vehemently till you meet me at Ṣafā."

When the slaughter of the Qurayshites reached its climax, Abū Sufyān appeared on the rôof of the Ka'bah and called out, "O Messenger of Allāh, the Qurayshite leaders are being annihilated. There will be no Quraysh after this day." Or he said, "They have been annihilated, whoever enters his own house is safe." The Prophet said: "Yes", Abū Sufyān further added, "Whoever throws away the weapon is safe, whoever enters the Ka'bah is safe, and whoever enters the house of Abū Sufyān is safe." The Prophet said, "Yes".

When the Prophet entered *[fo. 32-a]* Makkah or Minā it was reported to him that Ibn Khaṭal had attached himself to the covers of the Ka'bah. The Prophet ordered that he be put to death. He also ordered execution of two singing girls who used to sing satires against him. Meanwhile 'Uthmān brought 'Abd Allāh ibn Sa'd ibn Abū Sarah to take oath of allegiance (*bay'ah*) at the hands of the Prophet, whereupon the Prophet kept silent and 'Uthmān repeated his words to him, and continued till 'Abd Allāh took the oath of allegiance at his hands. The Prophet, then, said to his Companions, "Were there none among you to have killed him?" They said, "Would that you have given the signal for it." The Prophet replied, "It is not befitting for a Prophet to give signals."

Abū Sufyān ibn al-Ḥarith ibn 'Abd al-Muṭṭalib, the foster-brother of the Prophet, who used to satirize him as vile, came to the Prophet and said, "Peace be upon you, O Messenger of Allāh." The Prophet turned his face from him, then Abū Sufyān took a turn to face him and said, "Peace be upon you, O Messenger of Allah." The Prophet again turned his face from him. He again said, "Peace be upon you, O Messenger of Allāh", and went away distressed. He met 'Alī to whom he mentioned this. 'Alī asked him to go back to the Prophet and also advised him to tell the Prophet if the latter turned his face again, "O Messenger of Allāh, why do you not tell me as Joseph told his brother, 'This day let no reproach be (cast) on you. May Allāh forgive you, and He is the Most Merciful of those who show mercy' " (7: 92). Abū Sufyān did so. The Prophet said, "And you too, may Allāh forgive you and He is the Most Merciful of all, may Allāh give recompense of good to him who told you to say so."

The Prophet did not rouse the Makkan's anger concerning any property of the Makkans. They were either to accept Islam or to escape for life, because he had not accepted any ransom from them, nor were they condemned to slavery. They were either to accept Islam or to face the sword. This was done to show due regard to the (believing) Quraysh and to punish the disbelievers from among them.

It has been proved that the Prophet said, "There are seven allies *(Mawālī)* who have no ally accept Allāh: the Quraysh, the Anṣār, Muzaynah Juhaynah, Aslam, and Ashja' and Ghifār. The Prophet allighted at the narrow valley of Banū Kinānah, where the disbelievers had taken oath against Banū Ḥāshim. It was therefore said to him, "Will you not come down at your dwellings?" The Prophet replied, " 'Aqīl did not leave any dwelling for us." 'Aqīl had sold the dwellings before he accepted Islam, and the Prophet disliked to take back something which was affected for the cause of Allāh.

There has been disagreement concerning lease of the housses of Makkah for rent. Sufyān did not consider it lawful to let them nor would he take to task those who resided therein for stopping payment of rent therein. Mālik disapproved of renting out of their houses during the season of pilgrimage. Those who hold this view interpret the saying of Allāh: "Together, the dweller therein and the nomad" (12: 25). Some *'Ulamā'* allow the owners to do with the houses whatever they like in matters of letting these houses etc.

Ibn 'Idrīs thinks that Makkah was conquered by a peace treaty. It has been proved that the Prophet addressed the people at Minā in his Farewell Pilgrimage, and said: "Verily, Allāh has declared Makkah sacred but people did not observe its sanctity and overpowered it with the elephant or fighting. Makkah was, however, made lawful for me only for one hour of the day, then its sanctity was restored till the Day of Resurrection." He also added, "Its trees must not be cut off, *[fo. 32-b]* its vegetables must not be plucked and its lost property must not be considered lawful for anyone save for one who gives information of the lost property to others." 'Abbās said to the Prophet, "Except al-Idhkhir (Schaenantum) which is used for our houses and our graves." The Prophet added, "Except al-Idhkhir", meaning that unlike other places, gleaner of the lost property therein is allowed forever only to announce and make it known to others.

There has been disagreement concerning one who commits murder, injures somebody and then seeks refuge in the Holy Sanctuary. Mālik and many other *'Ulamā'* hold that this would not debar anyone from taking retaliation of murder nor would the Holy Sanctuary give shelter to a transgressor. Abū Shurayḥ al-Ka'bī, Ibn 'Abbās and 'Ubayd ibn 'Umar hold that he who takes refuge in the Holy Sanctuary will not be disturbed. Ibn 'Abbās says that the people would be forbidden to have transaction with him, to mix with him and to converse with him, till he is forced to get out of the place and thus the punishment will be inflicted on him.

Nu'mān says: "If he commits murder in the Holy Sanctuary, the retaliation for murder will be taken from him in Holy Sanctuary, but if he kills somebody in a place other than the Holy Sanctuary and then takes refuge in the Sanctuary, people should be forbidden to mix with him till he is forced to come out of it and thus the retaliation will be taken from him."

There has been disagreement concerning one who commits a crime in the Holy Sanctuary or during the Sacred Months. Mālik, his followers, and a group of the *'Ulamā'* hold that blood-money will not be imposed on him on account of the sanctity of the Holy Sanctuary and Sacred Months, and in all its affairs it will not be treated like the lands conquered by force nor will its rites cease till the two mountains of it vanish.

It has been confirmed by the Prophetic *Ḥadīth* that there will be pilgrimage at Makkah after (the appearance of) Gog and Magog. Another *ḥadīth* contains the words: "Perform pilgrimage before you are unable to perform it." If this is proved it means that the pilgrimage will discontinue, then it will be reinstated.

Whoever tried to violate the sanctity of the Holy House, was destroyed by Allāh. When Ḥuṣayn ibn Numayr besieged Ibn al-Zubayr and set up ballista under the care of one called al-Zubayr who started stoning Ka'bah, no sooner had he done so than a fire came and burnt the ballista as well as those who were in charge of it. This is what the poet means when he says:

> Verily it was a bad appointment when al-Zubayr was appointed. When he burnt the *Qiblah* and the place of the prayer. It was the *Qiblah* of those who perform pilgrimage and prayer.

They, however, installed another to which they hung up a copy of the Qur'ān just to seek refuge with it. They then threw burning tar and stones at the House till it caught fire and the roof fell down. Yazīd ibn Abū Ḥabīb says: "Nothing greater than three incidents was ever done by this community: their murdering the Caliph, burning of Ka'bah and taking *Jizyah* from the Muslims."

While Ḥuṣayn was busy with his siege, suddenly there came to him the death news of Yazīd. Soon he, along with his party, withdrew. Ibn al-Zubayr came out, became powerful, his domain extended and he was proclaimed as *Amīr al-Mu'minīn* (the Commander of the Faithful). He ruled over Yaman, Ḥijāz, 'Iraq, and appointed his brother Muṣ'ab, governor of 'Irāq, and himself looked after the pilgrimage for nine years continually.

'Abd al-Malik then proceeded to Iraq, defeated Muṣ'ab and killed him. He also killed his son 'Īsā; both were killed in the battle. This happened after they had rolled themselves up *[fo. 33-a]* into the court of Muṣ'ab. He took his seat on his throne and kept the sword on his thigh while nothing of him displayed any movement. He then asked his son 'Īsā to fight if he wanted to achieve anything. Whereupon, 'Īsā fought till he was killed.

Then Muṣ'ab stood up on his throne and fought till he was killed. The head of Muṣ'ab was then brought before 'Abd al-Malik who said, "Surely you have enjoyed our friendship and honour, but this country is barren." All of a sudden, a man bewailed and cried. 'Abd al-Malik asked him about the cause of his weeping. The man replied, "I was present in this very court when the head of Ḥuṣayn was brought to 'Ubayd Allāh ibn Ziyād, then in my presence here, the head of 'Ubayd Allāh ibn Ziyād was brought to al-Mukhtār ibn 'Ubayd Allāh, and again the head of al-Mukhtār in my presence was brought to Muṣ'ab, and now, the head of Muṣ'ab has been brought to you."

When the death news of Muṣ'ab reached 'Abd Allāh ibn Zubayr, he delayed in attending the prayer in the *Masjid al-Ḥarām* while he had never been behind time in the prayer. When he came out, he said: "I was not late due to grief and bewailment on account of Muṣ'ab; on the contrary, I recited the Qur'ān from the opening chapter to the end and prayed to Allāh to forgive Muṣ'ab." People then said, "May Allāh grant the prayer of the Commander of the Faithful."

Al-Ḥajjāj saw in his dream as if he was skinning Ibn al-Zubayr. He then mentioned it to Rawḥ ibn Zanbā' who mentioned the same to 'Abd al-Malik. 'Abd al-Malik, thereupon, sent al-Ḥajjāj to Ibn al-Zubayr whom he defeated and killed in the battle-field and crucified him. He then entered upon Asmā', the daughter of Abū Bakr, and mother of Ibn al-Zubayr, who was then one hundred years old, and expressed his grief for her. Whereupon, she said: "You express grief for me over what I met, Verily, the head of Yaḥyā ibn Zakriyāh, peace be upon them both, was presented to a prostitute."

Ḥajjāj was appointed governor over al-Ḥijāz. He burnt the holy Ka'bah, the roof of which fell down. Ibn al-Zubayr had built it after it was burnt by Ḥuṣayn and placed the black stone inside the Ka'bah. He opened in it two doors at the floor which al-Ḥajjāj demolished and restored it to its former construction and placed the remaining portion of (the Black Stone) inside the Ka'bah and on its door.

Once Ḥajjāj said to Ibn 'Umar, "Verily, Ibn al-Zubayr changed your *Qiblah*." On this Ibn 'Umar said to him, "Both Ibn al-Zubayr and you are too small to change our *Qiblah*." In the same year Ibn 'Umar died. His leg was pierced with a lance of some people of al-Ḥajjāj. Al-Ḥajjāj then called on him and enquired as to who had ill-treated him. Ibn 'Umar replied, "You". He said "How? may Allāh have mercy on you." He said, "Because you forced your weapon into the Holy Sanctuary and unsheathed your sword in a city in which it was not proper to unsheath the sword."

Chapter IV

ON THE STIPULATED WAGES (*JA'Ā'IL*) AND ON THE ALLOWANCES FIXED FOR THE FIGHTERS

'Umar organised the Register and kept on record the number of fighters of every land and fixed allowance for them. Whenever he sent any expedition, he charged every tribe with a specific number. Those who stayed behind offered some wealth to those who went out for war on *[fo. 33-b]* account of their participation in war. Makhūl says that the dreads of expeditions remove the dreads on the Day of Resurrection. Ibn Muḥayrīz says: "The recipients of allowances are better than those who offer allowances as they encounter the dreadful situations."

It was said to the Prophet, "Please give us legal verdict concerning one who offers and one who receives the wages." The Prophet said that the contributor will receive what he expects (of the reward) and the recipient will get the reward of the contributor as well as that of the recipient, meaning thereby that the latter will get the equivalent reward of what his companion offered him on his coming out for war as the similar act was his due and he will get himself the reward of his own act of going out for war.

When the warrior (*al-ghāzī*) is offered something without asking for it, and his coming out was not for this, whatever is offered will be lawful for him, no matter, whether he is rich or needy.

Whenever Ibn 'Umar gave anything to a warrior he would say to him, "When you reach Wādī al-Qurā', you take care of it", meaning that when he reaches the first stage of war, the object becomes his possession. If anybody is provided with horse in the way of Allāh and is killed by his combatant in the way of Allāh, and the horse upon which he mounted comes back, it should be bequeathed in the way of Allāh except when the owner disengaged it to the other person to do with the horse whatever he likes.

Once Ibn 'Umar brought forth something to give it to the fighters who refused to accept it. There was among them, 'Āmir ibn 'Abd Allāh ibn Zubayr who said, "By offering this, you cannot withhold the paradise from us, rather we shall accept it. If we require it we shall spend it and if we do not require it, we shall spend it according to its own way." He then accepted it and people also accepted it. Ibn 'Umar thereupon thanked him for this.

Abū 'l-Dardā' sent a few purses to be delivered to the soldiers. Then the person, with whom the purses were sent, came there and found a man keeping aloof from the people. He gave him a purse out of the lot. The man raised his head to the heaven and said, "O Allāh, you surely did not forget the deserving one. Now make the deserving one not to forget you." Abū 'l-Dardā' was informed of this. He said, its owner became the master of favours.

Whatever is given as additional share, *nafal,* by the chief of the army and commanders of fighting individuals, it will be agreeable for them and whatever is fixed for them will be lawful for them, except when their intentions of fighting in the war are for this, and in case when they are not given anything they would not have gone out. In this case their coming out in the war will be considered for the purposes they came out for.

Chapter V

ON *JIZYAH* AND BANŪ TAGHLIB

Allāh, the Exalted, says: "Fight against such of those who have been given the Scripture as believe not in Allāh, nor the Last Day; and forbid not that which Allāh hath forbidden by His Messenger, and follow not the religion of truth until they pay the tribute readily, being brought low." (9: 29)

It has been proved that the Prophet ordered to take *Jizyah* from the Magians. Moreover, it has been reported that during the life-time of the Prophet, *Jizyah* was realised at the rate of one *dīnār* from every adult, free or slave, male or female. 'Umar levied it on the *dhimmī*s at the rate of four *dīnār*s on every rich man, or forty *dirham*s, and did impose nothing on the women and the slaves; and he levied on those who were not rich at the rate of two *dīnār*s or twenty *dirhams* per head, and on those who were still not rich at the rate of one *dīnār* or ten *dirhams [fo. 35-a]* in case they belonged to the people of silver (*ahl al-Waraq*). To this rate he added bushels of olive oil and entertainment (hospitality) of Muslims for three days.

Mālik and his followers, therefore, follow the practice of 'Umar and interpret that his practice is not against the practice of the Prophet. 'Umar deviated from the early practice as mentioned earlier only on account of the wealth of these persons. So he levied on every individual according to his capacity. Undoubtedly this was the interpretation of 'Umar. Mālik and his followers hold that nothing is to be increased upon what is prescribed by 'Umar and I think they may be excused of entertainment which sometimes prove too much for them.

Ibn Idrīs opines that no *dīnār* is to be added to one *dīnār*. Another group of scholars holds that it is up to the Imām: If he thinks it proper to enhance it on account of their abundant wealth, he can enhance it as 'Umar enhanced.

It has been reported that Banū Taghlib, who were Christians, disliked to pay *Jizyah* before it was levied on them. They offered to pay one-fifth of their harvest as well as that of the produce of the land, and accordingly an agreement was concluded with them. Some of our authorities, however, refuse to accept this from them comparing the case with that of *Zakāh*, because *Zakāh* is realised only from the Muslims to purify them, and *Jizyah* is realised from the disbelievers to subdue them and the tradition has not been held by them as dependable.

This has been taken in the sense of a peace-treaty not in the sense of *Zakāh*. Had they been aware of the tradition mentioned above, they would not have surely opposed it, since, to conclude a peace-treaty on this term is permissible.

Chapter VI

ON THE PRESENTS OFFERED BY THE DISBELIEVERS TO THE MUSLIM RULERS; ON THE PRESENTS OFFERED BY THE RULERS; ON DEFRAUDING; AND ON PERMISSIBILITY OF TAKING FOOD AND FODDER

When any chief of the enemy or anyone from the disbelievers sends presents to the Imām before he invades the enemy-land while the former is not under the authority of the latter, the presents will belong to one to whom the presents have been sent. But, if the Muslim chief has invaded them, what is offered to him is to be treated like the wealth obtained as booty by the army (in common). If it is presented to him by a subordinate individual, be he a Muslim or a *dhimmī*, it will not be permissible for him to accept it.

The Syrians have reported that the Prophet used to burn by way of punishment the litter of one who defrauded the booty. The reports on this have spread out from them. The Prophet has said: "Defrauding is a shame, a fire and disgrace on the Day of Resurrection." He came upon a people who were addicted to defrauding and uttered *takbīr* on them as he used to utter *takbīr* on the dead. It was said concerning Mid'am, who had received a stray arrow; "May he be blessed with Paradise!" The Prophet said: "Surely not the small cloak which he had taken on the day of Khaybar and which was not divided, would certainly enkindle fire on him." The Prophet said, "Even a strap or two straps are pieces of fire." He also said, "You should return both the thread and the needle."

All that has been reported concerning the Prophet's burning *[fo. 34-a]* the litter of a fraudulent person is the example of his severe action taken on some occasions, not that it was a systematic ruling and Allāh alone knows it best, as it has been narrated that whoever refused to pay *Zakāh*, it (*Zakāh*) will be realized from him together with half of his herd. A certain man married a wife of his father, the Prophet sent someone to burn him, strike his neck and declare his property as a *nafal*. It is possible that the person who married, did so considering it lawful, he was, therefore, considered as a renegade.

It is permissible for the soldiers to take fodder and food without the permission of the Imām whether it was preserved by the Imām along with the booty or not, there being no harm if some of them exchanged some fodder with some food and some food with some other foods proportionately or disproportionately; because it was not a case of buying and selling. Companions only please each other with some of what they mutually possess. It is also permissible to take provision out of it in order to reach one's own family. After reaching his family if the surplus is considerable, he should retain a small portion thereof and give away the rest in alms, but if the surplus is negligible he may retain it.

There has been disagreement concerning the views of Mālik and his followers with regard to one who requires riding beast or needs a dress out of the booties in the enemy-land before the distribution. He considers it lawful and holds that as soon as he does not require it, he should return it to the booties, but if the army returns and (the soldiers) are dispersed, he should offer it in alms. He also says that he will not come near it and this is the most right and sound law of *Jihād*.

He was asked regarding one who picked up a ball of thread or something like this, whether he should return it to the booty. He said, "I am afraid, a thing like this might be mistaken as meaning that he should not bring it separately because it is insignificant. If, however, nothing falls into his hand except this he may throw it secretly in the booties or may leave it there where he found it."

There has been disagreement concerning fruits which some Muslim army cut off from their trees in *Dār al-Ḥarb* and also about things which they make from clay, like pottery, green jar pots, and what they pick up from their enclosures. Some say that all this will be put together in the booties; while others hold that these belong to one who picks them up. If some of the beasts of burden of the army die or become unable to carry their goods they belong to one who holds them.

Chapter VII

ON THE WEALTH OF THE MUSLIMS FOUND IN THE BOOTY; ON ONE WHO EMBRACES ISLAM WHILE HE HAS IN HIS POSSESSION THE WEALTH OF ANOTHER MUSLIM; ON ONE WHO EMBRACES ISLAM BUT FINDS IN THE HAND OF A MUSLIM ALL THAT WAS TAKEN AWAY FROM HIM AS BOOTY; AND ALSO ON A PERSON AS WELL WHO PAYS UP THE RANSOM FOR A MUSLIM OR OFFERS RANSOM FOR THE SLAVE OF A MUSLIM

A horse of Ibn 'Umar disappeared, and a slave of his ran away to the enemy, he afterwards found them out before they were distributed (as booty), *[fo. 35-a]* thereupon, Khālid ibn al-Walīd returned them to Ibn 'Umar.

It has been reported that (the Prophet said), "Whoever finds out his article before it is divided, has better claim over it. But if it is already divided, the owner can get it on payment of its price." The chain of narrators of this *ḥadīth* is not sound. The '*Ulamā*' have disagreed concerning this; our authorities adhere to what is in the context of the *ḥadīth*. Some say that he has better claim over the article without payment of price, even after its division.

It has been reported that before his accepting Islam, al-Mughīrah killed some disbelievers and brought to the Prophet their wealth and then accepted Islam. The Prophet said to him, "I have no corcern with anything of this wealth," and asked him neither to return it nor to remove it from his hand.

It has been reported that a man accepted Islam and informed the Prophet of the fact that some of his belongings were in the possession of a Muslim. The Prophet then asked the Muslim to return it. The meaning of the *ḥadīth*, and Allāh knows the best, is the fact that the Prophet requested him to return his wealth by way of recommendation and urged him to do so, not that the Prophet made it binding upon him to return his wealth, as the traditions have consecutively been narrated against this. 'Urwah has reported that the Prophet said, "Whoever accepts Islam holding something in his possession has right to it."

They have disagreed concerning one who gives ransom for a Muslim belonging to the enemy-territory or gives ransom for a slave of a Muslim. Our authorities and most of the *'Ulamā'* hold that he will turn (for the payment) to the freeman and to the master of the slave. Some others say that he will not get anything. The latter view has been narrated on the authority of Ibn Sīrīn, al-Ḥakam and others.

Those who hold this argue that the Prophet said, "You emancipate the slave". This is therefore obligatory on the Muslims alone and this will not turn to one on whom it is not binding. Others hold that this is obligatory for the Muslims. If their authority (*Sulṭān*) fails in discharging the obligation, the captive should not keep himself in the abode of disbelief and retain his wealth and the master of the slave cannot take hold of his slave without any price from one who sets him free because he could not set him free, and because had he accepted Islam, he had better claim over him.

Chapter VIII

ON THE INHABITANTS OF THE ENEMY-TERRITORY WHO ENTER THE MUSLIM TERRITORY WITH THE PLEDGE OF SECURITY WHILE THEY HOLD IN THEIR POSSESSION MUSLIM INDIVIDUALS FREE OR SLAVE; OR ON THOSE SOME OF WHOSE SLAVES EMBRACE ISLAM; OR ON THOSE WHO COME AS ENVOYS BUT LATER ON EMBRACE ISLAM AND WANT TO STAY BEHIND IN THE MUSLIM-TERRITORY

There has been disagreement concerning the inahbitants of the people of the enemy-territory who come to us with the pledge of security (*Amān*) while they hold in possession free Muslim individuals or some of their slaves accept Islam. Some say that they will be asked to redeem the free and sell the slaves. If they refuse, they will not be forced to do so. Some say that they will be taken from them on price. Some others say that if they make a condition that they will not be taken from them the condition will be fulfilled, otherwise *[fo. 35-b]* they will be taken from them on price.

They have also disagreed concerning an envoy who embraces Islam or wants to stay behind with us as a *dhimmī*. It is said, that this will be accepted from him, but some others hold that he will be returned to one who has sent him. As to one whose safety has been guarantteed and who dies among us, his wealth will be sent to his heirs. If a Muslim kills him, his blood-money will be sent to them. Some say it becomes *fay'*.

Chapter IX

ON INVITING (TO ISLAM) BEFORE FIGHTING; ON ENTERING THE ENEMY-TERRITORY; AND ON SETTLING AT FRONTIER-TOWNS

Anas says; whenever the Prophet went to a place at night, he made no raid upon them till the dawn. On the appearance of dawn, if he heard the call for prayer (*Adhān*) he would refrain, but if he did not hear any call for prayer, he raided.

The Prophet reached Khaybar at night, but he made no raid upon them. When it dawned, they came out with their implements of cultivation and date-baskets. As soon as they saw the Prophet they cried out: "Muḥammad, by Allāh, Muḥammad along with the entire army." The Prophet then said, "Allāh is great, Khaybar perished! Verily, whenever we alighted at the plain-space of any people, then, what a helpless morning is for those who are warned."

The Prophet used to give instructions to the commanders of his army and to those of the troops to invite to Islam whomever they met. If he (the non-Muslim) responds they should inform him of all the obligations incumbent on him: if he again responds he will be regarded as a Muslim, but if he refuses and happens to be included among those from who *Jizyah* can be accepted, they should ask him to pay *Jizyah*, if he refuses they will fight against him.

The invitation is to be accorded only to those who were not invited earlier, and to whom invitation did not reach, otherwise invitation is not required. The Prophet sent forth someone to Abū Rafī', Ka'b ibn Ashraf and Ibn al-Tayyāḥ to assassinate them unaware without inviting them to Islam.

If somebody asks concerning the saying of Allāh addressed to His

Prophet: "Say (O Muḥammad) O mankind: Lo! I am the Messenger of Allāh to you all." (7: 158): whether the invitation has been delivered to all of them? It will be said to him, that Allāh, the Exalted, has explained it by His saying: "And this Qur'ān hath been inspired in me, that I may warn therewith you and whomsoever it may reach." (6: 19) and by His saying "Whom they will find described in the Torah and the Gospel (which are) with them. He will enjoin on them that which is right and forbid them that which is wrong." (7: 157)

The Messenger of Allāh thus delivered invitation during his life to all those to whom he could convey, and his followers delivered in the past, are delivering at present and will be delivering in future the invitations to all those whom they were able and will be able to contact. As for others, divine books and Messengers have already reached them (bidding them) that Muḥammad would soon be sent to the humanity at large.

The plea is, therefore, substantiated against them and it became incumbent upon them to believe in the Messenger. Whoever, then, denies the Messenger, the argument is established against him. One who believed in the Messenger but his dwellings happened to be far away from the Muslims and had not been acquainted with the laws (of Islam) but the news reached him to the effect that the Messenger had been sent, it was incumbent upon him to visit the territory of the Muslims (*Dār al-Islām*) and know what laws (of Islam) were prescribed for him.

As for one to whom his message did not reach while he believed in the Messenger through the teachings and discussions that reached earlier and also believed in all Prophets without adhering to Judaism, Christianity or Sabianism or Manichaenism or *[fo. 36-a]* disbelief, considered lawful all that Allāh explicitly mentioned in the Qur'ān that He would soon make them lawful for all nations, consider unlawful all that was explicitly mentioned that He would soon declare them unlawful. All the preceding laws which had been incumbent upon him particularly would remain no more binging upon him as soon as he declared that Allāh is one, He has no partner with Him, and believed in His Prophets, and Messengers, Angels, Books and the Last Day.

Zayd ibn 'Amr ibn Nufayl had accepted Islam. Formerly he practised the religion of Abraham. He was a contemporary of the Prophet but he died before his call to Prophethood. The Prophet said: "On the Day of Resurrection, he will be raised as a single community." As the laws (of Islam) were coming down to the Prophet, it was not necessary for anyone to act according to these laws when he was not present with the Prophet at the time of the revelation since these laws would not reach him.

Somebody came to the inhabitants of Qubā' and informed them that the *Qiblah* had been shifted towards Ka'bah. So they moved round to face the Ka'bah and nothing fell incumbent on them for their past acts. Abū 'Ubaydah, Abū Ṭalḥah, Ubayy and Anas were informed while they were drinking wine that wine had been declared forbidden. They said to Anas, "Stand up and break these jars." They had not to give any explanation for their actions in the past, nor did anything occur in their hearts concerning any action of the past.

The Prophet himself used to come out in person and very often he sent troops and expeditions to the enemy-land. He often encountered opposition, and sometimes he did not. The Prophet did not face any opposition in the "Expedition of Hardship" (Tabūk) to which these Muhājirūn and Anṣār who had remained behind were reproved, and those who had attended the expedition were promised with the acceptance of their repentance. The Prophet asked Usāmah to go to Obna and burn it down.

Abū 'Ubaydah wrote to 'Umar mentioning to him what had frightened them on account of huge gathering of the Romans. 'Umar wrote to him; "Surely, a tough period shall not prevail over the two easy periods, and that whenever a hardship befalls a believer, Allāh enables him to derive out of it some ease and a way out. Verily, Allāh the Exalted, says, 'O Ye who believe! Persevere, outdo all others in patience and perseverance, be ready and observe your duty to Allāh in order that Ye may succeed.' [3: 200] He also said: 'Make ready for them all thou canst of (armed) forces and of horse tethered, that thereby ye may dismay the enemy of Allāh and your enemy.' [8: 60]".

The Prophet says: "The horse is a reward for a man, a shield for a man and a burden upon a man. As for one for whom it is a reward, it is the man who has saddled it for the cause of Allāh, has prolonged its tether in a meadow or a garden. Now, whatever it consumed in its tether in the meadow or the garden, all its foot-prints and dung shall be considered as good deeds for him. If his horse passes over a stream, drinks out of it while he intends it not to drink, its drink shall be considered as good deeds for him. Whoever ties his horse with saddle and bridle for becoming free from need and for abstaining from begging without forgetting the right of Allāh on its neck and back, it shall be a shield for him. Whoever ties it *[fo. 36-b]* up for pride, hypocrisy and opposition to the followers of Islam, it is then a burden upon him."

The Prophet said, "Horses will carry fortune in their forelocks up to the Day of Resurrection." He added, "There is no match, nor is there any equivalent act like *Jihād* in the way of Allāh." He also said, "The *Mujāhid* in the way of Allāh is like the person who does not break his fast nor does he cease from his prayer." He also said, "Allāh takes the responsibility of one who wages *Jihād* in His Way, and nothing takes him out from his house except the *Jihād* in the way of Allāh, and attestation to His words that he would make him either enter into the Paradise or return him to his dwelling from which he had come out along with the reward or booty which he obtained."

He also said, "Had I not felt it difficult for my followers, I would have surely desired not to remain behind from any expedition that had gone out in the way of Allāh, while I did not find any riding beast for them nor did they themselves find their own riding beast. Morover, it would be difficult for them to remain behind me (so I do not attend every expedition), otherwise, it is my desire to fight in the way of Allāh till I am killed, I am then restored to life and be killed and again I am restored to life and be killed again." He also said, "Nobody is injured in His way but he will come on the Day of Resurrection with his wound bleeding having the colour of blood and the fragrance of the musk."

It was said to the Prophet: "Which of the actions is most excellent?" The Prophet said, "The belief in Allāh"; he was again asked, "Then what?" he said, "Offering of prayer at its time." It was, again, asked, "Then what?" He said, "*Jihād* in the way of Allāh". Another *ḥadīth* contains the words of "belief in Allāh." He was again asked, "Then what?" He replied, "*Jihād* in the way of Allāh". It was again said, "Then what?" He replied, "A pious pilgrimage". There is no disagreement in the fact that if the prayer and the pilgrimage are both obligatory, the prayer is more excellent (of the two), but if the prayer is voluntary, then *Jihād* excells it.

All the battles (*Ghazawāt*) and expeditions (*Sarāyā*) undertaken by the Prophet were forty-five in number: eighteen battles (*Ghazawāt*) and twenty-seven expeditions (*Sarāyā*). The first battle was that of Bawāṭ and was called *al-'Ushayrah*. The Prophet personally attended eight battles: Badr, Uḥud, al-Khandaq, which was also called al-Aḥzāb. There was shooting of arrows for a part of the day, and on this occasion Sa'd ibn Mu'ādh received wound in the median vein of his hand which caused his death. (Other wars are) Banū'l-Mūṣṭaliq, Banū'l Qurayẓah, Khaybar, the conquest of Makkah, Ḥunayn with Hawāzin and al-Ṭā'if.

All these have been mentioned by Allāh in the Qur'ān; Allāh, the Exalted, said, "And Allāh had already given you victory at Badr when Ye were contemptible." (3: 123) He added, "And when thou settedst forth for day-break from thy housefolk to assign to the believers their positions for the battle" (3: 121). This concerns the day of Uḥud. He also said, "When they came upon you from above you and from below you" (33: 10). All these verses concerned the day of Aḥzāb. He also said, "And He brought those of the people of the Scripture who supported them down from their strongholds, and cast panic into their hearts. Some Ye slew and Ye made captive some." Upto the saying: "Allāh is very Able to do all things" (33: 26–27). These verses concern Banū Qurayẓah, Banū'l-Muṣṭaliq and the inhabitants of Khaybar. And the land on which he did neither tread nor did he run over at the time of conquest meant Banū Qaynuqā' and Banū al-Naḍīr.

As to Banū Qaynuqā', they possessed wealth other than landed property which the Prophet divided among his followers at once and then ejected them. When the Polytheists were defeated at Badr, they used to say, *[fo 37-a]* "Muḥammad thinks that we are like the Makkans, had we fought him, he would have surely known that we possessed strength (and bravery)", and thus they are those concerning whom Allāh revealed: "If Ye are driven out, we surely will go out with you and will never obey anyone against you." Upto His saying: "Then, they would not have been victorious." (59: 11-12).

Allāh has also revealed on the occasion of Khaybar: "Allāh promised you much booty that Ye will capture and hath given you this in advance" (48: 20). Afterwards He says, "When Allāh's succour and the triumph cometh" (110: 1). This concerns the conquest of Makkah. He also said, "And on the day of Ḥunayn when Ye exulted in your multitude." Upto His saying: "Lo, Ye turned back in flight." (IX: 25)

The Battle of Badr took place in the month of Ramaḍān in H 2, whereas Uḥud took place in the month of Shawwāl in H 3, al-Aḥzāb and Banū Qurayẓah in 4, Banū'l-Muṣṭaliq in 5, Khaybar in 6 or, it is said, in 7, the conquest of Makkah in 8, in which year the Ḥunayn and all that which followed it occurred. The battle of 'Usrah (Hardship), that is Tabūk, was the last battle in which the Prophet personally participated and in which there was no fighting.

He entered into an agreement with the people of *Ilah* on their coming out and came back (to Madinah). The last expedition is the expedition in which he appointed Usāmah as the commander who came out before his (Prophet's) demise but went to its destination after his demise during the Caliphate of Abū Bakr. The Muslims had desired Abū Bakr to detain the expedition, but he refused and said, "Let there not be the first knot which I would execute by undoing the last knot which was done by the Prophet. Even if the dogs run around the litters of the Mothers of the Believers (the wives of the Prophet) I would not withhold it." When Usāmah intended to move ahead, he urged Abū Bakr to give him instructions. Abū Bakr said, "The instruction will be the same as the Messenger of Allāh gave you."

Usāmah then wanted to know as to what orders he would give him. Abū Bakr said, "The order is the same as the Messenger of Allāh gave you." Usāmah thereupon marched ahead.

Abū Bakr directed Khālid ibn al-Walīd to meet the renegades, and thus the hopes of those who had aspired to march towards al-Madīnah on account of the death of the Prophet came to an end. They said that they were the people who were not shocked by the death of their master. Thus victory welcomed the Muslims. Allāh caused the death of Musaylimah, the liar, while Ṭulayḥah fled away and afterwards accepted Islam.

The Companions of the Prophet used to go out to participate in the battles and liked to settle down at frontier-towns. Here, for example, is Ibn Umm Maktūm who was a blind man and was seen in the land of the enemy holding his banner.

When Abū Bakr became Caliph, Bilāl consulted him seeking his permission to go to Syria but Abū Bakr refused to let him go. Bilāl, then said, "If you have freed me to serve you, I shall render you such a service which will never be performed by anybody, but if you had freed me for the sake of Allāh, let me go away." Abū Bakr thereafter allowed him to go out, and Bilāl went to Syria where he lived upto his death. Mu'ādh also settled in Syria.

Once, Suhayl ibn 'Amr, Abū Sufyān, and Ḥārith ibn Hishām came to the door of 'Umar and found Ṣuhayb, Bilāl and Salmān sitting (waiting for permission). Yarfa' informed 'Umar of their position but 'Umar asked him to let Bilāl, Ṣuhayb and Salmān enter upon him. Abū Sufyān got angry and said, "We are being deprived while these people enter." Suhayl pacified him saying, "Here they have preceded us a little only to the door of 'Umar. This is nothing. Don't you realize that they have gone far ahead. Let us then go to these frontier-towns where we may achieve some of what we want." They, thereafter, set out for Syria.

Suhayl gave his daughter into marriage to Ḥārith ibn Hishām who had eighteen children from her. After this, 'Umar used to send instructions to them *[fo. 37-b.]* They lived there upto his death. A number of the Companions of the Prophet like Ḥudhayfah, Abū'l-Dardā' settled in frontier-towns.

Bahz ibn Ḥakīm ibn Mu'āwiyah ibn Ḥīdah reported on the authority of his father, on the authority of his grandfather, who said, "I said, 'O Messenger of Allāh: grant me something.' " The Prophet made for him a sign toward Syria.

One day, while he was in a battle-field, Salmān saw a man forcing a *dhimmī* to carry for him the fodder of his animal but the latter refused, whereupon, the Muslim treated him harshly. Salmān asked him not to do this, whereupon, the man asked him to carry the burden himself. He took it from the *dhimmī* while the man did not know him. Then some people said to him: "This man is Salmān, do not let him carry." The man then apologised to Salmān, who said, "Well, there is no harm to you, I have acquired by this act three virtues, I helped you in the way of Allāh by carrying it, prevented an act of injustice and tested my soul whether any sign of pride has remained therein."

Mu'āwiyyah sent out his son Yazīd, who was very young, to command an army. This was disliked by Abū Ayyūb who stayed behind but afterwards repented. Next year he set out and said, "I shall fight for my share of the next world and everybody receives the benefit of what he performs." He, then, fell ill near Constantinople. Yazīd visited him in his illness and enquired about his need. Abū Ayyūb said, "When I die, please make my grave deep and conceal its place."

When he died, Yazīd took his body far away at night and buried him. Afterwards they passed over it with their horses in order to conceal its place. But lo! the people saw their action. When dawn appeared, the people said, "Certainly something grave happened to you last night." He replied, "Yes, a great Companion of our Prophet fell ill and died. We buried him in your land. If you do any mischief therein, no bell will be rung for you in the land of Islam, as long as we have authority over it." Afterwards, whenever they faced drought they visited his grave and then rain was supplied to them.

A man said to Mālik that he had killed a man, and that he was afraid of his guardians who might kill him any moment and sought his advice. Mālik advised him to go to the frontier-towns and to remain there till his death.

Chapter X

ON *AL-ZAKĀH*

Allāh, the Exalted, says in many verses: "And establish prayer and pay *Zakāh.*" (2:43) And mentions therein the obligatory character of *Zakāh.* He also says: "And they ask thee what they ought to spend? Say, that which is superfluous." (2: 219) It is said that *'afw* is that which their souls grant spontaneously, that is to say their souls bestow bountifully. Some say that *'afw* is anything which remains in excess (*faḍl*) after meeting one's basic needs of food (*qūt*). A cultivator is, therefore, expected to keep the provision of one year and offer the excess (*faḍl*) in alms. If he is an artisan, he will keep the provision of his day and will offer the excess in alms. This was the practice before the organization of the system of *Zakāh.*

Allāh, may He be glorified, says, "The alms are only for the poor and the needy and those who collect them and those whose hearts are to be reconciled and to free the captives and the debtors, and for the cause of Allāh, and (for) the wayfarer; a duty imposed by Allāh. Allāh is Knower, Wise" (9: 60). Allāh, the Glorified, has not thus left its divine duty to any other category.

There has been disagreement about (the meaning of) *Fuqarā'* and *Masākīn* as to who they are. It has been said, that a *Faqīr* is one who possesses means of subsistence and a *Miskīn* is one who posseses nothing. Some say that *Faqīr* is one who has nothing, and a *Miskīn* is one who has something. Some say that a *Faqīr* is one who has no wealth nor has he any physical disability, while a *Miskīn* is one who has physical disability. Some others say that a *Faqīr* is one who does not beg, while a *Miskīn* is one who begs. Yet, some others say that *al-Fuqarā* are those emigrants (*Muhājirūn*) who are needy, *[fo. 38-a]* while the *Masākīn* are those needy who are not emigrants. Some hold that *Faqīr* is a Muslim and *Miskīn* is a *Dhimmī.* This has been related from the authority of Ibn 'Abbās and has been held by some people of Kūfah.

As to *al-'Āmilūna 'Alayhā,* they are those who are employed to collect *Zakāh* and are given out of it by way of wages irrespective of their being rich or poor except Banū Ḥāshim, who are not to be employed for collecting *Zakāh*. This has been proved on the authority of the Prophet.

As to the *al-Mu'allifati qulubūhum,* they are the chiefs of Banū Muḍar and their leaders. Their attachment to Islam was required in order to induce those who were under them to accept Islam. They were, for example, Abū Sufyān ibn Ḥarb, his son Mu'āwiyah, Ḥakīm ibn Ḥizām, Suhayl ibn 'Umar, Ṣafwān ibn Umayyah, 'Ikrimah ibn Abū Jahl, Abū'l Sanābil ibn Ba'kak Aqra' ibn Ḥābis, 'Uyaynah ibn Ḥisn, 'Abbās ibn Mirdās including other people.

There has been disagreement about the time when the act of seeking attachment to Islam will be started; some say that it should be done before accepting Islam to allure them to accept Islam. Some others hold that it should be tried after their accepting Islam in order to endear belief to them. They were treated so during the life of the Messenger of Allāh, as well as the early phase of the caliphate of Abū Bakr. Abū Bakr, afterwards said to Abū Sufyān: "The monetary help has now been stopped. Allāh has now rendered Islam strong, and has discontinued this from them."

It is said that they enjoyed throughout the life of the Messenger of Allāh, that of Abū Bakr and the early phase of the caliphate of 'Umar who in his time, said to Abū Sufyān: "Allāh has now placed Islam in no need of your help and that of the people like you, you are only a Muslim like others, and then stopped the early practice."

There has been disagreement concerning the share as to whom it should be assigned. Ṣome say that it will be redistributed among the seven groups of people mentioned along with them in the Qur'ānic verse. Some others say that half of the share will be assigned to the building of the mosques and the other half will be assigned to all the seven groups mentioned therin.

They have also disagreed whether the like of it will recur if the Muslims face such a situation in which they need the similar practice. Many '*Ulama*', including Mālik and his followers, hold that this share has been stopped and hence it should be assigned to those who have been mentioned in the verse. 'Umar ibn 'Abd al-'Azīz and Ibn Shihāb hold that if a similar situation arises, the Imām can seek attachment to Islam from those whose attachment to Islam is required as the situation demanded in the past.

There has been disagreement concerning the meaning of *wa fi'l-Riqāb*.

It is said that the slaves who are under contract to redeem themselves (*al-Mukātibūn*) will be offered out of it to the extent of obtaining their freedom, but the slaves will not be purchased with it for freedom. Some others say, on the contrary, the slave under contract of buying freedom will not be given anything out of it since *walā'* (the right of succession to the freed man) is confirmed for those who have declared them *Mukātab*.

Some others say that the share will be spent particularly for all these groups. All these views have been recorded on the authority of Mālik. It has also been said that out of this share the ransom will be paid for the Muslim prisoners in order to obtain their freedom.

As for *w'al-Ghārimīna*, it means those who borrow for good purposes and not for the sake of an unlawful purpose, nor do they find anything for the payment of their debts. Some say that it means whoever is crushed by debt and has not incurred it for the sake of an unlawful purpose, will be given out of it, even if he possesses something to pay up his loan. They have obviously considered the apparent meaning of the verse and what has been reported on the authority of the Prophet: that *Ṣadaqah* is not lawful *[fo. 38-b]* for any rich man except for five persons; for a debtor, for a collector of it, for a man who purchases it with his money, for a man who has a needy neighbour to whom the *Ṣadaqah* is offered and the needy neighbour offers it to the rich man as a gift, or for one who fights in the way of Allāh.

As regards the words *Fī Sabīli'l-lāh*, they mean provision of riding-animal out of *Ṣadaqah* to those who have no riding-animal and provision to those who have no provision, and to seal the frontier-towns out of it. Horses, weapons, and riding-animals are to be purchased out of *Ṣadaqah* for making preparation in the way of Allāh. Some say it is permitted for the warrior (*ghazī*), whether rich or poor, to receive out of it in accordance with the apparent meaning of the Qur'ānic verse and the Prophetic tradition.

Ibn al-Sabīl is a wayfarer whose means of travelling are cut off in course of his journey, though he possesses wealth in his own town.

They have disagreed concerning the division of the *Ṣadaqah* (alms). Some hold that it will be divided into either eight shares in accordance with the number of the groups, or seven shares. It is also said that out of these groups, the needy groups will be given preference, and then it will be transferred to those from among them to whom the need is transferred. It has been narrated on the authority of the Prophet with good chain of narrators that the Prophet said, "*Ṣadaqah* is neither lawful for the rich nor for an artisan." *Dhū'l Mirrah* means one who is niggardly skillful in profession, or an artisan who earns his livelihood and maintenance of his living by his skill.

As for one who is deprived of earning and is unable to earn, as whenever he attempts to do anything he fails to earn his livelihood, deserves *Ṣadaqah*.

There has been disagreement concerning the limit to earning when it is not desirable for the earner to accept *Ṣadaqah*. Yaḥyā ibn Sallām narrates on the authority of some people of Kūfah that he who possesses fifty *dirhams* should not accept it. I do not think that it has ever been substantiated by those who possess authority. What has been proved from the authority is that he who possesses not so much coins as to incur *Zakāh*, nor has goods equivalent to it in price, can receive *Zakāh* because of the saying of the Prophet: "The *Ṣadaqah* will be taken from their rich and will be distributed among the poor." Thus, the Prophet has made a limit between the two groups. This was also the opinion of al-Mughīrah ibn 'Abd al-Raḥmān al-Madanī al-Makhzūmī.

There has been disagreement about the amount which may be given out of it (*Zakāh*) to the poor. Some say that a poor person may be given to the extent of incurring *Zakāh*. Some say that if this much can be given to him at a time, there is no harm in giving him more than the amount necessitating *Zakāh*.

He who possesses a house or a servant can be given *Zakāh* provided he would not have anything in excess after meeting his necessities if he sells the two, or purchases out of their price a house just to suffice him and a servant just to satisfy his need and then something surplus remains in his possession. Some of them hold that even he would be given out of *Zakāh* if he owns a house, a servant and a horse.

Chapter XI

ON THE WEALTH LIABLE FOR *ZAKĀH*; AND ON THE RATES OF *ZAKĀH*; AND ON OTHER DUES ON WEALTH

[fo. 39-a] It has been proved that the Prophet said: "No *Ṣadaqah* is to be realised from less than five *awqiyyah* of silver and less than five camels in number, and no *Ṣadaqah* is to be paid for what is less than five *wasaq*."

It has been related that the Prophet levied *Zakāh* on twenty *dīnārs* of gold. This is held by *'Ulamā'* in general. Al-Ḥasan says that no *Zakāh* is to be levied on gold till it reaches forty *dīnārs*. It has been related on the authority of Ibn Shihāb that he said: "Whoever possesses gold worth two hundred *dirhams*, has to pay *Zakāḥ* for it."

Mālik, his followers, and many *'Ulamā'* say that *Zakāh* is to be levied only on crops, ready-money and cattle. Al-Nu'mān says that *Zakāh* is to be levied on all wealth except straw (*tibn*) and wood (*ḥaṭab*). It has been proved that the Prophet said: "No *Zakāh* is to be levied on a Muslim for his slave or for his horse."

The Syrians are of the view that *Zakāh* is to be levied on honey. They relate in this connection a *Ḥadīth* traced back to the Prophet that he used to realise one water skin out of ten watersakins (full of honey), then he reserved it for them. If the *Ḥadīth* is established, our authorities hold that they offered it voluntarily. Some say that they offered this only because he reserved an exclusive place for them in their territory. The Messenger of Allāh has said: "There is no *Ḥimā* (reserved land) except for the sake of Allāh and for His Messenger." Hence, it became the price of that which was reserved for them. Mālik and his followers hold that there is no *Zakāh* on vegetables, on walnuts, on almonds, pistachio, pine-pitch, fig and all other kinds of fruits except date, grapes, seeds and olive. But Ibn Idrīs holds that no *Zakāh* is to be levied on olive. Ibn Ḥabīb holds that *Zakāh* is to be levied on vegetables.

They have agreed that *Zakāh* is not to be levied on sheep and goats (*al-ghanam*) till their number reaches forty. Out of forty, one goat is to be paid, there being only one goat upto one hundred and twenty. Two goats are only to be paid out of one hundred and twenty-one to two hundred goats. They have disagreed when the number exceeds two hundred by one goat. Most of them hold, and this is the view of Mālik also, that three goats will be paid; while some others hold that only two goats will be paid upto two hundred and forty. After this, one goat is to be paid for every one hundred goats.

They have agreed that one goat is to be levied on every five camels till they reach twenty-five, there being nothing extra for what lies inbetween the two prescribed numbers. One *bint-makhāḍ* (i.e. a female camel of one year) is to be levied on twenty-five camels. Now, *bint makhāḍ* is the she-camel in the womb of whose mother her youngling moves before the birth. If *bint makhāḍ* is not available, then one *ibn labūn* (a male camel of two years) is to be paid tupto thirty-five, *[fo. 39-b]* and then one *bint labūn* (a female camel of two years) from thirty-six upto forty-five camels. One *ḥiqqaḥ* (female camel of three years) from forty-six to sixty; one *jidha'ah* (female camel of four years) from sixty-one to seventy-five; two *bint labūn* from seventy-six to ninety; two *ḥiqqaḥ* from ninety-one to one hundred and twenty.

When the number reaches upto one hundred and twenty-one, the *Sā'īm* (the tax-collector) may take either three *bint labūn* or two *ḥiqqaḥ*. But some say that only three *bint labūn* are to be paid for one hundred and twenty-one, but others say that only two *ḥiqqaḥ* are to be levied on them.

Many *'Ulamā'* hold, and this is also the view of Mālik, that he will not go back to the prescribed *Zakāh* of sheep except when the number decreases so much so that it becomes less than twenty-five. It has been related on the authority of 'Alī that when the number exceeds one hundred and twenty by five then one goat is to be paid for five; similarly one goat is to be levied on every five sheep above the number from ten to twenty. A group of people followed him on this point.

They have agreed that one *tabī'* (female calf of one year) is to be paid for thirty *baqar* (i.e. all bovine animals viz. cows, bulls, oxen and buffaloes etc.), and one *musinnah* (female calf of two years) for forty. *Musinnah* is a female calf having all her milkteeth fallen. They have disagreed concerning those that are below thirty. Most of the *'Ulamā'*, including Mālik, hold that nothing is to be paid for less than thirty as has been reported on the authority of Mu'ādh. Some say that one goat is to be levied on every five *baqar*. But the *'Ulamā'* in general hold that only one *musinnah* is to be paid for fifty. It has been related on the authority of al-Nakh'ī that one *musinnah* is to be paid for fifty *baqar*.

They have disagreed concerning al-Khulaṭā (co-partners) who possess so much cattle which, when they are kept separate, everyone from among the owners is not liable to pay *Zakāh*. Mālik, his followers and a group of the *'Ulamā'*, are of the opinion that when the whole lot is taxable nothing is to be levied on him whose share is not taxable with *Zakāh*. Rabī'ah, al-Layth and a group of the *'Ulamā'* hold that when the whole lot is taxable *Zakāh* is to be realised. Mālik says: "If the tax-collector does according to this, the partner would make claims for restitution each upon the other due to difference of opinion and it will be regarded as a case in which rulings differ."

They have disagreed concerning the nature of *al-Khulaṭā*: the majority of the *'Ulamā'* explains that this occurs when everyone of them brings his own sheep in which the shepherd, watering-pail and resting place are common. Ṭā'ūs and 'Aṭā' hold that *al-Khulaṭā* are no other than share-holders, but this is against the tradition, since the two co-partners make claims for restitutioning the surplus, each upon the other equally, whereas the share-holders have no scope for doing so. Some say that when the shepherd is common, they are *Khalīṭ*, since in this case stallion is common, so both will be regarded as co-partners irrespective of realising taxes. Some say that if they are combined in both ways, they are *Khalīṭ*. They are, however, regarded as *al-Khulaṭā' [fo. 40-a]* when the owners of cattle permit this sort of union. When they herd together before the end of the year, they are co-partners except if the year happens to be very near, and similar is the case when they are separated.

They have disagreed concerning the meaning of the *Ḥadīth*: "Those who are separate will not be combined and those who are combined will not be separated out of the fear of *ṣadaqah*." Mālik says that it is, for example, in the case when two or three persons have forty sheep each, now, when the tax-collector appears to them they gather these together so that they are to pay only one goat, for example; or a person who has one hundred goats, and another has one hundred and one goats, now, when the tax-collector appears to them they separate their herds and thus either of the two will be liable to pay one goat each.

Ibn Idrīs says: "The meaning of the *Ḥadīth* 'The combined are not to be separated', means that either of the two co-partners possesses forty goats, the tax-collector is not then allowed to divide them and take one goat from each of them. He who differs from us in the interpretation of the word, does not differ from us in holding the view." What he says is the view of Mālik except that the interpretation of Mālik appears to be more suited to the external meaning of the words, because, his expression: *Khashyat al-Ṣadaqah* (for fear of *Ṣadaqah*) is to be understood in respect of one who pays it and not in respect of one who collects it.

The *'Ulamā'*, in general, hold that what is obtained as accruing from apparent properties is not subject to *Zakāh* until a year passes over it. Ibn 'Abbās says that *Zakāh* should be paid immediately and then after every year. The same meaning has been expressed by Mu'āwiyyah in taking *Zakāh* out of the allowances given to the people.

They have disagreed concerning the *Zakāh* of ornaments, 'Ā'ishah and many Companions of the Prophet hold that ornaments are not liable to *Zakāh*. This is the view of Mālik and his followers. Some Companions of the Prophet and a section of the *'Ulamā'* hold that the ornaments are liable to *Zakāh;* some others hold that if it is lent, its lending will be treated as *Zakāh*.

They have disagreed about the *Zakāh* of the wealth of the minors. 'Umar and a number of the people of the early period hold that *Zakāh* is to be levied on these and this is the view of Mālik and his followers. Some people of 'Irāq hold that no *Zakāh* is to be levied on them. Al-Thawrī says: "The guardian will maintain an account of that which falls due to him every year and when he hands over wealth to him, he should inform him of his due." Those who hold that *Zakāh* is not to be levied upon them argue that it is so, because prayer, fasting, pilgrimage and punishments are not incumbent upon them except when they reach the age of puberty. As to those who hold this (i.e. *Zakāh* is to be levied upon them) argue that *Zakāh* is levied on wealth and not on persons.

They have disagreed concerning the *Zakāh* of the wealth of slaves. So those who think *[fo. 40-b]* that a slave owns (wealth) hold that no *Zakāh* is to be levied upon him and those who do not consider him to be an owner, say that he himself is the property of his master and the master is to pay the *Zakāh* for him. The first view is the view of Mālik and his followers. They argue on the basis of the Qur'ānic verse in which Allāh, the Exalted, says: "And whoso is not able to afford to marry free believing women, let them marry from the believing maids whom your right hands possess. Allāh knoweth best (concerning) your faith. Ye (proceed) one from another. So wed them by permission of their folk, and give unto them their portions." (4: 25)

He thereby ordered to gave their dowry, and also with what al-Layth related on the authority of Bukayr on the authority of Nāfi' on the authority of Ibn 'Umar that the Prophet said: "Whoever sells a slave who owns property, his property belongs to the seller except in the case when the purchaser makes a condition." So he (the Prophet) allowed the purchase of a slave together with his property and he did not exclude any known or unknown thing or property on cash or on credit, nor that which cannot be sold, as he declared the property part and parcel of the slave. The disagreement of those who oppose us in this case when it is not permissible to exclude the property of the slave when it is unspecified and something which is not to be sold is no proof, since, when something has been substantiated on the authority of the Messenger of Allāh, disagreement of those who opposed it is no proof. Since disagreement does not affect the genuine proofs.

When they did not find anything objectionable in the chain (of narrators) of the *Ḥadīth* of al-Layth they charged that 'Ubayd Allāh ibn Abū Ja'far exceeded the limits in it, but this is an expression without any proof. Again, one who intends something against *Sunnah* has no right to advance arguments without proof that what refutes it.

The *'Ulamā'* in general hold that no *Zakāh* is to be levied on *al-mukātab* (the slave under contract to earn his freedom), and this is the view of one who considers him as slave so long as something of the term of *Kītabah* remains due to him. Ibn 'Abbās used to hold that when the scribe wrote the terms of *Kitābah*, the slave becomes free and the terms of *Kitābah* are a debt, on him, so according to his view, he is liable to pay *Zakāh*. Some say that if he pays one-fourth of the term, he becomes free. Some say that if he pays his entire price, and some say that he is free to the extent of what he has paid. Some say that, when he pays in instalments (he is free). 'Alī used to hold that he who sets free partly will inherit him and will inherit to the extent of freedom in him. This necessitates that *Zakāh* will be levied in the like manner, Ibn 'Abbās did not favour to split the freedom into parts and whenever someone freed a slave he asked to free the rest of the slave.

They have disagreed concerning the case when a woman gives her *Zakāh* to her husband. It has been proved that the Prophet permitted Zaynbab al-Thaqafiyyah, the wife of Ibn Mas'ūd, to give her *Zakāh* to him and to her son from him. Abū 'Ubayd says: "Verily it is the case of Ibn Mas'ūd together with his son from other than Zaynab. *[fo. 41-a.]* He (Abū 'Ubayd) says: "Because they have agreed that a woman cannot give something from her *Zakāh* to her own son."

The opinion of (Abū 'Ubayd) that it is an *Ijmā'* (consensus) is surely not so, because Mālik and his followers hold that whoever is not responsible for the maintenance of a person, can give his *Zakāh* to that person and because of their view that it is not incumbent upon the mother to bear the maintenance of her children whether they are minor or adult. Of course, there has been disagreement concerning the view of Mālik whether it is preferable (*Mustaḥab*) for one to give *Zakāh* to the near relations or not. Once he disliked it because it removes from him the duty showing favour (*Ṣilah*) to them and once again he (Mālik) allowed it. In either of his views it is not found that in case he gives them, it will not suffice him. He liked that one should not be in-charge of distributing his own *Ṣadaqah* because by it he earns praise and escapes thereby from blame. He preferred also to give *Zakāh* secretly like the voluntry alms, while some people may follow each other and vie with each other in good deeds.

There has been disagreement about the person who pays his *Zakāh* in advance before it falls due to him. Mālik thinks that it will not suffice him like the one who performs prayers before its time, except in case when it (paying of *Zakāh*) happens only a few days earlier since that would be regarded as its exact time. Some of the *'Ulamā'* have permitted it saying that some performances cannot be compared with one another.

They have argued with the *Ḥadīth* in which it has been reported that it was said to the Prophet that 'Abbās, Khālid ibn al-Walīd and Ibn Jamīl refused to pay *Zakāh*. The Prophet said, "As for 'Abbās, he will get it as well as the like of it, and as for Khālid, you are certainly doing injustice to him, he has dedicated his coats of mail and his men for the cause of Allāh, and as for Ibn Jamīl, he did not refuse except for the reason that Allāh, and His Messenger made him rich, out of Allāh's bounty." So they have interpreted that 'Abbās and Khālid paid their *Zakāh* in advance.

In this connection they have again offered the argument that the Prophet ordered the women to come out for the *'Īd* prayers so that they may attain to the good action and be present at the feast of the believers. They then came out so much so that the newly grown up girls and the veiled women came out; or he said, the newly grown up veiled girls. When he performed the prayer, he came upon them accompanied by Bilāl. He then delivered sermons before them and asked them to offer *Ṣadaqah*, whereupon, they started throwing the ornaments in the clothes of Bilāl. The prophet then did not ask them, whether one year had passed or not as the possessions of the people may very.

Those who hold that *Zakāh* is to be levied on the ornaments argue with this, and those who allow the actions of women without the permission of their husbands also argue with this, because the Prophet did not ask them whether they were unmarried or married. Here is also given argument in favour of the view of Mālik who held that *Zakāh* is to be levied on the wealth of the children, because the Prophet did not ask them whether they were adult or minor or whether they were offering alms voluntarily or compulsorily.

They have disagreed about the person who buys his own *Ṣadaqah* and gives *[fo. 41-b]* articles (*al-'urūḍ*) in exchange for cash. Mālik dislikes all these and taking articles in exchange for cash is most abhorrent to him except in case when he is forced to do so and he does not think that to pay articles will suffice him. Some people allowed this and they argued with the example of purchasing *Ṣadaqah*, because it has been proved by the Prophet who said concerning one upon whom *Zakāh* became incumbent and he brought an animal younger than the required age of the animal of the *Zakāh*. It and two goats more will be accepted from him if these two are convenient for him, or twenty *dirhams* and if he brings an animal older than the required animal of *Zakāh*, it will be accepted from him and he will be given two goats." In this case, there is a sort of purchase and this is contrary to the voluntary charity the purchase of which the Prophet forbade. 'Umar, and he (the Prophet) said: "One who takes back his charity is like a dog who swallows its vomit."

They have argued in favour of giving articles in payment of *Ṣadaqah* with what has been reported on the authority of Mu'ādh that the Prophet said to him, when he sent him to al-Yaman, to collect *Ṣadaqah*: "Bring to me the garments called *Khamīṣ* or *labīs*, because it is more convenient to you and more useful for the emigrants (*Muhājirūn*) residing at al-Madīnah".

They have disagreed concerning coming out of the collector of *Zakāh* in a year of drought. It is said that this will be delayed till the next year, so he will realise the *Ṣadaqah* for two years. Some say that this cannot be delayed; and both these views have been held by Mālik.

They have also disagreed about the person who possesses forty young lambs (*sakhlah*), none being big. Mālik says that the owner should bring a big she-goat or such a big he-goat which may be allowed for payment of *Ṣadaqah*. Some say that one will be taken out of them. Some say that the price of one will be taken because it is not permissible to take younger than the *Jidh'a*. Some say that nothing falls due in it.

They have differed whether the tax-collector will divide the whole lot of the goats into three parts. Mālik says that he cannot do so, and whatever the owner brings and whatever he pays as his due, the collector should accept it. Ibn Shihāb says that the whole lot will be divided into three parts and the owner will choose two-thirds out of it and the tax-collector will choose the other one-third aiming the required age necessary for him.

They have disagreed concerning one to whom a goat falls due, then he slaughters it and distributes its flesh. Ibn al-Qāsim says that this will not suffice him and Ashhab says that this will suffice him.

There has been disagreement concerning the view of Mālik regarding the two co-partners, one of them has five camels while the other nine. He said that one goat is to be paid by each and they will not reimburse among them. Afterwards he said, rather they should reimburse among themselves concerning the two goats according to the number of his camels. He says that this is the meaning of the *Ḥadīth* and this is held by his followers.

They have disagreed concerning the case of one who says that the tax-collector had been absent from him for a number of years. Some say that he will have to pay the *Zakāh* of that which he finds with him for the years that had passed *[fo. 42-a]* except in the case when this reduces the number after the collection of *Zakāh* for some years, then *Zakāh* will not fall due in it and this *Zakāh* will be waived from him. Some say that he will be asked about the number of the camels he had with him every year so he will have to pay *Zakāh* accordingly.

They have disagreed concerning a man whose cattle was taken away forcibly from him and then it was restored to him after a number of years. Some say that he will pay *Zakāh* for one year only and some say that he will have to pay *Zakāh* for all these years which have passed. 'Umar ibn 'Abd al-'Azīz wrote concerning the wealth (cattle) which was taken without any right, that it should be returned to its owner and its *Zakāh* should be taken for all the years which had passed. Then he sent another letter immediately after the first asking to take *Zakāh* for one year only. Others say that a year will be counted for him in advance.

They have disagreed concerning the person who exchanged sheep with sheep or cow with cow or camel with camel and he took animals in which *Zakāh* falls due. Some says that *Zakāh* will be taken out of what he took in the first year, and some say that he will wait with it for one year more.

They have disagreed concerning the case when one exchanged goat with camel or cow and camel with cow but whatever he took was not liable to *Zakāh*. Some say that *Zakāh* falls due in it at the first year, and some say that a year will be counted for him in advance.

They have disagreed concerning the oxen used for water-wheel and the working camels and the domesticated and minor younglings of sheep. Mālik and his followers say that *Zakāh* will be levied on all these when they constitute *niṣāb* (taxable limit). Some say that no *Zakāh* is to be levied on any cattle except on the pasturing animals.

They have disagreed about the sheep of a trader who constantly exchanges his sheep; when he completes the years his wealth (cattle) is found invested in the articles of trade. Mālik and his followers hold that no *Zakāh* is to be levied on them till they are sold. Some of the people of Kūfah say that these will be evaluated at the end of each year.

They have disagreed concerning a man who constantly exchanges his merchandise. Some people say that no *Zakāh* is to be levied on them till the goods are exchanged in cash money and then it will be evaluated provided a year passes over it. Some say that it will be evaluated at the end of every year as 'Umar asked Ḥammās tō do.

They have disagreed about a person who neglected the payment of his *Zakāh* till he died. Mālik and most of his followers hold that it is not incumbent upon his heirs to pay it on his behalf except when he enjoins (for its payment) then *Zakāh* will be paid from one-third of his properlty. Ibn Shihāb says that *Zakāh* will be paid from his entire property whether he enjoins or not and the debt of the people are not more obligatory than *Zakāh*.

They have disagreed concerning the person whose *Zakāh* fell due on his death-bed but he could not pay it and died. Mālik and most of his followers hold that if he enjoins, it will be paid from his entire property but if he does not enjoin, it will not be incumbent upon his heirs to pay it except when they desired to do so. Shihāb says that it is to be paid from his entire property (capital) whether he enjoins or not.

They have differed about the person who raised from his crops some cereals in the like of which *Zakāh* is to be levied while he owed the similar quantity of cereals, or the one has the *niṣāb [fo. 42-b]* of cattle while the like of it is due to him. Ibn Sīrīn says, and this is also the view of Mālik and his followers, that no obligatory *Zakāh* will be waived from him on account of this. Some say it will be waived.

They have disagreed concerning a person whose slave came to him on the day of *'Īd al-Fiṭr* while he is to pay the *Ṣadaqah* of a slave like him; some say that *Ṣadaqah* will not be waived from him on account of this; some say it will be waived from him.

They have also differed about the payment of *Ṣadaqat al-Fiṭr* on behalf of one's wife. Mālik and his followers say that it is incumbent on him and similarly he is to pay on behalf of her servant. Some say that he is to pay *Ṣadaqah* on behalf of her more than one servant if she is a lady of distinction. Some say that he is not to pay *Ṣadaqah* on her behalf nor on the behalf of her servant.

They have disagreed concerning a serving-slave. Some say that his *Ṣadaqah* is to be paid by his master and some say that it is incumbent upon the one who enjoys his service.

They have differed about the case when the *Khawārij* conquered a city and collected *Zakāh* from the inhabitants. Some say that it will be sufficient for them and some say that it will not suffice them.

They have disagreed about the person who gave his *Zakāh* to a rich man without knowing him. Some say that he is to pay the *Zakāh* again while others say that nothing falls due to him.

They have disagreed about a grown up and healthy son to whom his father gives something from his *Zakāh.* Those who hold that maintenance is not binding upon the father because of his puberty say that it will suffice him and those who hold that maintenance is incumbent upon the father as the Prophet said to Hind when she said to him saying that Abū Sufyān was a niggardly fellow, should she take something from his wealth secretly? Whereupon the Prophet said: "You can take that which is sufficient for you and for your children with justice," and he did not exempt adult from minor.

They have disagreed concerning the allies of Banū Ḥāshim in matters of receiving the voluntary alms.

They have disagreed concerning the meaning of Allāh's saying: "And pay the due thereof upon the harvest day." (6: 142) Some say that it means the prescribed *Zakāh.* Some say that the beggar should be given at harvest-time and also at the time of gathering the crops and also a handful (*Qabṣ*) at the time of gathering on the threshing-floor. *Qabṣ* means plucking something with forefingers and *Zakāh* will be given when wheat is threshed out.

They have differed about the meaning of God's Saying: "And they refuse small kindness" (107: 7). Some say that it means *Zakāh.* Some say that it is lending of rope, watering-pail and pick-axe.

They have disagreed as to how much of wheat is paid for the *Ṣadaqat al-Fiṭr.* Mālik and his followers say that one *Ṣā'* from every human being (will be taken), according to the statement of Abū Sa'īd al-Khudrī: "We used to pay one *Ṣā'* from food". Ibn Idrīs says that *Ṣadaqat al-Fiṭr* is half of one *Ṣā'* and on this concern a *Ḥadīth* has been narrated which requires consideration in its chain of narrators.

They have differed about the payment of *Ṣadaqat al-Fiṭr* on behalf of slaves. Some say that the master is to pay on their behalf, and some say that he is not to pay. There has been disagreement concerning a slave who is half-free. Some say that *Ṣadaqat al-Fiṭr* will be paid on his behalf by one who owned him partly. Some say that it is to be paid in proportion to his freedom and in proportion to his being a slave. According to the view of Ibn 'Abbās, some of the parts of a human being cannot be partly free and partly *[fo. 43-a]* slave. The *Ṣadaqat al-Fiṭr* according to his view is, therefore, to be levied on the man.

They have disagreed concerning the embryo, whether the *Ṣadaqat al-Fiṭr* is to be paid on its behalf. The *'Ulamā'* in general hold that this is not incumbent, and Ibn Ḥanbal says that *Ṣadaqat al-Fiṭr* is to be paid on its behalf.

They have disagreed about the payment of *Ṣadaqat al-Fiṭr* on behalf of one who was born on the day of *'Īd al-Fiṭr*. Some of them consider it as preferable (*Mustaḥab*) without any obligation, while Ibn Ḥanbal makes its payment obligatory (*Wājib*). They have also differed about the payment of the *Ṣadaqat al-Fiṭr* in the form of a cost-price (*thaman*). Most of them hold that it does not suffice, so they disagreed while some of them permitted this.

They have disagreed concerning the measurement of the *mudd* as recorded from the Prophet. The people of the two Sacred Cities have agreed that it is one *raṭl* and the third of it. The *raṭl* consists of one hundred and twenty-eight *dirhams*. To this Abū Yūsuf had agreed when he argued with Mālik on this matter in the presence of the Caliph, the Commander of the Faithful, and this is also held by Abū 'Ubayd. The people of 'Irāq say that *mudd* consists of two *raṭls*.

And in wealth there are dues other than *Zakāh* as well. Among them is the emancipation of their prisoners. It has been made compulsory for the Muslims to redeem them. It has been narrated on the authority of the Prophet that he said: "You emancipate the prisoner (*al-'Ānī*) and *al-'Ānī* means prisoner. Aṣbāgh says that this is incumbent upon the Muslims (even if it costs all their wealth). Another case is that of a person who does not find anything which could strainghten his affairs, so it then becomes incumbent upon one who comes to know this from him, to give him that which may straighten his affairs and he (the needy person) can take it by force and even he can take away by hiding himself, if he is unable to overpower him, except by this way. Another case is to give to a beggar if he comes across a prepared thing by chance. It becomes then incumbent upon him to give to the beggar out of it. But if he does not find anything available but knows that the beggar does not possess anything which can strainghten his affairs, it becomes incumbent upon him to give him that which is helpful for him. If he does not know his condition, he should speak to him justly.

It is the duty of one who reaps the crops or plucks the fruits to entertain those who are present with some of it. It has been mentioned that this is the meaning of God's saying: "And pay the due thereof (*Ḥaqqahū*) upon the harvest day," and this *Ḥaqq* (due) is other than *Zakāh*.

Some say that it is incumbent upon him to leave that which has been missed by the reapers. Some people live on it. It has been narrated that the Prophet forbade reaping the harvest at night, because it will deprive the needy of the kind treatment. This is the interpretation of the verse of the Qur'ānic chapter *Nūn wa'l-Qalam*, by those who hold this view. Some say that he forbade this out of the fear of snakes and reptiles of the land.

THE THIRD PART COMES TO AN END WITH THE PRAISE OF ALLĀH AND HIS ASSISTANCE

PART FOUR

Chapter I

ON THE WEALTH THE OWNERS OF WHICH ARE NOT KNOWN; ON THE USURPED WEALTH; AND THOSE WHOSE OWNERS ALL OR SOME ARE EXILED; *[fo. 43–b]* ON DEALING WITH USURPERS; TRANSGRESSORS; AND THOSE WHO ARE FORCED TO SETTLE AT USURPED LAND; AND ALSO MEANS OF EARNING DISAPPROVED AND LAWFUL

It has been said to Aḥmad ibn Naṣr that the rulers levy a number of taxes in the name of *Kharāj;* often they levy a tax according to the price of land and trees and sometimes impose it according to water and canals and some other times according to the number of trees as strictly agreed upon by the chiefs of these places. This practice has continued from generation to generation and nobody knows the actual position whether the land and the cities were under *Kharāj* or tax was realized from them unjustly. This happened in the land of al-Maghrib.

He says: "Saḥnūn reports that he had investigated into the affair of the land of Ifrīqiyyah but could not establish whether the land was conquered by force or by a peace treaty, or whether the inhabitants embraced Islam on the condition of retaining the land. What is agreed upon by the inhabitants of the cities is that they have inherited (these lands) and it is known through ages and accepted by all and sundry that they possessed these lands as usually lands are owned and that they did therein all sorts of acts as the owners of lands usually do with their lands viz. sale, offering as charity, gift, mortmain, mortgage, loan, dowry and all other transactions. No ascetic needs there to refrain from this except in some other places called as *al-Akhmās* and known so essentially and some other places which were usurped from their owners and turned into exclusive estates (*ṣāfiyah*) and a long time has since passed over it, its owners are not known and also some other places the inhabitants of which emigrated on account of oppressions meted out to them, and a long period has since passed over it, the owners are not known and other places as well where this happened on account of wars that broke out among the inhabitants and their neighbours.

"In some places out of these categories, some other people settled down therein, nevertheless the circumstances of the place were known; it was known to the entire population who knew that land that the inhabitants of these lands were ejected from these, and that these other people alighted at the land by way of transgression. Some of them hold that in the past, a group of people had alighted at the land by way of oppression. Anyone belonging to all these descriptions who recognises his companions whose number may be counted although they do not know as to how these lands belonged to them, will be reconciled therein as the like. But if they refuse and are serious while nobody from among them claims to know of anything he demands, the ruling will be deferred therein till they are reconciled. But if they are at law therein, they will be treated according to legal procedure. But if some of them claim of knowing while the others show ignorance saying that they have no knowledge, the land will belong to one *[fo. 44-a]* who claims it, some say that the claims will be confirmed with oath, while others hold that they need no oath, if there was none to dispute over it.

"If some people say that they have rights (over the land) but they do not know them due to their long absence from the lands as well as due to long absence of their predecessors whom they have inherited and that the land is not also in their possession but others claim the knowledge of what they claim as their right; the lands will belong to those who claim the knowledge accompanied with an oath to the effect that the lands belonged to them and that they were not aware of others' right therein.

"But if the owners are known but their number is not known and it is not known as to who from among them are present and who are absent and also who had something therein out of those and who had nothing and again they did not know if their possession was scanty or in plenty, nor did they recognise these exactly, nor how did the inheritance circulates among them, due to passage of long span of time, such lands will be treated like the property left behind by a man whose heirs are neither known for, nor knowledge about them is expected. These will be spent for the welfare of the Muslims and should not be abandoned in desolation.

"There has been disagreement as to the fact whether these lands will be treated like *Ṣadaqāt* or like the *fay'*. But what is sound by consideration is the fact that it should be treated like *fay'*, since they have all agreed on the view that one whose heir by lineage is not known, he is to be inherited by the right of relationship (*walā'*), so it has been treated like the *fay'* as the *Ṣadaqāt* are neither meant for the definite individuals nor for the wealthy people. Further, it is also known that every mortal being surely has an heir and if the heir is not known, some heir must be there to meet him in accordance with the knowledge of Allāh.

"But if it is held that often a reunited lineage is cancelled on the ground of illegal bed (illegitimacy), it will be said that this view of yours is not sound for a number of reasons; the objects are to be understood according to their apparent meanings and consideration will be taken therein as I have mentioned.

"The other reason is that every human being save Adam, Eve and Jesus Christ must have a father and for this reason Allāh, the Exalted, has addressed us saying: "O children of Ādam". Again the *'Ulamā'* have agreed on the view that an illegitimate child inherits his mother and there is no difference between father and mother. Those who hold that the fornicator will not inherit the child who is born of his fornication, oppose because the fornicator does not know the fact as to whether the child is born of him or of somebody else. So, when he does not have any legal bed and his affairs remain dubious, he cannot be accepted as heir on account of their denying that.

"It has been related on the authority of 'Umar that where legal bed was not available he used to join the children born during the days of ignorance to those who wanted them affiliated to them during the days of Islam. This view is also held by Mālik and his followers. They argue with the story of the son of the slave-girl of Zam'ah who had a legal bed, but when bed and fornication join together, the legal bed will be given preference. Al-Nakha'ī, al-Nu'mān and Isḥāq hold that he who wants an illegitimate child affiliated to him, the child becomes affiliated to him when he has no legal bed.

"Isḥāq also argues with the fact that they have agreed on appointing the mother as heir. And the other argument to the effect that this will be treated like *fay'* *[fo. 44-b]* is the fact that they all agree with the view that one whose heir by lineage is not known, he is to be inherited by the right of relationship (*walā'*) so it has been treated like the *fay'*. Because as for *Ṣadaqāt,* the Prophet, peace be upon him, told a man who asked him about a goat which he found in the desert that it belonged either to the man or to his brother or to the wolf. Further, he found a date lying, whereupon he said, had he known that it was not out of *Ṣadaqah,* he would have surely eaten it up."

Aḥmad was asked as to whether he advises one to exempt himself from the payment of this tax called *Kharāj,* imposed by the ruler, if he can do so. He replies in the affirmative, and holds that he is allowed to do this much only. Again, he was asked about the fact that if the ruler had imposed it on the people of a town, realized it from them at the rate of a fixed amount and the people paid them against their properties, whether one is allowed to exempt himself from its payment if he can do so. But when he does so, the authority will realize the total amount imposed on them from the entire people. He replies that he can do so.

This is further corroborated by the opinion of Mālik concerning a tax-collector who realizes one goat from the goats of one of the partners though the total lot of the goats is not taxable: "That it has been taken wrongfully, accruing to one for whom it is collected and not to be used upon one from whom it is collected who in turn is not entitled to make a claim for anything upon his co-partners and in this case, I shall not accept that which has been recorded on the authority of Saḥmūn, because there should not be any model in doing wrong nor is it incumbent upon anybody to insert himself into injustice lest injustice might be doubled for others. Allah, the Exalted, says: 'The way (of blame) is only against those who oppress mankind' (42: 42)."

It is said to him that there are a people who have to pay this tax according to the number of their trees which are irrigated by the water of the canals, and in water their ownership is known; some of them have little and some have much water as Allāh blessed them it. Sometimes they make transaction of water and not that of tree as a result; some of them have plenty of trees but little water or trees without water or plenty of water but few trees while no tax is levied on water. So the chiefs of the local people all agreed on sharing the entire water of the locality according to the number of trees, so water became little for those who had plenty of it and plentiful for those who had little of it and water was also given to those who had no water on account of the quota of his trees.

So, some people abstained from using water that fell in their share while most of them used that and those who abstained from using water had to pay the tax levied to the extent of their share in that. The affair continued for long so much so that neither the nature of their ownership was determined, nor was it known who from among them did own something therein and who did not. Afterwards all or some of them wanted to adopt the best way.

Aḥmad says: "If they are counted, there being no absentee—orphan or light-witted individual, they should come to an agreement among themselves on that water as they liked; and if the officer in charge finds in that case any way to act equitably, he should defer the rulling till they come to an agreement. But if the owners are not present *[fo. 45-a]* the owners being absentees and orphans, and the number of absentees from among them is not determined nor are their whereabouts known, the water thereof will be treated like the property the owners of which are not known, as I have mentioned earlier.

"If the Imām so desires, he may bequeath it as an endowment so that the use of water may be offered for sale on dialy, monthly and annual basis and also exercise his own discretion to use it for the welfare of the Muslims, he can do so. But if he thinks of selling itself, dividing it in many parts among the owners of those trees and of using them for the welfare of the Muslims, he can do so. But if there is no just authority to employ it for the very purpose, the just Muslims shall administer it on behalf of the Imām, whoever from among them undertakes the task, his action will be considered sufficient."

The inhabitants of a certain territory said to him that under some convenants (with some other people) they received water by which they watered their land. On the authority of their forefathers, their forefathers had informed them of the fact that water originally did not belong to them and that water in fact belonged to some people whom they did not know. He replies that this case, too, is like the one as he has mentioned about the decision of the Imām or that of the just Muslims if the just Imām is not available to sell it on time basis and one who undertakes the administration can do so and will employ the price for the benefit of the Muslims, and if he thinks it proper to sell itself, he can do so. But if there is none to undertake any of these, whoever receives water out of it should give the price in alms and use it for the benefit of the Muslims.

He was asked about a people whom the ruler had ejected from their localities and seized their landed properties. They had proprietary right over the canals in which they had other partners who had not given up their proprietary rights over the canals. The canals were common among them and they shared these together according to some definite parts without having any fixed day which they cannot turn away. Now, whether it is allowed to take his own share for one who is not prevented from taking his share without having any claim of the deprived people upon him. He replies that he cannot take that but if he takes only to the extent of his share he should share it along with the deprived people in proportion to their shares in the canal, and in case of their absence he should consider therein for them.

It was said to him that if the canal was shared by the owners, each having a definite day of the week; Friday for one group, Saturday for another and Sunday for still another. Afterwards, some owners gave up their own proprietary right thus enabling some others who had not given up their rights to take a day other than his and give up his own day, now whether it would be lawful to take it. He said, "No, except that he is able to take his own day exactly, and it would not be lawful for him to take anyother day."

He was asked about the people of a certain town, in which the ruler levied heavy taxes on them for their landed properties while there were some other people who had no landed property. As this continued for long with the owners of the landed properties and fell heavy on them, a group from among them made agreement with the rulers to allot all the lands lying outside their town among them all on condition that the unlawful taxes would be levied *[fo. 45-b]* on the (newly) allotted lands and thus everyone, whether he had owned any land or not was included therein. They then turned their scattered holdings into common property.

They remained on it for a period till knowledge of all about the origin of the lands and also about the ownership was forgotten. Later on, they were ejected from their town and the town as well as the adjoining places which were left in their possessions became desolate so much so that a long time passed by, every one forgot his own right and it was not known as to who had something and who had not. As their number increased and all spread over the lands it was not possible to note the present from those who remained absent. He says, "This case, too, will be like the one I have described earlier with regard to the places in which the inhabitants are not known and the place will be treated like the article lost and picked up; the Imām or the just Muslims will decide the case therein according to what would be deemed best for the Muslims."

It was asked about one who had obtained produce of the land or gained benefit out of some of these places. He replies that he will have to pay the price of the rent of what he benefitted; if the land is worthy of rent or the rent of the fruits if he benefits by the fruits provided the measure of the fruits is unknown, or he will pay the price in case the measure is not known and fruits belong to somebody who is not known. If its owner is not known and knowledge about him is not expected, it should be given in alms or be spent for the welfare of the Muslims.

It is said to him that the inhabitants of this town were at war with their neighbours and fighting broke out among them, then the elders of the town made peace with the people who fought them on having half of the valley by which they irrigate their land while the entire valley belonged to a large number of people most of whom were neither consulted nor their consent was taken. Will this agreement be considered lawful? He says, "No, except in case when the recipient desires to take the shares of those (only) who entered into the agreement provided they did not enter into the agreement under injustice or oppression nor did they exceed the limits into their main affairs while everybody from among them demanded that much only to which he was entitled to."

He was asked about certain people whom the ruler drove away from the entire land and then a long time passed by till it was not known how the holdings were owned originally or how the aggrieved parties shared the land among themselves. He replied that it would also be treated like the properties which he had mentioned, that the owners thereof are not known and their trace is not expected.

It is said to him that there lived a people who had a river and it was the custom among them that the powerful people used water and with held the water as long as they needed it, and as soon as they were not in need of water, another powerful people would come and take water after the former had taken so the weak people could not reach it as long as the strong people needed water and they were not aware of the original holding of every one of them. Later on, they wanted to do the best and some of the people expected to obtain their due. What is to be done in this case? He replies that if those who preceded them had informed them of the fact that the land belonged to all of them *[fo. 46-a]* except that their powerful people prevailed over their weak till they siezed it as you have mentioned and they do not know as to what their holdings are they should make peace on the terms they so desire. But if they refuse, water should flow from the highest to the next highest; the highest one should keep back (water) in his land upto two ankle-bones and then relase it for the next till water reaches the last one.

He was asked about a people who were ejected from their places and were forced to live in a town alongwith their offspring in spite of the opposition from the inhabitants of the place. The ruler took an undertaking from them that nobody from among them would go away from it and whoever leaves the place from among them fears the punishment from the authority.. Now what is about one who wants to do the suitable? He says: "If he finds anyone from among the inhabitants of that city to get the land legalised from him, he should do so, and whatever is made lawful for him viz, dwelling, harvest or crops, will be treated as such.

"But if he does not find that and the inhabitants are known, he should live in the place according to the minimum requirement for himself and for his family and pay the rent to the inhabitants provided he knows them, or to the poor if he does not expect to know them. Mostly, he should dwell in the mosques and other places, where nobody prevents others from living, like the present thoroughfares and the lands belonging to none.

"However, if he has something else because of which he is in no need of these things, he should not come near other's property except with the consent of the owner. As to that which is made lawful by the owner upto a definite period or upto the life of the owner or upto that of the donee, will be regarded as lawful. And what they donate him from the root and the donee was able to receive it before the death of the donor, the thing belongs to him, but if he was able to receive only after the death of the donor, according to Ibn al-Qāsim the endowment will be null and void. But Ashhab and most of our authorities hold that the occupation of the donee will be deemed as that of a usurper.

"Those who alighted at other's places are allowed to use the thoroughfares of that town, mosques and the public places as they like. They, like the original inhabitants, can gather wood from the places from where the common people gather wood, and bring under cultivation those lands only which lay uncultivated by the people of the locality. Similar is the case in respect of their use of the drinking water of the local people. So whatever property which remains common among the people he can take from it like others but whenever he finds any other alternative while the abode was not made lawful for him he should not settle at that place."

He was asked about a people whose lands were grabbed (by some other people) and were afterwards able to obtain their due while the usurper tilled the land for a period and they found standing crops therein. He says as to that which they found in the season of harvest, they have the right to take it without offering anything to the usurper except that it belongs to the usurper when he reaps the crops and throws on the ground *[fo. 46-b]* the price. The usurper will have to pay to (the owner) the price of it being reaped after deducting the wages of the reaper of the harvest and in case when he had crops before hand, account will be settled with him according to that price. But if they are not able to obtain the due and the season of the harvest lapses, there has been disagreement concerning the view in it and the '*Ulamā*' have also disagreed in this; some saying that the usurper has to pay the rent while the crops will belong to him and some others hold that crops will belong to the owner of the land.

Preference will be given to this view on account of a Prophetic tradition traced back to the Prophet: "One who plants or sows wrongfully has no right (in the land)", and also for the consensus of the '*Ulamā*' that whoever has begotten the child to an abducted slave-girl, her master will be better entitled to her child, so, what the usurper had obtained out of his cultivation in this land will fall under this category.

It was enquired of him: whether the poor can receive the tithe of this land if the usurper pays it. He says: "Yes, the poor can receive this, because the grain either belongs to the cultivator or to the owner of the land and in either case he is liable to pay *Zakāh* therein, and *Zakāh* is the right of the poor as well as of the beneficiaries of *Zakāh,* so they can receive it in whatever way they get it."

It is said: "Is it allowed to purchase food from the usurper?" He says: "I have already informed you of my view that the crops belong to the owner of the land. How can it be allowed to purchase from someone a thing in which others have better claim except in the case when he settles his affair with the owner of the land on lawful terms, and in such a case it is lawful to purchase from him. Those among our companions who think that the crops belong to the usurper and he is to pay the rent of the land, disapprove of purchasing from the usurper till he pays the dues to the owner of the land or till he makes it lawful for him from the owner." He further says, "Whatsoever the usurper adds (on the land) like plantation of trees, and what he does wrongfully, fall under the category of what has been raised out of cultivating the land according to their difference of opinions.

"But when the land is restored to the owner, he is to pay to the usurper the price of the tree thrown on the ground after deducting the wages of the reaper and the account will be settled out of his past dues for him and similar is the case of the constructions in the usurped land. Now if the usurper sold anything usurped exactly and purchased in its exchange cattle which brought forth younglings or purchased a slave-girl which gave birth to children, what he purchased in exchange of the price will be lawful for him, in case dues were realised from him or he himself paid up the dues, provided he sold the usurped thing for ready commodity and the bargain of what he purchased was done verbally and afterwards handed over the ready mony. But if he sells the usurped thing in exchange of articles and then sells the article in exchange of another article, the person usurped of will be given choice, either he can accept his article if he finds it and cancel both the transactions provided both the articles are intact, or he can accept the article in exchange of which his article was sold while other transactions will be null and void, or he can allow both the transactions and accept the other article.

But if he does not find his article he will be given choice, he can accept the price of his article of the day it was usurped according to our authorities *[fo. 47-a]* while others hold that he will get the entire price as it would be evaluated from the day it was taken from him forcibly upto the day he missed it; or if he so wills, he can accept the article which has been received in exchange, and cancel the third deal, and if he so wills, he can accept the third deal, and all the transactions will be recognised because, some of the '*Ulamā*' allow him only to accept his article if he finds it or the price, if it is lost.

"But they do not allow him to recognise the transaction of his article in any bargain. But if he sells the usurped article or *dīnār*, ready money, and afterwards purchases an article on condition of the same ready money, then the article was claimed, according to our authorities, the option will be given to the claimant, he can receive his article while the buyer will turn to the usurper for the price, and if he so wills he can allow the sale of his article and accept the equivalent price of the article sold. But if the price is ready mony, according to them as well as to others, the claimant cannot accept what he purchased for its price.

"And our opponents hold that he has no right to allow the sale of its substitute on condition that he will accept the price, and one who purchased the substitute for its price, cannot own what he purchased. And they consider all the transactions as null and void, because according to them, to have the claim of ready money is as good as to have the claim of the goods at a time when the condition is stipulated to accept the ready money itself while the bargain was not executed by the word and afterwards he handed over that ready money."

He was asked about a man who forcibly carried away oxen and slaves and then tilled the land with the help of those slaves and oxen at his lawfully owned land with lawful means, whether it will be permissible to purchase the crops he raised?

He says: "It is undesirable to purchase it from him as long as his affair is not sound with regard to slaves and oxen but its gradation of undesirability will not be like that of one who forcibly took away some grains which he sowed, because, I do not know of anyone holding the view that the corns belong to the owner of the oxen and the slaves and the force of undesirability (therein) is not like the one who grabbed a land, then tilled it.

"So purchasing from its grain is more undesirable than (to purchase) the raised and usurped grain due to the strong difference of opinions on it and on account of paucity of those who hold that whoever sows usurped seeds, the raised seeds belong to the person usurped from, notwithstanding the fact, that in all these cases it is undesirable to purchase anything from the usurper till his affair is settled with the one from whom he usurped.

"As for the person, who usurps wool, linen, cotton or soft hair and then makes clothes out of these, according to all our authorities and the people of Kufah, he is liable to pay the equal in quality of what he has usurped, if he knows the measure (weight). Further, our authorities hold that it will not be lawful to purchase what is made out of it till he pays dues to the owner. Some of the *'Ulamā'* hold that the person usurped from, can accept what is made of it if he so wills or its price entirely as it amounted on the day of usurpation, *[fo. 47-b]* and similar will be the case of the person who wrongfully takes away gold or silver and then changes or melts it, or copper or iron and then makes pots or swords or knives and other objects out of it. When they are changed fromd their original forms according to their difference of (substances), so whoever holds that the owners are to accept them does not allow its sale.

"As for one who does not like them to accept, disapprove of its sale and does not cancel it if the price is abated except that our authorities find the gradation of undesirability very severe in that and take it as a defect for which the buyer can return the article.

"According to our authorities, if any person carries away forcibly an eatable animal, slaughters it, and afterwards the owner seizes it as uncooked meat, the owner will be given option between accepting the meat or receiving the price of the animal, while others hold that he will get the meat as well as what falls short in the price. But if the meat is cooked, then according to our authorities and the people of Kufah, the claimant will receive only the price of the usurped animal.

"Some *'Ulamā'* hold that he will receive his animal exactly. I do not know any disagreement in the case of the animal slaughtered by the thief and found by its owner or the latter's acceptance of the price that the slaughter in it is lawful slaughter except according to the views of Ṭā'ūs and 'Aṭā' who hold that it is not a lawful slaughter.

"As for that which has been made defective by any usurper, transgressor or a thief out of fruits, milk or wool or a hired land, a house or a dwelling place, will be regarded as indemnity against them. However there has been disagreement on this issue with regard to the views of Imām Mālik and those of his followers; and this is the most correct view of all the views held on it so far.

"When, in the custody of the usurper, the female animals and other cattle give birth to younglings and afterwards, the mothers die leaving behind the younglings or the younglings die and mothers live, according to many of our authorities, the owners will be given option between receiving the remainder without receiving anything for the dead animals or receiving the price of the usurped animal to be evaluated on the day of usurpation. Some others hold that he will get the remainder as well as the price of the dead animals and this is the most sound in consideration. As for the younglings and their mothers eaten or being offered as gifts or being benefitted, they all agree that the owner will receive whatever he finds (on the spot) as well as the price of what has been destroyed on account of the usurper."

He says: "Whoever has been robbed of *dīnārs* or *dirhams* or food or anything which he is not able to recognise when it is kept hidden from him, and afterwards the thing is mixed with similar things before it goes out of the hands of the usurper. The owner will receive the equal measure or weight whether the usurper is bankrupt or one who is liable to pay back the dues which he owes on account of his oppression, because by accepting this the person is not doing any harm to the other party.

"There has been disagreement among our authorities concerning the transaction with a person who mingles his wealth (cattle) with unlawful thing while the major portion is lawful. Ibn al-Qāsim allows the deal without any binding *[fo. 48-a]* except in the case when he knows it as unlawful and in that case he should keep away from it. And similar is the case with regard to taking his food and receiving his gift as long as claims upon him do not overwhelm his lawful and unlawful possession, because very few people can avoid such deals. Ibn Wahhāb disapproves of this, saying that it should neither be sold nor should his gifts be accepted.

"Our authorities unanimously agree that when the unlawful object dominates over the object he holds in his possession, the possessor is not allowed to make any deal unless he purchases the lawful commodity, and then there is no harm in purchasing from him. But if the man offers it as gift and is aware of the fact that all that is left in his possession is enough to cover the claims against him, then there is no harm in accepting it from him provided he knows that it origin is lawful because by his acceptance no harm is done to anybody."

It was said to him that Abū'l 'Āfiyyah relates on the authority of Faḍl ibn Salmah from Ibn Abū Īsā' ibn Ṣiddīq and Ibn Ḥabīb to the effect that whoever purchases a lawful commodity in exchange of unlawful property, there is no harm in accepting the gifts from him if he is overburdened with the responsibility for transferring (changing) the ownership.

He says: "Abū'l 'Āfiyyah is an obscure man whose report cannot be considered and had it been established, from who you have mentioned, they would neither be followed nor did any argument stand in accordance with their view. This is also contrary to the view of the people of 'Irāq that they allow the endowment of the borrower though nothing remains at his disposal to pay up his credit.

"It has been established that a man declared that his slave would be free after his death. The Prophet then sold the slave and gave to the man his price. It has been said that debt was due to the man, so the Prophet asked him to pay up the loan. Had he sold the slave without any debt due to him, his sale would have been more emphatic on account of debt, because possessions of the people are inviolable except for their dues. As for their saying that "the ownership has bneen (transferred or) changed" is difficult to understand from the word, because, when the properties are usurped without a (valid) reason, the properties belong to the real owners, wherever the properties are because, there is no disagreement among the *'Ulamā'* that whoever has proved an article to be his own, he is entitled to accept it wherever he gets the object, without any consideration of its present shape and possession.

"A person asked the Prophet for something which was not permissible for him. At this, the Prophet became angry and said: 'He begs of me something which is not good for me and nor is for him. If I do not give, it will displease me; if I give it to him I will thus give him a thing which is not good for me as well as for him.' So, the Prophet has informed of the fact that it is not good to receive anything giving of which is not good on the part of the giver and this refutes what they have argued. The questioner adds that they argue with the fact that 'Umar ibn 'Abd al-'Azīz used to give from the official treasuries that came at his disposal and that the pious people used to receive it from him. This is really a careless point from one who argues with it, because 'Umar ibn 'Abd al-'Azīz repaired the wrongs and as such all that remained at the official treasury became good and lawful, since no unjust object reamined in it and the receipt of the similar object is lawful when it is spent in its right way."

He adds: "Abū'l 'Āfiyyah mentions *[fo. 48-b]* from a man whom he mentioned by name that two gold coins (*dīnārs*) were brought before Saḥnūn from a certain place. He disliked them. So he sent for someone from whom he got these exchanged." He says: "This is not an authentic report about Saḥnūn who is most immune from it. I have already informed you that the report of a person like Abū'l 'Āfiyyah would not be worth considering. However, if it is proved authentic, Saḥnūn hand disliked its coin on account of its inferior quality, so he got them exchanged lawfully with superior quality of gold but not for the reasons that the coins were not lawful."

It has been related from him, that a certain Abū Dā'ūd, one of

Saḥnūn's reliable friends, gave evidence before him. So he charged Ḥamdīs al-Qaṭṭān with the task of investigating into the names of the witnesses which included the name of Abū Dā'ūd. Ḥamdīs then wrote in the report that he was not a reliable man and this frightened Saḥnūn as soon as he looked into it. It is then enquired of Ḥamdīs as to who had remarked about Abū Dā'ūd in that way. "I", he replied. It is again asked; where from?

He replied: "(Once) I accompanied Abū Dā'ūd while he had with him a slave; then a policeman appeared and purchased some clothes from the slave. The report was communicated to Abū Dā'ūd once Ḥamdīs passed by him, he asked Ḥamdīs whether the *Qāḍī* had charged him with any probe. 'Yes', replied Ḥamdīs. 'Was my name entered therein?' He asked. 'Yes', he replied. 'What did you enter in that?' Abū Dā'ūd asked. 'That you are not reliable one,' Ḥamdīs replied. 'How do you know that?' Abū Dā'ūd again enquired. 'Because I was with you on such and such day along with your slave and then a policeman appeared and purchased some clothes from the slave.' Ḥamdīs replied. At this, Abū Dā'ūd announced: 'O man, the slave will not belong to me, he is free and I disown what he holds in his possession.' At this Ḥamdīs became glad and he then came back to Ṣaḥnūn and narrated to him what Abū Dā'ūd had said." This in turn pleased Ṣaḥnūn. He praised Allāh on this occasion as he was aware of reliability of Abū Dā'ūd.

He adds: "As for the property of one which has been usurped by the bankrupt, one who compelled him to sell it on his behalf, or some one took the initiative and sold it on behalf of the bankrupt one or on behalf of one whose presents are not legally accepted on account of exces of claims of injustices on him, so he engaged for it a surety and the surety is one whose transaction is considered lawful, or he purchased a lawful commodity and transferred it to the bankrupt, this is lawful, because he did not throw any spot on the debtor of the bankrupt, he did only turn one responsibility into another or undertook a responsibility for another."

He was enquired of the view as it has been reportedly held by Abū 'l-Zahrā and al-Ḥasan about a man who dies leaving behind wealth some of which contains these (irregularities), that his heirs are entitled to receive the wealth. He replies: "I do not consider this view to have been firmly established by them and had this been proven from them, the explicit meaning of the Qur'ān would have repudiated it, because Allāh, the Glorified, says: 'After any legacy that may have been bequeathed or debt' (4:II). There being no disagreement as to the fact that whenever property of others falls at the disposal of one not in a proper way; either through usurpation, transgression, usury or any other unlawful means, it will be like the debt due to him as the saying of Allāh, the Glorified, goes: 'And eat not up your property among yourselves in vanity' (2: 188). And he says on usuary: *[fo. 49-a]* 'And if ye repent, then ye have your principals (without interest), wrong not, and Ye shall not be wronged' (3: 179). So whatever is considered as debt due to the occupant, his heir will not have better claim to it than the debtors, because, debt is more binding than inheritance, by the Qur'ān, the Prophetic practice, and the consensus of the community. So, the suggestion for transferring the ownership from the deserving one was put forward without any deliberation at all and hence should not be accepted.

"There is no disagreement regarding the fact that had this dead man been summoned during his lifetime, his wrongs would have been repaired to or denied by him, so, neither his death nor excess of demands upon him will remit that from his wealth. But if these claimants are not known due to their abundance, in comparison to those who made the objects which were held in their possession out of that as lawful for his heirs. As for one who belongs to this category and does not expect to count his claimants, whatever he leaves behind, will be treated like the property lost and picked up in which the trace of the owner is not expected and wherein the gleaner declares himself immune from it and like the treatment of the property of a dead person whose heirs are not known."

He was asked about one to whom innumerable claims are due and afterwards he inherited lawful wealth (cattle), whether it is lawful to accept some of these as gift or whether one is allowed to purchase that wealth (cattle) from him, or if it is permissible for him to eat it. He replies: "As for his purchase from him, it is permitted, because had he purchased a lawful commodity in exchange for unlawful commodity it was permitted to purchase from him, and this is evidently a sound view. As for his offering it as gift or eating out of it, it is not lawful, because then he will stand on the way of obtaining justice from him."

It is again said: whether it is lawful to accept this property if he married in its exchange or paid up with it his loan. He replied, "No".

It is said: does he not hold the power of transaction in his properties while he knew this property exactly as lawful? He replies: "The person holding the same position is one whose acts are lawful as long as his property is not bequeathed and witheld for him as well as one who does not prevent others from realising their dues from him and one who allows others to obtain the justice from him, and also one who by the official power annuls the just decree by way of injustice and power of putting an obstacle while he was in such a state or condition that he was within the jurisdiction of enforcing the decree on him. The authority (*sulṭān*) of Allāh is above the authority of His servants."

He was asked about the person who desired to repent and (renounce) the unlawful properties which he held in possession. He replies: "If he had earned the properties through usury he should return the earned property to one on whom he practised usury, and if the debtor is not present he should be traced out. And in case he is not expected to be found alive, the property should be spent in alms on his behalf. He should do like-wise in the case of those on whom he committed injustice."

He was asked as to how to deal with the property the real affair of which is confounded with him and he is unable to know how much wealth in his possession is lawful and how much is unlawful, and whether it suffices him to take a portion out of his property for spending it in alms (there being no other way for this man except to select that). He says: "Spending a fixed portion of his possession in alms by a man whose state of affairs is like this is not reasonable *[fo. 49-b]* but the man should select such a portion of his possession the return of which was necessary for him so that the remainder will be undoubtedly pure for him. He then can restore out of that which he renounced to those who are known and were subjected to injustice or usury and the people who remained should be traced out for the return of the rest of the property. But if the existence of the remaining people is not expected the property should be spent in alms on their behalf."

He was asked about giving in alms by one who is overtaken by the claims of the acts of injustices out of the properties the owners of which are not known to him because the thing exactly will not be recognised when it is kept hidden from him. And he knows that the man giving in alms will never do justice on account of his huge claims upon him and large number of claimants, while he can neither meet these all nor enable others to realise their dues from him. He replies: "As to that which the man gives in alms on behalf of the owner by way of repentance and withdrawal, the recipient thereof is allowed to receive it but as to that in which the man gives in alms on his own behalf, he cannot give it in alms on his own behalf and will not receive any reward in it. And the safest act for the recipient is not to receive it. But if its recipient believes that the property belongs to the destitutes so he accepts it as a debt transferred to him it would be a possible course. But if one for whom charity is not lawful accepts it for running the affairs of the Muslims while it is allowed for him for that purpose to receive something from the *Bayt al-Māl* of the Muslims, it is right. Because had he given up what is in his possession, he would have asked to spend it on that account; so the act done by him would not be more troublesome than the circumstances called for by him."

It is enquired as to the nature of repentance by one who is overwhelmed by the acts of injustice. The man knows also that he will never be able to pay up their dues incumbent upon him. The enquiry is made also as to whether his evidence in the law court will be accepted. He replies: "The nature of repentance on his part will be to withdraw from everything he had held in his possession and to hand it over either to the destitute or to one who looks after the welfare of the Muslims so much so that nothing rmains in his possession except less than the dress that suffices him in his prayer; that is to say, that much which covers his body from his navel upto his knees and the food of that day, because this is the amount which he is allowed to take from other's properties when he is constrained to it though the possessor does not like it. According to our view, the insolvent is here different, because the properties of the people do not come to the insolvent by way of transgression, the people themselves carry the property to him; so, according to our view that which covers him as well as that which constitutes the shape of his dress will be left out for him.

"But Abū 'Ubayd holds that nothing of the dress will be left out for the insolvent except so little as to suffice him in prayer; that is to say, that much which covers him up from his navel down to his knee and then whatever remains in his possession he should dispose it of and must not retain anything out of it except that which I have mentioned till he as well as one who knows his condition come to know that the man has paid up his dues.

"Whoever acquires undersirable wealth secretly, should remove them away and disposssess himself also secretly. But as to that which he acquired openly and people at large know that, the guilt will not vanish from him in this case except with evidence *[fo. 50-a]* of his payment of dues. But as to the property which he got legalized from the real owner and received from him through his free will without subjecting him to fear while it was not acquired by bribe at giving a decree, and imposing a right against any claimant, nor any soothsayer's fee, nor the dowry of a prostitute, nor the earning of a singer, nor that of a hired wailing woman. As for one earned through transgression and usury, the permission of the oppressed one will acquit him of his sin."

He was asked about a man who accompanied a story-teller and used to earn on it some *dirhams* wrongfully and afterwards one of them desired repentance. He suggests to the one who desired repentance that if "he were in charge of the receipt or had benefitted out of it, he should give back the amount to one who had paid him together with fine, but if he was neither in charge of it nor had benefitted out of it the due falls on the other man. But if the owners are not available and are not known, or their trace is not expected, it should be given in alms."

He was asked about something given away as a gift by a man of this type, whether it is lawful to purchase the thing from him while the thing was given to them as a gift only for the dues upon him. He says that it is prohibited and not lawful for anyone by purchase or gift. He asked if the donor permits the object for the donee out of that which he gave him and, afterwards, the donee repents, whether it will be lawful? He replies: "It would not be lawful, he must offer it in charity and should not return it to its donor. Now if the object is lost at the hand of the donee he shall have to offer the like of it in charity provided the object has the equivalent, otherwise its price. But if nothing remains in his possession it will be treated like a debt due to him which he will offer in charity except the donations which perished before his arrival and there he will not have to pay anything for that."

He was asked about one who was entrusted with some deposit which he employed in trade and earned profit out of it. He replies: "According to the view of Mālik, Ibn al-Qāsim and most of our authorities, what he has done in respect of taking loan from it is despairing and the profit will belong to him. Ashhab recommended him to offer the profit in charity while Ibn 'Umar and Nāfi', his freed slave, hold that the profit belongs to the depositor; and according to Ibn Idrīs, and al-Marwazī, if the man had purchased with the same goods, the sale will be cancelled and the deal will not be confirmed with it, but if he had purchased it verbally without any fixed commodity, and then he completed the sale and afterwards handed over the goods, the profit will belong to him."

He was asked about someone who held in his possession some disagreeable goods whether the possessor can perform pilgrimage and take part in the holy war with it. He forbade him to do that.

He was asked about a person who was subjected to injustice, then a man averted the acts of injustice from him, afterwards the oppressed man offered something as a gift to his benefector, whether it will be lawful for him. He replies: "If it was offered for his averting injustice from him, its receipt will not be lawful for him."

He was asked about the judge who distributes wealth among a people on condition that he will receive some remuneration. He replies: "If he happens to be the same judge who decides the cases among them, it would not be lawful for him, but if the judge is somebody else and receives the remuneration only for his engagement with accounts, it will be lawful."

He was also asked about a person who held in his possession some properties which he considers *[fo. 50-b]* to have sequels containing goods of different nature, and, therefore, desires to offer the property in charity while he had dependants or no dependant at all. He replies: "If he had laid hands on the properties on the prohibition of which there exists explicit text from the Book of Allāh, established Prophetic Practice or Consensus of the Community he should dispossess that and if it had owners, the property should be restored to them, otherwise he should offer it in charity. But if there is neither an explicit text nor Consensus of the Community concerning it and the property which he held in possession be enormous, or he desires to give up some of it, he should do that.

"But if he maintains a large family having dependants, he should keep it back for them so that it does not incite him to commit crimes and lest he might be unable to endure and fall into a more dangerous situation. But if he is a righteous bechelor and is immune from the direction of his motive he can do so, and it is best for him to retain some of it.

Sufyān al-Thawrī who was a jurist, may Allāh have mercy on him, says: "An earning which contains something is better than begging from some people and wherever the soul of man urges him to a sure good he should not lose time in doing it lest his soul might pull him off from it. But if the soul urges him to a thing in which peril is apprehended though at the moment some good is visible in it, he should refrain from it as far as he can, except in the case when he comes to know with certainty that it will not change on account of diferent situations and demands on him to do his part righteously, wherever is found way of success one should hasten to do it.

"Whoever entrusts any deposit and it becomes known that the deposited object reached the depositor by way of excess or that the depositor happens to be a non-bailiff, he should return the object to the owner if he knows them or offer it in charity if he does not know them when he returns the object to the depositor.

"Once one of the companions of Saḥnūn was seated by the Qāḍī Ismā'īl at Baghdād, a man brought a valuable pearl that came out from the treasury of the king. The people then started turning it in their hands. Some one asked the companion of Saḥnūn if he had noticed it. He replied in the negative. Ismā'īl then urged him to extemporize on the point. He said: 'If it had reached my hands it would come under my surety.' This pleased Ismā'īl and he liked it."

It has been reported that a man found a bead at the hands of a plunderer. He considered it suitable for the neck of his wife, and purchased it from the plunderer for seven *dīnārs*. He paid up the price to the plunderer and put the bead in an evelope. Afterwards it appeared to him that the bead did not suit his wife, so he demanded rescission of the sale from him who in turn rescinded the sale and gave him back all the *dīnārs*, and the plunderer received the bead. The jurists of al-Qayruwān who were present gave the juridical verdict that "the price which was incumbent upon him should be offered by him in charity and in exchange of the commodity, he shall have to offer all the *dīnārs* in charity as well" and in that they did not use deceit. This happened when Ibrāhīm ibn Aḥmad conquered Tūnis.

Aḥmed says: "This answer (verdict) was given without due consideration. The man shall not have to pay anything for the bead *[fo. 51-a]* nor for the *dīnārs*. Had it been so, one who purchased some goods in the market of the Muslims by lawful way and later on it appeared to him that it was an usurped article which perished not due to him or he purchased a slave-girl with whom he had sexual intercourse, he would have been charged with the payment of the price of the article perished and punishment for his having sexual intercourse.

"As for one whose property has been mingled with unlawful property, should receive his property per weight. The Prophet, peace be upon him, says: 'Whoever takes over any tract of land (unlawfully) Allāh will put around his neck the seven Earths on the Day of Resurrection.' " He adds: "The acts of injustice are darknesses on the Day of Resurrection." He further adds: "Whoever has committed acts of injustice should expiate them before the Day when there would be no *dīnār* and *dirham.*"

As to that which has been reported that he said: "If anyone of you is unable to be like Abū Ḍamḍam whenever he (Abū Ḍamḍam) comes out of his abode, he says, 'O Allah, I have offered my honour in charity among the people.' The *'Ulamā'* have disagreed on the question of legitimization (*Taḥallul*); Ibn al-Musayyib does not permit anyone in respect of honour and property while Sulaymān ibn Yasār used to permit (others) in respect of honour and property. Mālik approves of giving permission to others in respect of wealth but not in respect of honour.

"The Prophetic tradition has been established that when the people would cross the Path of Heaven on the Day of Resurrection, they would be detained till some of them obtain their dues from some others.

"Some *'Ulamā'* say that all the evil acts will move in between the servant (of Allāh) and Allāh, the Glorified, either the wronged person will take away the good acts of the oppressor or he will ascribe to the oppressor his evil acts, or he will forgive him or Allāh will be pleased with the wronged man and forgive the Muslim wrongdoer and afterwards the affair of the servant will return to Allāh, the Exalted.

"Some of the *'Ulamā* hold that whoever is dealt unjustly and his property is taken away, will get the reward of what has been witheld from him upto his death and then the reward will go to his heir and thus to more deserving one, because the property remains after the death of the survivor and this is sound on deliberation. According to this view, if the usurper of property dies before the man to whom the wrongs were done without leaving anything behind or that he left behind some properties in which the heirs were not aware of his wrong acts, the claims of the wronged will not be transferred to his heirs, because nothing remained for the wrongdoer which the heirs of the wronged could demand.

"But when the claim is due upon the man to whom the wrongs were done for the property, his claims will not be inherited except after the payment of his dues, because the claim to his property is prior to his debt which in turn is prior to the heir and Allāh has calculated this, taught it and taught as to whom it belongs."

Chapter II

ON SOLICITATION OF AID (*MAS'ALAH*)

Allāh the Exalted says: "The unthinking man accounteth them wealthy because of their restraint. Thou shall know them by their mark. They do not beg of men with importunity" (2: 273). The Prophet, may peace be upon him, says: "Whoever from among you begs while he owns one ounce of silver *[fo. 51-b]* or its equivalent, surely, he begs with importunity." He adds: "Surely, it is better for anyone of you to take his rope, pick up firewood and carry the wood on his back than to approach a man whom Allāh has given out of his bounties and beg of him whether the latter gives him or not."

He further says: "The upper hand is better than the lower hand, and begin with those whose maintenance is due to you." He also says: "The best of alms is that which is offered over and above the level of sufficiency that keeps him in no need, and begin with those whose maintenance you owe." He also says: "The destitute is not the one who rambles and whom one or two morsels or two dates send back; the real destitute is he who does not have enough sufficiency to satisfy his wants, nor does he come out to beg publicly."

Ḥakīm ibn Ḥizām says: "I asked the Messenger of Allāh, may Allāh bless him and grant him peace, for some thing; whereupon, he gave me, I again begged of him and he gave me. I asked him again and he again gave me, and then said to me, 'O Ḥakīm, how unsparing is your begging; verily, this wealth is sweet and fresh; whatever one receives out of this with generosity of the soul, he is blessed with it and whatever one receives out of this one receives with the greed of the soul, he is like one who eats but does not feel satiated and surely, it is good for you not to take anything from anybody.' " I said: "And even not from you, O Messenger of Allāh," "No, not even from me," the Prophet replied. I rejoined, "By Allāh, I shall not take anything from anybody". And he then gave up begging. Whenever, later on 'Umar offered him his allowances, Ḥakīm said that he had given that up during the time of one who was greater than him, meaning the Prophet, may peace be upon him. At this, 'Umar replied: "I ask you to bear witness, O congregation of the Muslims [The Prophet, may peace be upon him, has said this to Ḥakīm when he noticed in the latter greediness leading to begging]."

The Messenger of Allāh, may Allāh bless him and grant him peace, has said: "Verily, Allāh recommends for you three things and disapproves of three things for you; that you serve Him, and do not associate anything with Him, hold fast the rope of Allāh unitedly, and give sincere advice to one whom Allāh entrusts with your affairs. For you He disapproves of wastage of wealth and importunate begging." It is reported that he said, as it has been related in another Prophetic tradition: "Allāh forbids you to do three things; burial of female children alive, disobedience to mothers, and withholding and begging." As for importunate begging, it is said the Prophet meant begging by a person from the people as to whatever is in their hands. Some say that this means that a person must not ask about the problems which do not concern him.

It has been reported that the Prophet, may peace be upon him, said: "On the Day of Resurrection begging will appear on the face of any one of them like the marks of scratching, wrinkling or lacerating." The prohibited begging is the begging by one who acts as a beggar while he is not a beggar or who exhibits his wants more than his actual want. And an undesirable begging is one in which a person begs while he owns one ounce of silver. However, it is not forbidden for him, because the Prophet, may peace be upon him, gave alms to Ḥakīm several times though he had possessed more than one ounce. Neverthless, he was from among those who deserved charity as he was one of those whose hearts needed reconciliation. Had it been forbidden for him, the Prophet would not have given charity to him although he disliked it for Ḥakīm. Moreover, 'Uthmān ibn 'Affān *[fo. 52-a]* and Jubayr ibn Mūṭ'im prayed to the Prophet to grant them out of the one-fifth along with Banū 'Abd Shams and Banū Nawfal when the Prophet gave out of it to Banū Ḥāshim and Banū'l Muṭṭalib.

There is no harm if a person who possesses less than forty *dirhams* begs in an agreeable way. Whoever is constrained to beg, it then becomes incumbent upon him to beg and the donor will not be considered superior to the donee because, Moses and al-Khiḍr asked the inhabitants of a village to give them food. Again, begging is lawful if one begs in an agreeable way due to reasons other than poverty; due to an incident, that happened to him, a want that overtook him, a burden that he bore, a blood money that fell due to him, or a compensation he owed. In these cases the donor will not be superior to the donee. The Prophet, may peace be upon him, once went out to Banū Qaynuqā', the Jews, to seek their help for payment of blood money that fell due to his two Companions. He entered and food was brought to him. At this, the Prophet said: "Did I not notice the cooking pot boiling with meat?" It was replied that it was charity offered to Barīrah and he did not eat charity. "For her it is charity but for us it is a gift", the Prophet retorted.

The Prophet offered something to 'Umar who enquired if he had not said that it was better not to take anything from anybody. The Prophet replied that it was in the context of begging. As for that which comes without begging, it is only a sustenance offered to him by Allāh. Thereupon, 'Umar declared: "By Allāh, I shall neither beg of anybody for anything nor shall I refuse to accept anything that comes to me without begging." The Prophet, may peace be upon him, said to his Companions: "You intercede, you will be rewarded. Allāh decrees whatever He wills through the tongue of His Prophet."

Once Abū Mūsā came to the Prophet along with a group of the Ash'arites with a request to provide them with beasts of burden and found him busy. Prophet then swore by Allāh three times that he would not provide them with the beasts of burden. No sooner had they departed than thirteen young she-camels were brought before him. He, then, called them back and offered them out of these animals. When they went their way, they discussed among themselves saying, perhaps the Prophet had forgotten his oath that he would not provide them with the beasts of burden but afterwards he provided them with. They later on came back to the Prophet and said: "O Messenger of Allāh, you swore that you would not provide us with any beast of burden but later on you did provide us with [them]." The Prophet replied: "By Allāh, I did not provide you with the beast of burden nor was I to provide you with the beast of burden, it is Allāh who provided you with the beast of burden, by Allāh, whenever I take an oath, and then find something else better, I offer the atonement for my oath and do what is better."

When the Prophet was distributing the booties out of one-fifth among the Banū'l-Muṭṭalib as well as Banū Hāshim, 'Uthmān and Jubayr ibn Muṭ'im came to him, may peace be upon him, and said: "O Messenger of Allāh, we acknowledge the superiority of Banū Hāshim on account of their relation to you, but you gave Banū'l-Muṭṭalib and neglected us, although they and we in relation to you stand on the same footing." The Prophet replied: "Surely, Banū Hāshim and Banū'l-Muṭṭalib are one." And he knitted together his fingers.

This is an instance of permissible begging and they both intended therein to be blessed with. The Prophetic tradition has already been mentioned in its proper place. Moreover, when the Prophet gave Aqra' and 'Uyaynah one hundred camels each and fifty to 'Abbās *[fo. 52-b]* ibn Mirdās, the latter composed those peoms which had been mentioned earlier and the Prophet then increased his share. This is also an instance of agreeable begging because, by this he wanted to be blessed with and hence became importunate and the Prophet, therefore, increased his share. Had it not been lawful, the Prophet would not have made it allowable to him.

Chapter III

ON SUFFICIENCY, POVERTY AND WEALTH

Aḥmad ibn Naṣr says that there are some explicit texts on the description of sufficiency (*kafāf*), poverty (*faqr*), and wealth (***ghinā'***) which provide explanation and satisfaction for the *'Ulamā'*. Surely superiority goes to sufficiency while poverty and wealth are the two divine trials and tests by which the best servants of Allāh are tried so that the endurance of those who endure, thankfulness of the thankful, rebellious nature of the insolent, and greediness of the greedy are tested. However, ambiguity will remain only for the ignorant and the negligent, and those who do not contemplate among the strong ones. Allāh, the Exalted, says: "And if they had referred it to the Messenger and such of them as are in authority, those among them who are able to think out the matter would have known it" (4: 83). He also says: "And none will grasp their meaning save the wise" (29: 43). He also says: "Will they then not meditate on the Qur'ān, or are there locks on the hearts?" (47: 24)

Some people, therefore, compiled works giving preference to wealth over poverty, while others composed books giving preference to poverty over wealth. Thus they became unmindful of the required encouragement and recommendation and in it they committed exaggeration. Some of them blamed others and criticised among them. I hope for one whose argument is sound, intention is sincerely for Allāh, and discourse is directed for the sake of Him while he has enough knowledge befitting his discourse and bringing out the conclusion, that Allāh will cover him with his forgiveness, reward him for his intention and turn away from his fault because, the human beings are not infallible. Sometimes they inevitably commit errors and become neglectful. Allāh, the Great and High, helps whomsoever and in whatsoever circumstances He wills to assist by rendering the circumstances favourable for him. I hope also that this community by His grace will never agree on misguidance.

Allāh, the High, and Exalted, says; "Lo! we have placed all that is on the earth as an ornament thereof that we may try them: which of them is best in conduct" (18: 7). And He says: "And we shall try you with evil and with good for ordeal. And unto us ye will be returned" (21: 35). And He says: "And when we make life pleasant unto man, he turneth away and is averse and when ill toucheth him he is in despair" (18: 83). "Then he aboundeth in prayer" (41: 51). And He says "Lo! man was created impatient, fretful when evil befalleth him, and, when good befalleth him grudging" (70: 19–21).

And He says: "As for man, whenever his Lord trieth him, by honouring him, and is gracious into him he saith: 'My Lord honoureth me.' But whenever He trieth him by straitening his means of life, he saith: 'My Lord despiseth me,' " (89: 15–16) upto His saying: "And you love wealth with abounding love" (89: 20). That is to say, you are neither honoured by wealth nor despised by poverty. He adds: "And if Allāh were to enlarge the provision for His slaves, they would surely rebel in the earth but He sendeth down *[fo. 53-a]* by measures as He willeth. Lo! He the Informed, Seer of His bondmen" (42: 27). And He says: "And were it that mankind would have become one community, We might well have appointed, for those who disbelieve in the Beneficent, roofs of silver for their houses and stairs (of silver) whereby to mount," (43: 33) upto His saying: "for those who keep from evil" (43: 35). And He says: "Nay, but verily man is rebellious, that he thinketh himself independent" (96: 6–7). And he says: "Lo! man is an ingrate unto his Lord and Lo! he is witness unto that. And is in the love of wealth, he is violent" (100: 6–8).

Some say, *al-Kanūd* means *al-Kafūr* i.e. denial of faith, while some others hold that it means *al-Jaḥūd* i.e. aburation of faith. Some others comment on His saying: "Verily he is violent in the love of his wealth," that is to say, he is violent lover of wealth; and others hold that he becomes emaciated due to love of wealth. The Prophet, peace be upon him, says: "Whoever wants to remain chaste, Allāh keeps him chaste, and whoever wants to be self-sufficient, Allāh keeps him self-sufficient. And nobody has, ever endowed with anything better and more capacious than preseverance."

He further says: "Sufficiency is not achieved through abundance of goods: it is achieved only by the wealth of the soul." He says: "It does not make him cheerful to have gold to the size of the mountain of Uḥud while after three days, he is reduced to a state in which he possesses nothing except that which he has as the balance of payment for debt."

Abū Dhar says: "I have heard the Prophet saying, 'By the Lord of Ka'bah, they surely possess little.' 'Who are they, O Messenger of Allāh?'

I asked. 'They are those who possess enormously except one who uttered in the property such, such, such and such,' and he pointed out by both of his hands, to the right, left, front and the back. And he says: 'This property is like sweet and verdant herbage except the ripest of the herbage eaten up (by the cattle), so much so that when both of its flanks were filled, its size was reduced and it faced the sun. Afterwards it threw thin dung, made water and then pastured.' Some said 'O Messenger of Allāh, does good come from evil?" He replied: "The good does come only from good, the good does come only from good, the good comes only from good and whatever plants the autumn causes to grow does kill, or nearly kills, by swelling of bellies.' "

The Anṣār heard of the wealth that was brought to the Prophet from Baḥrayn so they gathered around him in the morning prayer. When the Prophet performed the prayer, he looked at the multitude and said smilingly: "I think, you have heard of the arrival of Abū 'Ubaydah and of the fact that he has brought something." They said "Yes". He said: "Then cheer up and be filled with what cheers you up. By God, it is not the wealth which I fear for you but I fear the world for you which will be opened for you after me as it was opened for the people before you. So you would quarrel among you for it as they did quarrel for it and it would destroy you as it did destroy them." And the Prophet, peace be upon him, used to pray as follows: "O Allāh, I seek refuge with you from the trial of grave as well as from that of wealth (*ghinā'*)."

Whatever we have recited and quoted so far proves that over and above the level of sufficiency (*kafāf*), there is a trial from which nobody is safe except one whom Allāh keeps safe. It has been reported in a Prophetic tradition that what is little and sufficient is better than what exceeds in number and is earned by appropriating (other's right).

When the wealth of Khusroes was brought before 'Umar, he along with the other illustrious Companions of the Prophet spent the night with the wealth in the mosque. In the morning, when the light of the Sun fell on it, the crowns presented wonderful scene. At this, 'Umar began to weep, whereupon, Ibn 'Awf reminded 'Umar that it was not the time for weeping, rather it was to moment for thanksgiving. 'Umar replied that he thought that whenever Allāh favours any people with this, they invariably shed their blood and break with their blood-kindred.

And he added: "O Allāh, we are not able but to clear the way with what is in my power, O Allāh, give me power to exhaust it in the right cause." He added: "O Allāh, verily, you have denied it to your Prophet as a token of honour to him but favoured me with it just to put me to trial: O Allāh, guard me against its allurement." Or the words to that effect. The

Prophet, peace be upon him, says: "The poor will enter Paradise but the wealthy people will be detained to account (for their deeds)."

Once a man wrapped in fillings passed by the Prophet, the Prophet then enquired of his Companions as to what they thought about the man. They replied: the man was fit to be rejected in a marriage proposal if he proposed for marriage and he would not be given entrance if he seeks admittance. Afterwards, another man wrapped in a beautiful cloak passed by the Prophet who again asked them about their opinion of him. They replied that the man was worthy of being accepted in a marriage proposal if he proposed and would be given admittance if he sought it. At this, the Prophet remarked: "Verily, this man is better than the earth filled with the other like one."

And all these prove the preeminence of the state of sufficiency (*kafāf*) and not that of poverty (*faqr*), and the case is not as it appeared to them. Poverty and wealth are both trials. The Prophet used to invoke divine protection against both trials. In addition, the divine expression supports this: "And let not thy hand be chained to thy neck nor open it, with a complete opening, lest thou sit down rebuked, denuded" (17: 29). And He says: "And those who, when they spend, are neither prodigal nor grudging; and there is ever a firm station between the two" (25: 67). And He says: "Give not unto the foolish (what) is in your (keeping of their) wealth, which Allāh hath given you to maintain; but feed and clothe them from it; and speak kindly unto them" (4: 5). And He says with regard to the guardian of the orphan, "Whoso (of the guardians) is rich, let him abstain generously (from taking of the property of orphans); and whoso is poor let him take thereof in reason (for his guardianship)" (4: 6).

So, some say, he should live on his own property reasonably, so that he does not require the property of the orphan. Some others hold that he should live on some property of the orphan reasonably in return for his looking after it; while others hold that he should borrow from the wealth of the orphan reasonably, and others say that he along with the orphan should lay his hand (on the property). He says: "And let those fear (in their behaviour toward orphans) who if they left behind them weak offspring would be afraid for them. So, let them mind their duty to Allāh, and speak justly" (4: 9). That is to say, whoever attends a testator, he should advise him not to hinder his heirs (from the property) as he himself would have liked, hand the heirs been his own.

What we have so far said has further been corroborated by the story of Ka'b ibn Mālik when Allāh had accepted his repentance. He addressed the Messenger of Allāh, saying: "Surely my repentance entails that I should be stripped of my wealth, and sacrifice it for Allāh and His Messenger and that I should not say except truth." The Prophet then said to him: "You should keep back for you some of your property and that would be good for you."

Sa'd had sought permission from the Prophet to bequeath two-thirds of his wealth, whereupon, the Prophet forbade him. Sa'd then asked permission for one-third, whereupon, the Prophet replied that one-third was also a big amount. He added: "It is better for you to leave behind you heirs self-sufficient than to leave them destitute begging alms from the people. So this kind of wealth (*ghinā'*) is not excessive. Had every surplus been better, *[fo. 54-a]* the Prophet would have forbidden him to bequeath anything. The hands of people fell short of giving in alms and spending in the way of Allāh though that would have led to a different situation.

Fāṭimah, the daughter of Qāys, told the Messenger of Allāh that Mu'āwiyah and Abū Jahm both asked her in marriage. The Messenger of Allāh remarked: "As for Mu'āwiyah, he is a poor man and does not possess any property." The Messenger of Allāh would not have censured a condition which was good. The Messenger of Allāh said to 'Amr ibn al-'Āṣ: "Shall I send you in an army, may Allāh keep you safe and sound, grant you booty, and shall I make you interested in some wealth?" He ('Amr) replied: "My migration is not for the sake of wealth rather I migrate for the sake of Allāh and for His Messenger." The Prophet said: "Bravo! a good wealth is for a good man." He, therefore, could not encourage anyone to do anything which reduced his share with Allāh. So, it is not lawful to say that either of the two conditions is superior to the other because both of them are trials.

One who holds this view says: the loss of two hands of a human being is better with Allāh than the loss of a leg; and again, the loss of hearing is better than the loss of an eye. So there is no point of superiority, rather here is the point of trials by which Allāh subjects His servants to test so that those, who persevere and thank Allāh, are distinguished from others.

As far as we know, no Prophetic tradition has come down to the effect that the Prophet, peace be upon him, used to invoke poverty (*faqr*) for himself nor did he ever invoke poverty for anybody whom he wished well; rather he used to pray for self-sufficiency (*kafāf*) and invoked divine protection against the trials of poverty and wealth. Moreover, the Prophet did not invoke wealth (*ghinā'*) for anyone except with a condition which he would mention in his prayer.

There is, however, a Prophetic tradition in which it is reported that the Prophet used to say: "O Allāh, keep me alive as a destitute (*miskīn*) and put me to death as a destitute and resurrect me in the group of the destitutes." If this tradition is established to be correct through its transmission, it would mean a stage which does not exceed the limits of self-sufficiency (*kafāf*) or that the Prophet desired to become humble before Allāh, the Exalted. The soundness of this interpretation has been corroborated by the fact that the Prophet left behind (after his death) the properties of Banū 'l-Naḍīr, his share in Khaybar and Fadak. So, it is not logical to think of the Prophet that he would pray to Allāh so that nothing remains in his possession, and he was able to remove the things from his possession through spending in alms.

In another tradition, it has been reported that the Prophet said: "O Allāh, decrease the wealth and children of those who believe in me and hold as true what I have brought." This tradition is not authentic through the way of transmission as well as in consideration. Had his prayer been only for the wealth, it was possible that he would have prayed for their sufficiency (*kafāf*), but as to his prayer with regard to the children, how can he pray for decrease in the number of Muslims, since the ruination of a generation results in reduction of the Muslims and their destruction. But what raises the size of the family has been traced back to the Prophet, peace be upon him, *[fo. 54-b]* the traditions which do not contradict (this point).

How can he censure the poverty of Mu'āwiyah when at the same time he asks Ka'b ibn Mālik and Sa'd to keep back the wealth as mentioned with the remark that it was good and then he opposed that? It has been established that the Prophet prayed for Anas ibn Mālik and said: "O Allāh, multiply him in wealth and progeny and bless him in what You have given him." Anas Says: "My daughter has counted that I presented before Ḥajjāj at Baṣrah about one hundred and twenty living beings coming from my progeny on account of the prayer of the Messenger of Allāh, may Allāh bless him and send down His peace on him." He lived for a number of years after this and other children were born to him. Even after him, the prosperity of his family continued. So, the Prophet not only prayed for the abundance of his wealth but conjoined it with his expression: "And bless him in what you have given him."

Now if the question is put, of the two men which one is better, the one put to test with poverty or the one tried with wealth, provided the condition of either of them is otherwise sound. It is said, the question about this does not stand, because this man can have besides this trial, other acts in which he is better than the other man, whereas the other man may have acts by which he excells his equal in the similar situation. Again, this man whose condition is sound in poverty, often may not remain so in wealth, while the condition of the other man may remain sound in both poverty as well as in wealth. So the conditions of both may be different in other similar acts.

It may be argued that the condition of either of them remains sound in both the circumstances, while besides this, they have equal acts; the poor man does the acts incumbent on him in his poverty, like fortitude, restraint, and contentment, the rich man does the acts incumbent on him, like spending in alms, generosity, gratitude, and humility. So, of the two which one is better? The knowledge about it rests with Allāh, notwithstanding the fact, that a group of people prefer poverty (*faqr*) on account of the Prophetic tradition which we have mentioned: that the poor will enter the Paradise while the owners of fortunes will be detained to give accounts.

Others reject this interpretation. They say that only those who boast and vie in accumulating wealth will be detained; but as for one who pays up the dues of Allāh in his property and does not vie with others by his wealth in boasting and accumulating wealth, and spends out of it as for as he realises to be his duty and lays aside the remainder for fulfilling his needs. In this circumstance, the others will not be considered superior to him in anything. This is further corroborated by that which has been proved correct from the Prophet, may Allāh bless him and send him peace, who says: "There must not be any envy except with two persons; a man whom Allāh gives wealth and then empowers him to exhaust it in (the way of) truth, and a man whom Allāh favours with wisdom with the help of which the man decides the cases and teaches it (to some others)."

In another Prophetic tradition, it has been reported in some other words: "A man whom Allāh gives wealth and then empowers him to exhaust it in (the way of) truth and a man whom Allāh favours with the Qur'ān by which he abides day and night." So, the Messenger of Allāh has explained that there is no more dignified position than these two positions. *[fo. 55-a]* He is the only one who can explain on behalf of Allāh and give juridical verdict of what He wills. Had one who had this position been superceded in the world Hereafter, the Messenger of Allāh, peace be upon him, would not have encouraged him to stick to his act nor would he had described it with this description nor would he urge Ka'b ibn Mālik to turn to the position which would lead him to Paradise and no more.

What we have so far mentioned is enough including the Prophet's saying: "The horse will be a reward for a man, a shield for another and a burden upon another, so the man for whom it is a reward is one who has saddled it for the Path of Allāh," upto the Prophetic tradition that has been previously mentioned. The man for whom it is a shield is one who saddled it for becoming free from want and for acquiring self-restraint without forgetting Allāh's due on its neck and back, the man upon whom it is a burden is one who saddled it out of hypocrisy, boastfulness and opposition to the Muslims, and this man belongs to the group of people who would be detained for giving accounts if Allāh so wills, and the first two belong to the states of self-sufficiency (*kafāf*) in two cases.

Ibn Shihāb says: "An ascetic is one in whom neither the lawful things exhaust his gratitude (for Allāh) nor do the prohibited things exhaust his patience." It has been confirmed from the Prophet who says: "You look at the one who is inferior to you and do not look at the one who is superior to you."

It has been reported that Ḥudhayfah said: "O Allāh, no one can be raised in dignity except by dint of actions and no action is possible except with the help of property and no property is acquired except out of your bounty, so keep me free from want with your abounding mercy. O Allāh, I cannot do with a meagre amount nor is it enough for me."

It has been established that when Allāh asked Prophet Ayyūb [Job] to take bath so that he was cured of his desease, lo! a swarm of golden locusts passed by him. At this he started collecting these in his clothes while he was naked. Allāh then sent down revelation to him (saying): "Can you not do without these?" "Who does not need your mercy, O my Nourisher?" He said, or used a similar expression.

Moreover, verily, Allāh, the Exalted, says: "Nor unto those whom, when they come to thee (asking) that thou shouldst mount them, thou didst tell: 'I cannot find whereon to mount you.' They turned back with eyes flowing with tears for sorrow that they could not find the means to spend" (9:92). Now in the circumstances in which they were, if priority goes to one whom others do not match, they would not have grieved when they did not get beast of burden inferior to that. Had they overlooked that and thought that the other would be superior, Allāh certainly would have explained that.

Nevertheless, the dangers of wealth are many while those who are saved from them are very few, because scarcely people escape its danger except one who is infalliable (*ma'ṣūm*) and for this reason, the position of the infalliable one in it is great as the devil allures him either in receiving (wealth) without his right, in spending (wealth) inappropriately, depriving a person of his right, showing oppression and transgression (in acquiring) wealth, or little thankfulness for it or in aspiring to it and other similar situations which canot be described. So great is the gratitude and patience of one whom Allāh granted safety from it.

All praise belongs to Allāh for His favour He conferred upon us through His Book before *[fo. 55-b]* and behind of which falsehood does not come—a revelation from One Wise and Praised and also through the Practice (*Sunnah*) of the Messenger of Allāh, may Allāh bless him and grant him peace and keep it alive among us after His Prophet, so, nobody other than one who is doomed will destroy them. May Allāh send down blessings on Muḥammad, His Prophet, peace be upon him and his family.

THE BOOK IS COMPLETE BY THE GRACE OF ALLAH AND HIS HELP, BLESSINGS BE ON MUḤAMMAD, HIS PROPHET AND SERVANT

The transcript of it was finished on Saturday the 23rd Ṣafar in the year 677. May Allāh give benefit with it. Muḥammad ibn Muḥammad ibn 'Abd al-Raḥmān al-Maghīli undertook its transcription in the beginning and completed it himself.

APPENDIX

Ahmad abu Rafar Araudi.

Tractatus Juridicus de praedis, ac de divisione illarum juxta legem Alcorani et Unanimem Doctorum Consensum facienda/Ubi nimiam regum aviditatem, ac licentiam in praedis, Civiumque fortunis usurpandis acriter impugnal, Sugillatis.

Agit etiam de tributo aequo rebus imponendo, Ubi excipit omnia commestibilia quaeque ad victus rationem necessaria; asseritque venationem, piscatumque non posse licite prohiberi nec reservari; plura de decimis; de lucre licito, ac illicito, dę bello licito queq requisitis contra Christianos, ubi plura de militum licentia, Ibidem decet Chrianos posse retinere sua bona, quae jure possidebant in regnis in ditionem Mauritanorum redactis et solum teneri, Singulos viros, exceptis pueris Mulieribusque Tribitum, Singulis annis solvere, quod testaticum Vocamus, posse etiam sine ullo impedimento suam profiteri religionem, eam lebere exercere, qd Andulusorum Christianorum Mauritanis subjectorum Tune temporis nune temporis Confirmat.

equiv. 677

TRANSLATION

Aḥmad Abū Ja'far Dā'ūdī,

Juridical Treatise on booty and how the division of booty has to be made according to the law of the Qur'ān and the unanimous consensus of Doctors (of law).

He criticises in strong language, the excessive greediness of the kings and their indulgence in booty, while misusing to their own benefit the fortunes of the civilian population. In the book he also deals with equitable imposition of taxes and makes exceptions for all eatables and things which are necessary for a reasonable livelihood. He asserts that hunting and fishing cannot in a legitimate way be prohibited, nor (its products) be conserved.

He (teaches) more about tithing, about legitimate and illigitimate earnings, about legitimate warfare and the things which can be charged against Christians. In this section he says more about what soldiers are allowed to do and what not. In the same place, he teaches that Christians can keep their (earthly) goods under their own control, the goods they possessed legally in those territories which were brought under the sway of the Muslims and that only the individual men (with the exception of young boys and women) will be held responsible to pay tribute every single year. We call this head-money. He teaches that the Christians can profess their religion and practise it without hindrance, which (right) he confirms for the Christians under the Muslim rule for the past and present.

It was written in 677.

SELECT BIBLIOGRAPHY

(Books referred to in this work)

Abū 'Abd Allāh Muḥammad ibn Aḥmad ibn Qāsim ibn Sa'īd al-'Uqbānī al-Tilimsānī, "Kitāb Tuḥfat al-Nāẓir wa Ghunyat al-Dhākir fī Ḥafẓ al-Sha'āyir wa Taghyīr al-Manākir", Damascus (Institute Françäis de Damas, *Bulletin d' études orientales*, Tome XIX (1967), Années 1965–66).

Abū Aḥmad Ḥumayd ibn Zanjawayh, "Kitāb al-Amwāl", Maktabat al-Ẓāhirīyyah MS, Damascus, No. 223 (II) "*Ḥadīth*", Parts XIII–XIV.

Abū Bakr Aḥmad ibn 'Alī al-Khaṭīb al-Baghdādī, *Ta'rīkh Baghdād*, 14 vols. (Cairo, 1349/1931).

Abū'l-Faraj Jamāl al-Dīn 'Abd al-Raḥmān ibn 'Alī ibn Muḥammad ibn 'Alī ibn al-Jawzī, *Kitāb Ṣifat al-Ṣafwah*, Ist ed., 4 vols. (Hyderabad, Deccan, H 1355–1357).

——, *Sīrah 'Umar ibn 'Abd al-'Azīz.*

Abū'l-Faraj Qudāmah ibn Ja'far, *Kitāb al-Kharāj wa Ṣinā'at al-Kitābah.*

Abū'l-Falāḥ 'Abd al-Ḥayy ibn al-'Imād al-Ḥanbalī, *Shadhrāt al-Dhahab fī Akhbār man Dhahaba*, 8 vols. (Cairo, H 1350).

Abū 'Ubayd, al-Qāsim ibn Sallām, *Kitāb al-Amwāl*, ed. Muḥammad Ḥamīd al-Fiqqī (Cairo: Maktabah al-Tijāriyyah Kubrā, H 1353).

Abū Yūsuf Ya'qūb ibn Ibrāhīm al-Anṣārī, *Kitāb al-Kharāj*, 3rd ed. (Cairo, H 1382).

——, *Kitāb al-Radd'alā Siyar al-Awzā'ī*, ed. Abū'l-Wafā al-Afghānī (Cairo, 1357/1938).

Aḥmad Tawfīq al-Madanī, *al-Muslimūn fī Jazīrah Ṣiqilliyah wa Janūbī Iṭāliyyah* (Algeria, H 1368).

Al-Balādhurī, Abū'l 'Abbās Aḥmad ibn Yaḥyā ibn Jābir. *Kitāb Futūḥ al-Buldān,* ed. M.J. De. Goeje (Leiden, 1866).

Ben Shemesh, A. *Taxation in Islam* (Leiden: E.J. Brill. vol. I, 1958; vol. II, 1965).

Brockelmann, C. *Geschichte Der Arabischen litterature,* 2 vols. (Leiden: E.J. Brill, 1938).

——, *Zweiter Supplement band,* 3 vols.

Al-Bukhārī, Abū 'Abd Allāh Muḥammad ibn Ismā'īl. *Al-Jāmi' al-Ṣaḥīḥ,* 4 vols., ed. Ludolf Krehl (Leiden, 1862–1908).

Al-Busṭānī, Buṭrus. *Kitāb Dā'irat al-Ma'ārif,* 11 vols. (Beirut/Cairo, 1876–1900).

Al-Dhahabī, Abū 'Abd Allāh Shams al-Dīn. *Tadhkirat al-Ḥuffāẓ,* 4 vols. (Hyderabad, n.d.).

——, *Sirat A'lām al-Nubalā,* ed. Dr Ṣalāḥ al-Dīn al-Munajjid (Cairo, 1955).

——, *Ta'rīkh al-Islām,* 6 vols. (Cairo, H 1367).

The Encyclopaedia Britannica, ed. Walter Yust (London, 1951), 25 vols.

The Encyclopaedia of Islam, 4 vols., eds., M. Th. Houtsma, T.W. Arnold, R. Basset and R. Hartmann (London: Luzac and Co., 1913).

Fuād Sayyid, *'Fihrist al-Makhṭūṭāt al-Muṣawwarah Ma'had Iḥyā' al-Makhṭūṭāt al-'Arabiyah,* 2 vols. (Cairo, 1957).

Ḥamīd Allāh al-Mustawfī, *Nuzhat al-Qulūb* (Leiden, 1919).

(Ibn 'Abd al-Barr), Abū 'Umar Yūsuf ibn 'Abd Allāh ibn Muḥammad ibn 'Abd al-Barr ibn 'Āṣim al-Namarī, *al-Istī'āb fī Ma'rifat al-Aṣḥāb,* 2 vols., ed. 'Alī Muḥammad al-Bajawī (Cairo, n.d.).

Ibn 'Abd Rabbihi Abū 'Umar Aḥmad ibn Muḥammad al-Andulusī, *Kitāb 'Iqd al-Farīd,* 7 vols. (Cairo, 1359/1940).

Ibn al-'Ādhārī al-Marrākushī, *Kitāb al-Bayān al-Mughrib fī Akhbār al-Andalus wa'l Maghrib,* 3 vols., ed. G.S. Colin and E. Levi-Provençal

(Leiden: E.J. Brill, 1948).

Ibn al-'Asākir Abū'l Qāsim 'Alī ibn al-Ḥasan ibn Hibat Allāh, ibn 'Abd Allāh al-Sibtī al-Shāfi'ī, *Tahdhib Tārikh Ibn 'Asākir,* 2 vols. (VI, VII) (Damascus, H 1349/1951).

——, *al-Ta'rīkh al-Kabīr Rawḍat al-Shām* (H 1329, 1332, 1332) (I, II, III, IV, V).

Ibn al-Athīr, Abū'l Ḥasan 'Alī ibn Abū'l Karam Muḥammad ibn Muḥammad ibn 'Abd al-Karīm ibn 'Abd al-Wāḥid al-Shaybānī, 'Izz al-Dīn, *Tārīkh al-Kāmil,* 12 vols. (Cairo, H 1290).

Ibn Bakshkuwāl, Abū'l Qāsim Khalaf ibn 'Abd al-Mālik. *Kitāb al-Ṣillah,* 2 vols. (Cairo, 1347/1955).

Ibn Farḥūn, Burhān al-Dīn Ibrāhīm ibn 'Alī ibn Muḥammad, *al-Dībāj al-Mudhahhab* (Cairo, H 1351).

Ibn Ḥajar al-'Asqalānī Shihāb al-Dīn Aḥmad ibn 'Alī, *Tahdhīb al-Tahdhīb,* 12 vols. (Hyderabad (Deccan), H 1325).

——, *al-Iṣābah fī Tamīz al-Ṣaḥābah,* 4 vols. (Cairo, 1385/1939).

Ibn Hishām, Muḥammad 'Abd al-Mālik ibn Hishām, *Ṣīrat al-Nabī,* 4 vols. (Cairo, H 1356).

Ibn Kathīr 'Imād al-Dīn al-Fidā, Ismā'il ibn 'Umar al-Dimashqī. *al-Bidāyah wa'l Nihāyah,* Ist ed., 14 vols. (Cairo, 1351/1932).

Ibn Khaldūn 'Abd al-Raḥmān, *Kitāb al-'Ibar wa Dīwān al-Mubtadā wa'l Khabar fī Ayyām al-'Arab wa'l 'Ajam wa'l-Barbar wa man 'Aṣarahum Min Dhawi'l Sulṭān al-Akbar,* 7 vols. (n.d.).

Ibn Khallikān, Abū'l 'Abbās Shamsud-Dīn Aḥmad ibn Muḥammad ibn Abū Bakr, *Wafayāt al-A'yān,* 6 vols., ed. M. Muḥī al-Dīn 'Abd al-Ḥamīd (Cairo, 1948).

Ibn Khayr Abū Bakr Muḥammad ibn Khayr ibn 'Umar ibn Khalīfah al-Umawī al-Ishbelī, *Fihrist Ma Rawāhu 'an Shayukhihi min al-Dawāwin al-Muṣannafāt fī ḍarūb al-'ilm wa Anwā'i al-Ma'ārif,* 2nd ed. (Beirut, 1382/1963).

Ibn Manẓūr, Abū'l-Faḍl Jamāl al-Dīn Muḥammad ibn Mukrim, *Lisān al-'Arab*, 15 vols. (Beirut, 1374/1955).

Ibn Rajab, Abū'l Farāj 'Abd al-Raḥmān ibn Rajab al-Ḥanbalī, *al-Istikhrāj li Aḥkām al-Kharāj.*

Ibn Rushd, Abu'l Walīd Muḥammad ibn Aḥmad ibn Rushd, *Kitāb al-Muqaddimāt al-Mumahhadāt li-Bayān Mā iqtadathu Rusūm al-Mudawwanah min al-Aḥkām, al-Shar'īyyat wa'l-Taḥṣīlāt al-Muḥkamāt li Ummahāti Masā'liha'l-Mushkilāt*, 2 vols. (Cairo, H 1352).

Ibn Sa'd, Abū 'Abd Allāh Muḥammad. *Ṭabaqāt al-Kubrā*, 8 vols. (Beirut, 1376/1957).

Qāḍī 'Iyāḍ, Abū'l Faḍl 'Iyāḍ, ibn Mūsā ibn 'Iyāḍ. *Tartīb al-Madārik wa Taqrīb al-Masālik li Ma'rifat A'lām Madhhab Mālik*, 2 vols. ed., Muḥammad ibn Tāwīt al-Tunjī (al-Rabāt, 1983/1965).

———, *Tartīb al-Madārik Ṣādiqiyyah*, MS Grand Mosque No. 5132, 6509–10–11, quoted by Abdulwahab (H.H) and F. Dachraoui in article, "Le regime foncier en Sicile au Moyen Age (IX e. Etxe Siecles), Edition et traductiond' un chapitre du Kitāb al-Amwāl d' al-Dā'ūdī", Etudes D' Orientalisme DEDIEES A LA MEMOIRE DE LEVI-PROVENÇAL, Paris (1962), Tome 11.

Khayr al-Dīn al-Zarkalī, *al-A'lām*, 10 vols., 2nd ed.

Al-Khushanī, Abū 'Abd Allāh Muḥammad ibn Ḥārith ibn Asad. *Quḍāt al-Qurṭubah* (Cairo, 1373).

Al-Qutubī, Muḥammad ibn Shakīr ibn Aḥmad, *Fawāt al-Wafayāt*, 2 vois., ed. Muḥammad Muḥi al-Dīn 'Abd al-Ḥamīd (Cairo, 1951).

Lane, E. *An Arabic-English Lexicon*, 8 Parts (London, 1863).

Mālik ibn Anās, *al-Muwaṭṭa'*, 2 vols. (Cairo, 1370/1951).

Al-Maqrīzī, Abū'l-'Abbās 'Ahmād ibn 'Alī ibn 'Abd al-Qāḍīr. *Kitāb al-Khiṭaṭ al-Maqrīzīyyah* (Cairo, 1324).

Al-Mas'ūdī, Abū'l Ḥasan Alī ibn al-Ḥusayn ibn 'Alī. *Marūj al-Dhahab wa Ma'ādīn al-Jawhar*, 2nd ed., Muḥyī al-Dīn 'Abd al-Ḥamīd (Cairo, 1367/1948).

Al-Māwardī, Abū'l Ḥasan, 'Alī ibn Muḥammad ibn Ḥabīb. *Kitāb al-Aḥkām al-Sulṭāniyah,* ed. M. Enger. (Bonn, 1853).

Muḥammad Murtaḍā al-Ḥusaynī al-Zubaydī, *Tāj al-'Urūs,* 9 vols., ed. 'Abd al-Sattār Aḥmad Faraj (Kuwait, 1380/1060).

Muḥammad Ṭāhir, *Majma' Biḥār al-Anwār,* 3 vols. (Lucknow, H 1283).

Muslim, Abū'l Ḥusayn Muslim ibn al-Ḥajjāj al-Qushayrī al-Nishāburī. *Ṣaḥīḥ,* 5 vols. (Cairo, 1374/1965).

Marmaduke Pickthall, *The Meaning of the Glorious Qur'ān: Text and explanatory Translation* (Dacca, n.d.).

Al-Qurṭubī, Abū 'Abd Allāh Muḥammad ibn Aḥmad al-Anṣarī al-Qurṭubī, *al-Jāmi' li Aḥkām al-Qur'ān,* 20 vols. (Cairo, 1948).

Ṣaḥnūn ibn Sa'īd al-Tanukhī, *al-Mudawwanat al-Kubrā,* 16 vols. (Cairo, H 1332).

Ṣalāḥ al-Dīn Khalīl ibn Aybok al-Ṣafadī, *al-Wafī fi'l Wafayāt,* 4 vols. (Istanbul, 1931).

Al-Shāfi'ī, Muḥammad ibn Idrīs, *Kitāb al-Umm,* 7 vols. (Cairo: Būlāq H 1325).

———, *Musnad al-Shāfi'ī,* 2 vols. (Cairo 1369/1050).

Al-Subkī, Tāj al-Dīn. *Ṭabaqāt al-Shāfi'yat al-Kubrā,* 6 vols., 1st ed. (Cairo, H 1324).

Al-Ṭabarī, Abū Ja'far Muḥammad Ibn Jarīr. *Kitāb Ikhtilāf al-Fuqahā.* Ed. J. Schacht (Leiden, 1933).

———, *Jāmi' 'l-Bayān' an Tāw'il al-Qur'ān,* 15 vols., ed. Maḥmūd Muḥammad Shākir (Cairo, 1958).

———, *Tārīkh al-Rusul wa'l-Mulūk,* 13 vols. (Cairo, H 1336).

Al-Tirmidhī, Abū'l-'Iṣā Muḥammad ibn Īsā Sawrah. *al-Jāmi' li'l-Tirmidhī,* 2 vols. (Kanpur, n.d.).

Al-Ya'qūbī, Aḥmad ibn Abū Ya'qūb ibn Wāḍīḥ al-Katīb. *Kitāb al-*

Buldān, 3rd ed. (Najaf, 1377/1957).

Yayḥā ibn Ādam al-Qarashī, *Kitāb al-Kharāj* (Cairo, H 1347).

Yāqūt, Shihāb al-Dīn Abū ʻAbd Allāh Yāqūt al-Ḥamawī. *Kitāb Muʻjam al-Buldān*, 10 vols., 1st ed. (Cairo, 1323/1906).

Al-Zubayrī, Abū ʻAbd Allāh al-Muṣʻab ibn ʻAbd Allāh ibn al-Muṣʻab. *Kitāb Nasab Quraysh* (Cairo, H 1353).

Al-Zurqānī, Muḥammad ibn ʻAbd al-Bāqī, *Sharḥ al-Zurqānī ʻalā Muwaṭṭa ʼl-Imām Mālik*, 4 vols. (Cairo, 1373/1954).

INDEX*

A

*Prepared by Iftikhar ul Hasan Mian

B

C

G

H

J

K

L

M

N

S

T

U

W

Y

Z

***